D1591270

SOUTHERN BIOGRAPHY SERIES

Titles in the SOUTHERN BIOGRAPHY SERIES

Edited by Fred C. Cole and Wendell H. Stephenson

FELIX GRUNDY, *by Joseph Howard Parks*
THOMAS SPALDING OF SAPELO, *by E. Merton Coulter*
EDWARD LIVINGSTON, *by William B. Hatcher*
FIGHTIN' JOE WHEELER, *by John P. Dyer*
JOHN SHARP WILLIAMS, *by George Coleman Osborn*
GEORGE FITZHUGH, *by Harvey Wish*
PITCHFORK BEN TILLMAN, *by Francis Butler Simkins*
SEARGENT S. PRENTISS, *by Dallas C. Dickey*
ZACHARY TAYLOR, *by Brainerd Dyer*

Edited by T. Harry Williams

JOHN BELL OF TENNESSEE, *by Joseph Howard Parks*
JAMES HARROD OF KENTUCKY, *by Kathryn Harrod Mason*
ARTHUR PUE GORMAN, *by John R. Lambert*
GENERAL EDMUND KIRBY SMITH, *by Joseph Howard Parks*
WILLIAM BLOUNT, *by William H. Masterson*
P. G. T. BEAUREGARD, *by T. Harry Williams*
HOKE SMITH AND THE POLITICS OF THE NEW SOUTH,
    by Dewey W. Grantham, Jr.
GENERAL LEONIDAS POLK, *by Joseph Howard Parks*
MR. CRUMP OF MEMPHIS, *by William D. Miller*
GENERAL WILLIAM J. HARDEE, *by Nathaniel Cheairs Hughes, Jr.*
MONTAGUE OF VIRGINIA, *by William E. Larsen*
THOMAS MANN RANDOLPH, *by William H. Gains, Jr.*
JAMES LUSK ALCORN, *by Lillian A. Pereyra*
ROBERT TOOMBS OF GEORGIA, *by William Y. Thompson*
THE WHITE CHIEF: JAMES KIMBLE VARDAMAN, *by William F. Holmes*
LOUIS T. WIGFALL, *by Alvy L. King*
L. Q. C. LAMAR, *by James B. Murphy*
BRECKINRIDGE: STATESMAN, SOLDIER, SYMBOL, *by William C. Davis*
JOSEPH E. BROWN OF GEORGIA, *by Joseph Howard Parks*
DAVID FRENCH BOYD: FOUNDER OF LOUISIANA STATE UNIVERSITY,
    by Germaine Reed
CRACKER MESSIAH: GOVERNOR SIDNEY J. CATTS OF FLORIDA, *by Wayne Flynt*
MAVERICK REPUBLICAN IN THE OLD NORTH STATE: A POLITICAL BIOGRAPHY OF
    DANIEL L. RUSSELL, *by Jeffrey J. Crow and Robert F. Durden*

Maverick Republican
in the Old North State

Daniel Lindsay Russell, Jr.,
Governor of North Carolina, 1897–1901

Maverick Republican

in the Old North State

A Political Biography of

Daniel L. Russell

JEFFREY J. CROW and ROBERT F. DURDEN

LOUISIANA STATE UNIVERSITY PRESS

Baton Rouge and London

Copyright © 1977 by Louisiana State University Press
All rights reserved
Manufactured in the United States of America
Designer: Albert Crochet
Type face: VIP Primer
Typesetter: Graphic World, Inc., St. Louis, Missouri
Printer and binder: Kingsport Press, Kingsport, Tennessee

LIBRARY OF CONGRESS CATALOGING IN PUBLICATION DATA

Crow, Jeffrey J
  Maverick Republican in the Old North State.
  (Southern biography series)
  Includes bibliographical references and index.
  1. Russell, Daniel Lindsay, 1845–1908. 2. North
Carolina—Governors—Biography. 3. North Carolina—
Politics and government—1865–1950. 4. Reconstruction—
North Carolina. I. Durden, Robert Franklin, joint
author. II. Title. III. Series.
F259.R87C76   975.6'04'0924 [B]   77–3657
ISBN 0–8071–0291–1

This book is dedicated to D.O.C., G.M.C., M.O.D.R., and M.F.D.—
and the fine tradition of dissent in the Old North State, a land where
more than just vacations have long been varied.

Contents

Acknowledgments

WE OWE OUR primary institutional debts to the ever-helpful staffs of the Manuscript Department of the Perkins Library, Duke University; the Southern Historical Collection, Wilson Library, University of North Carolina, Chapel Hill; and the North Carolina Division of Archives and History, Raleigh. Among colleagues and friends who have helped us in various ways, including doing critical readings of all or portions of our manuscript, we thank Donald Butts, William McKee Evans, Paul Escott, Raymond Gavins, Larry Nelson, William Price, and Richard Watson. We appreciate the secretarial contributions of Vivian Jackson, Gladys Hogan, and Dorothy Sapp; and we are also grateful to the Research Council of Duke University for its support of various phases of this study.

Portions of the manuscript were previously published in two articles: "'Fusion, Confusion, and Negroism': Schisms Among Negro Republicans in the North Carolina Election of 1896," by Jeffrey J. Crow, in the Autumn, 1976, issue of the *North Carolina Historical Review*; and "'Populism to Progressivism' in North Carolina: Governor Daniel Russell and His War on the Southern Railway Company," by Jeffrey J. Crow, in the August, 1975, issue of *The Historian*. We gratefully acknowledge permission to reprint this material herein.

Introduction

DANIEL LINDSAY RUSSELL, Jr., portly and proud heir of one of North Carolina's relatively few great slaveholders, always dreamed of serving as governor of the Tarheel state. Born in 1845 and raised a Whig in the Wilmington area before the Civil War, he became a lifelong, defiant Republican—one of the scalawag minority so despised by southern Democrats—as soon as the Grand Old Party which had "saved the Union and freed the slaves" appeared in North Carolina in 1867. The election of Russell to the governorship in 1896—the only Republican to hold that office between Reconstruction and the 1970s—came about partly through the strange, complicated political situation created in North Carolina by the Populist revolt and partly through Russell's own talents as a politician and his long labors in the Republican vineyard.

Through circumstances largely beyond his control Russell's governorship turned into something of a nightmare for him. The Populist allies of the Republicans in the state legislature fell into a bitter quarrel that drastically weakened Governor Russell's political base. Intent upon achieving certain progressive economic reforms, especially in the area of railroad regulation, Russell alienated conservative, probusiness elements of his own party. Then the Tarheel Democrats, the "white man's party" since Reconstruction days, thwarted Russell's progressive initiatives by appealing to the racial fears and fantasies of the white majority in the violent white-supremacy campaigns of 1898 and 1900. This attack was especially ironic in Russell's case, for he had long tried to steer a middle course through the South's racial troubles.

Russell's maverick tendencies surfaced early in his career. A hot-headed young officer in the Confederate army, he fell seriously afoul of military regulations and midway in the war joined his father in outspoken defiance and criticism of the Richmond government and President Jefferson Davis. Saved from the clutches of Confederate authorities through election to the state legislature and the intervention of Governor Zebulon B. Vance, Russell showed himself early to be a man whose individuality kept him from being predictable.

After reading law Russell put his brilliant mind, impressive oratorical skill, and social prestige as one of the largest landholders in eastern North Carolina into the service of the Republican party. Never insecure about his own status or social standing, he held frankly paternalistic views toward the blacks who were in the majority in many eastern North Carolina counties and who formed a major element of the Republican party there. He came to accept and champion the civil equality of blacks, as embodied in the Fourteenth and Fifteenth amendments to the Constitution, while insisting that the fear of "social equality" was a mere bugaboo dreamed up by southern Democrats who refused to learn the lessons of the Civil War.

Elected as a judge of the superior court in 1868, when he was only twenty-two years old, Russell proceeded to establish a reputation as an outstanding legal mind as well as a fearless Republican who fully accepted the emancipation of the blacks and their incorporation into the body politic as legal equals. In his "Wilmington opera house" decision, discussed in Chapter II, he infuriated white Democrats who wished to bar Negroes altogether from various types of public places; but he also interestingly anticipated by more than two decades the decision of the United States Supreme Court in 1896 that upheld separate-but-equal accommodations for blacks as meeting the requirements of the Fourteenth Amendment.

After his six-year term as a judge, Russell served briefly in the state legislature and one term in Congress as a Greenbacker. But the governorship was clearly the capstone of his career. If he left that office early in 1901 as a man who had been soundly trounced by the Democrats and whose private financial resources were seriously strained, he was by no means knocked into passivity and silence. Having specialized for many decades in combating southern Democrats, he had one more large salvo to fire against the Tarheel Democrats, and that was the once-famous South Dakota bond suit.

Always a bitter opponent of repudiation of debt by a state government, Russell hit upon a scheme whereby he hoped to punish the Democrats who had repudiated much of North Carolina's debt in 1879 and to make some much-needed money for himself. The Eleventh Amendment to the United States Constitution prohibited private bondholders as individuals from suing a sovereign state. Russell's plan, pushed to a dramatic and constitutionally significant outcome in the Supreme Court of the United States, was to have private bondholders donate some of the bonds to a state (to South Dakota, as it turned out) and to have that state sue North Carolina in the Supreme Court, which has original jurisdiction in controversies between states.

Such was Russell's last foray, and a rich, fitting climax it was to his turbulent career as a dissenter in the Old North State. It is the thesis of this study that Daniel L. Russell represented a significant dissenting tradition in the post-Civil War South, a tradition that offered a viable alternative to the racial and economic dicta of the Bourbon Democrats. In the last analysis, however, Russell's unique blend of Old South paternalism toward blacks with New South radicalism concerning currency and railway reform challenged too many taboos of race, class, and party. His political career ended in failure—but the nature of that career and the reasons for the failure shed much light from an unusual angle on the South between 1860 and 1908 when Russell died.

Russell's contemporaries were struck by his hot temper and by his massive size—he weighed nearly three hundred pounds in his later years. He earned and apparently relished his reputation for being arrogant and irascible, yet he was a more complex man than his public image suggested. Formal and mannerly in a way that was increasingly old-fashioned as the twentieth century began, he was gentle with children and, more importantly, possessed a genuine social conscience.

Perhaps the best description of the mature Russell was provided in his last years by his young law partner: "Ponderous in body (56 inch waistline), leonine head (7-½ hat), large, protruding, light blue eyes, small nose, a jaw not too square, a wide thinlipped mouth, firm set, expressive of determination, small feet and legs, little hands (indicating lack of manual labor in youth), a linen duster over-all in summer, a wide brimmed straw hat, roguishly tilted, a heavy walking cane, a deep, roaring, yet musical voice,—he was all in all the prototype of the antebellum Southern Planter."

Maverick Republican
in the Old North State

Chapter I

To the Manor Born
Russell's Youth and
Civil War Experience

DANIEL LINDSAY RUSSELL, Jr., embodied some of the finest and some of the worst traits of the elite among antebellum southern planters. He was remarkably intelligent, well educated, proudly independent, and keenly sensitive about his personal honor and the obligations that accompanied his privileged position in society. On the other hand he possessed an unruly temper that he never conquered and that got him into much trouble throughout his life; his sense of dignity and honor slipped into arrogance, if not contempt, toward those whose mental processes moved more slowly than his own. Russell was, in short, a paradoxical figure.

He was, moreover, a maverick Tarheel, if there ever was one, in his public career. Born into a small aristocracy of great planters in a state that had comparatively few large slave owners, Russell became an ardent Republican soon after the Civil War. Holding various public offices, as his Whiggish father and grandfathers had done, he embraced a series of highly unorthodox causes throughout a career that was climaxed by his election as governor of North Carolina in 1896. As a perceptive kinswoman aptly said of him later, Russell never, as long as he lived, gave himself "the relaxation of conformity."[1]

---

1 Alice Sawyer Cooper, in collaboration with Louis Goodman, "Daniel Lindsay Russell: A Family and Friend's Memoir" (MS in the Daniel L. Russell Papers, Southern Historical Collection, University of North Carolina, Chapel Hill), hereinafter cited as Cooper, "Memoir." The late Mrs. Cooper was Russell's great-niece and lived for a number of years as a child with the Russells.

Born on August 7, 1845, at Winnabow plantation in Brunswick County, North Carolina, some fourteen miles below Wilmington and across the Cape Fear River, Russell was the son of Daniel L. Russell, Sr., and Elizabeth Caroline Sanders of nearby Onslow County. Russell, Sr., had moved from Onslow to Brunswick County some twenty-five years earlier and become the largest slave owner on the lower Cape Fear. With more than two hundred slaves, he produced not rice, as did many Wilmington planters, but cotton and naval stores (turpentine, tar, and rosin). When Wilmington was the world's capital for exports of naval stores, Russell, Sr., ranked as one of the largest individual producers.[2]

A staunch Whig from the 1830s when that party coalesced around Henry Clay and other such leaders—and against "King Andrew" Jackson—Russell, Sr., served for many years as the presiding magistrate of the justices of the peace in Brunswick County. A man of acknowledged ability and considerable wealth, he benefited from the deference to position that characterized much of antebellum southern society and was, thus, "reelected year after year for many years."[3]

Because young Dan Russell's mother died a few weeks after his birth, he was wet-nursed by a black woman named Celia, one of the twenty-five slaves Mrs. Russell had brought with her as part of her dowry. When young Dan was six years old, Russell, Sr., who had remarried, took him to live with his maternal grandfather, David Ward Sanders, in Onslow County. Death had claimed the last of Sanders' three children. Not only would young Dan Russell be a comfort to his grandparents, but he stood to inherit from his Grandfather Sanders extensive wealth in the form of cotton lands and slaves.[4]

Little is known of young Russell's life at Palo Alto plantation a few miles above Swansboro, North Carolina, on the White Oak River in Onslow County. As the designated heir of great wealth and the chief joy of his grandparents, Russell no doubt received much attention. Some of it seems to have backfired, for a story survives that while he was attending a neighborhood school, young Dan Russell observed

2 James M. Clifton, "Golden Grains of White: Rice Planting on the Lower Cape Fear," *North Carolina Historical Review*, L (October, 1973), 382, *n*. 63; W. McKee Evans, *Ballots and Fence Rails: Reconstruction on the Lower Cape Fear* (Chapel Hill: University of North Carolina Press, 1966), 14.
3 Walter G. Curtis, *Reminiscences* (Southport, N.C.: Herald Job Office, 1905), 12.
4 Cooper, "Memoir," 1–7.

that he was the only pupil to whom a servant brought a warm lunch each day. Annoyed by the distinction Russell announced that "if the other boys could eat cold lunch so could he"—or else he would not attend school.[5]

In 1857 when Russell was twelve years old, his Grandmother Sanders died, and his family then sent him to the famed Bingham School in Orange County, North Carolina. Featuring stern discipline and rigorous examinations, some of which allegedly required ten hours to write, the Bingham School occupied a proud place among the South's private academies in the nineteenth century.[6] After three years of this demanding training, Russell was probably ready to enter the University of North Carolina at Chapel Hill in 1860, though he was only fifteen years old. With John Brown's raid on Harper's Ferry occurring in the fall of 1859 and the presidential campaign that resulted in the election of Abraham Lincoln taking place as he enrolled at the university, Russell's college training was destined to be cut short.

Like many other old-line Whigs, Daniel Russell, Sr., and David Ward Sanders, who died in 1860, strongly opposed secession. Indeed, the great majority of North Carolinians clung desperately to their hopes for the Union and scorned secession—until after the Confederate forces at Charleston, South Carolina, opened fire on Fort Sumter in mid-April, 1861, and President Lincoln issued his call for troops to suppress the "rebellion."

Young Dan Russell may or may not have initially shared the political views of his father and his Grandfather Sanders. If he did at first oppose secession, he, like so many southerners who were swept along by the rush of events and forced to change their views, became a fire-eating "Southron" after mid-April, 1861, and he burned to fight for the Confederacy.

With eight or ten students leaving Chapel Hill everyday by late April, 1861, the remaining students petitioned in vain for a total suspension of classes. Once the actual battles began matters grew even worse at Chapel Hill. The town was several miles from the nearest railroad and lacked telegraphic lines. "Imagination not corrected by facts,

---

5 Joseph Parsons Brown, *The Commonwealth of Onslow: A History* (New Bern, N.C.: Owen G. Dunn, 1960), 113.

6 Charles Lee Raper, *The Church and Private Schools of North Carolina* (Greensboro: J. J. Stone, 1898), 76–78.

fed itself with fancied triumphs or dismal forebodings," the historian of the early university wrote. "Partial successes were exaggerated into 'glorious victories,' and inconclusive defeats into complete annihilation."[7] Young Dan Russell, at any rate, finally fled from the university in 1862. At his own expense he organized an artillery company of men from Brunswick County, was elected captain, and prepared to fight for the southern cause.[8]

Young Russell's Confederate career proved both colorful and abortive. It was also highly illustrative both of the man and of certain peculiarities and difficulties that plagued the Confederacy. Stationed initially at Fort Fisher, which stood on the tip of Cape Fear and guarded the river below Wilmington, Russell and his men found their principal excitement in watching the blockade-running ships move to and from Wilmington. Wearied by repeated denials of his request to be transferred to Virginia, Captain Russell finally hired a boat, loaded his men into it, and proceeded up the river to Wilmington in order to entrain for Virginia. He was arrested for acting without orders, but his youth and his family connections enabled him to get off with only a reprimand. His next scrape would not end so happily or easily for him.[9]

By 1863, if not sooner, Daniel Russell, Sr., like many other old-Whig Unionists who had opposed secession, made no secret of his thoroughgoing hostility toward the Confederate government in Richmond. It not only ignored states' rights in its conscription and other laws, he thought, but it was headed by Jefferson Davis, a longtime Democrat who had come to embody Confederate centralization and southern nationalism.[10] Other Confederate states, even in the Deep South, saw a resurgence of dissent, especially after the significant Confederate defeats at Gettysburg and Vicksburg in July, 1863. North Carolina, however, was a special hotbed of Confederate dissent, with William Woods Holden leading a growing contingent of those who clamored for peace—in another war in the following century a com-

---

7 Kemp P. Battle, *History of the University of North Carolina* (2 vols.; Raleigh: Edwards & Broughton, 1907), I, 737–39, 745.

8 Cooper, "Memoir," 9–10.

9 *Ibid.*, 10.

10 The problem posed for the Confederacy by persistent or reoccurring Unionism is discussed in Carl N. Degler, *The Other South: Southern Dissenters in the Nineteenth Century* (New York: Harper & Row, 1974), Chaps. 5 and 6, esp. pp. 168–69, 179.

parable group would be called "doves"—and with an old Whig and former Unionist, Zebulon B. Vance, elected governor in 1862.

By early 1864 the younger Russell had come to share his father's views about President Davis and his policies. Writing to Edward J. Hale, editor and publisher of the widely read Fayetteville *Observer*, Russell, Jr., declared that he and the men in his command "despised" the Confederate administration. Russell continued: "The soldiers expect to see you speak out boldly against the outrageous propositions that now agitate the country—to reconscript the army, for instance, without the privilege of reorganization; to give the president the right to say that his favorites and favorites of his subalterns throughout the country shall be exempt and none others; to suspend the writ of *habeas corpus*; to make civil offenses answerable to military courts—in a word, to make the government one grand consolidated military despotism to which the government of Abraham Lincoln is not a circumstance."[11]

Russell, Jr., had initially kept his political views at least semiprivate, but his father opposed the Confederate conscription law so vehemently and publicly that the older man fell under the observation of a Confederate enrolling officer in Wilmington, Captain William M. Swann. Young Russell ran afoul of Captain Swann when the former claimed to have taken four volunteers into his North Carolina militia company before Swann enrolled them for compulsory service in the Confederate Army. Swann reported to his superior officer that when he called upon young Russell to surrender the four men who had volunteered after the new conscript law had become operative, Russell "became very insolent, defied the authority of the Commandant [of] Conscripts, and says he will refuse under any *circumstances* to deliver them up." Swann added that both young Russell and his father had mixed with the assembled crowd and spoken freely of "the injustice and oppression of the Conscript Law." In fact, Russell, Sr., according to Swann, had invariably attended "enrollment days and sneered at and interfered in the carrying out of my instructions."[12]

11 Russell to Edward J. Hale, January 12, 1864, in Edward J. Hale Papers, North Carolina Division of Archives and History, Raleigh. The authors wish to thank Marc Kruman for calling their attention to this letter.
12 Russell to Wm. M. Swann, August 29, 1863, and copy of Swann to Peter Mallett, October 12, 1863, in Russell Papers.

Swann preferred charges against Russell, Jr., for disobedience of orders and conduct unbecoming an officer and prejudicial to good order and military discipline. Russell denied that the soldiers involved had been enrolled by Swann before he, Russell, had enlisted them; young Russell went on to note that "strictly speaking, I had no right to use the language referred to in as much as he [Swann] was engaged in the execution of the duties of his office." But, Russell added, "I should not have done [so] had I not been provoked by his unparalleled mendacity."[13]

If Captain Russell had limited his defense to words, even angry ones, he would have been spared much trouble. But he had come into possession of the letter Swann had written concerning his father and himself; he was only eighteen and no doubt aflame about the challenge to their "honor." Accordingly, on January 21, 1864, he armed himself with a hickory stick and a pistol and sought out Captain Swann. Swann, according to his later account of the incident, was seated at his desk in the Wilmington courthouse when young Russell marched in and, in a manner reminiscent of Congressman Preston Brooks' famed attack on Senator Charles Sumner, proceeded to whip him with the stick. Bystanders stopped the fray and seized both men, but Russell broke away and was about to shoot Swann when a third party deflected his arm and sent the bullet into the wall.[14]

Promptly arrested and confined to camp, young Russell found himself in a serious predicament. When a general court martial in late February, 1864, found him guilty of Swann's charges, as well as of refusing to submit to arrest, he was sentenced "to be dismissed from the service, and on account of his extreme youth, the court recommends the said Capt. Daniel L. Russell, Jr., to the clemency of the Commanding General."[15]

The commanding officer, Major General W. H. C. Whiting, finding nothing in the evidence adduced to justify a change in the sentence, declared that "Captain Russell's offense strikes at the very foundation

13 Charges and Specifications against Russell, submitted to Mallett by Swann, November 18, 1863, and Russell to R. M. Booker, January 12, 1864, *ibid.*
14 Swann's statement in the Raleigh *Daily Conservative*, September 12, 1864, in the Daniel Lindsay Russell Scrapbook, North Carolina Collection, University of North Carolina, Chapel Hill; see also Charges and Specifications against Russell, in Russell Papers.
15 General Order Number 25, from Headquarters, Department of the Cape Fear, Wilmington, February 27, 1864, in Russell Papers.

of military discipline and subordination, and is inexcusable." In consideration of the court's recommendation of clemency, however, and "especially from the very good character Capt. Russell has always borne as an officer," General Whiting ruled—and here he significantly differed from the court's sentence of dismissal from the service—that young Russell should be "allowed the privilege of selecting the company in which he will be enrolled."[16]

The Russells, both father and son, had no intention of accepting such a sentence. Aided by Governor Vance as well as by various high-ranking military and civilian friends in Richmond, they proceeded to lead the Confederate military authorities in Wilmington and Raleigh on a merry chase. Granted a leave of thirty days young Russell sought out General Whiting only to be reprimanded for approaching a commanding officer "without previous permission" and using language that "can be excused only from the fact that excited by the peculiar and difficult circumstances in which you were placed, you mistook an order for an insult." Vainly attempting to counsel and calm Russell, General Whiting added: "I give you the advice of an old soldier, go quietly to your company without *for the present* making any attempt to have your sentence changed. Show by your behavior that you can serve as faithfully and efficiently as a private as heretofore as an officer and your prospects will be much more favorable. Control yourself above all, [and] you will be sooner able to control others."[17]

Whiting's fatherly advice may have been sage and reasonable, but young Russell had neither the time nor the patience for it. Whether he, his father, or Governor Vance devised the next move is not known, but the magistrates of Brunswick County in early March, 1864, appointed Daniel Russell, Jr., county commissioner under the act of the General Assembly of North Carolina to receive and distribute money appropriated for the relief of wives and families of indigent soldiers from the county. Moreover, Governor Vance defiantly announced: "I claim the exemption of Daniel L. Russell, Jr., the county commissioner of Brunswick County, from Conscription as an officer necessary to the civil administration of the State Government."[18]

16 *Ibid.*
17 W. H. C. Whiting to Russell, March 7, 1864, *ibid.*
18 Brunswick County action of the magistrates, March term, 1864; and statement of Zebulon B. Vance, March 11, 1864, with notation of military authorities on back, *ibid.*

Foiled, at least temporarily, by the Russells and Governor Vance, General Whiting could only refer the matter to the War Department in Richmond. While Russell, Jr., went about his duties as commissioner for relief in Brunswick County, Vance, who had become a hardened veteran of conflicts with the Confederate government, exchanged strong words with the Confederate secretary of war, James A. Seddon. "In the first place I am unwilling to conclude that the exemption of State officers depends upon the action of Congress," Vance declared, "believing as I do that each State has the unqualified right to exempt from military service such officers as the General Assembly may declare necessary for the due administration of the Government and laws of the State." Ignoring Confederate military regulations providing that officers dropped from the rolls were to be enlisted under a sweeping conscription law of February 17, 1864, Vance insisted further that the court martial had only sentenced Russell to be dismissed from the service. Next the governor emphasized the court martial's recommendation of clemency because of Russell's extreme youth. "Upon consideration of the whole case," Vance avowed, "my conclusion is, that by the sentence of the Court, Mr. Russell was dismissed from the service, and became liable to be enrolled as a conscript; that before his enrollment he was duly elected to an office which I deemed necessary."[19]

When the War Department rejected the argument of Governor Vance and General Whiting ordered Russell to report for duty with whatever company he might choose, Governor Vance informed Whiting that no official reply to the governor's letter had come from the War Department. "I therefore notify you," Vance warned General Whiting, "that your offer to arrest Mr. Russell or to disturb him in the discharge of his official duties will be taken as a deliberate and unwarranted usurpation of authority and will be resented accordingly."[20]

To complicate further an already tangled affair, Richmond M. Pearson, chief justice of the North Carolina Supreme Court and another persistent Unionist, ruled on July 25, 1864, that Russell's appointment as county commissioner effectively exempted him from military service. Since the Confederate government, Pearson declared in time-hallowed states' rightist language, was "a creature of the states,

19   Vance to James A. Seddon, May 19, 1864, *ibid.*
20   James H. Hill to Russell, June 29, 1864, and copy of Vance to Whiting, July 5, 1864, *ibid.*

it is absurd to suppose that the intention was to make a grant of powers which would enable the creature to destroy the creator."[21]

Pearson's writ of habeas corpus discharging Russell was itself challenged by Confederate authorities, but the Russells next played their trump card: the voters of Brunswick County elected Daniel L. Russell, Jr., to the North Carolina legislature, from whence no Confederate authority could possibly take him. Russell, Sr., explained the move to an old friend: "I am now going to try to get the people to elect Dan'l L. Russell Jr. and not myself. I hope they will do so and [we will] see if that will have the effect to keep Jeff Davis and the petty tyrants under him from disturbing [us] any further. . . . You may depend on it, my Dear Sir, that my son did not want to leave the service and after he was dismissed said he had rather be restored than to be President of the Confederate States, but since he has been persecuted as he has, he wishes to be clear of the military authority if he can. He knows now the great blessing of personal liberty."[22]

The Russells, with the aid of the electorate in Brunswick County, had triumphed. Complete exoneration for the youthful captain came in October, 1864, when George Davis, the Confederate attorney-general and a native Tarheel and Wilmingtonian, conveyed word that President Jefferson Davis had reviewed the case and found inadequate grounds for the application of "doubtful principles to uphold a very severe sentence against a young officer who had, by all the testimony, manifested great zeal and fidelity in the discharge of his duties." Accordingly, an order would be issued remitting the sentence against young Russell. "But I must be permitted to tell you further, in a spirit of friendly candor," the attorney-general continued, "that this decision of the President has been made with a full knowledge of the settled and bitter hostility of your Father (with which you are understood to sympathize) towards himself personally, and towards his whole administration. This was communicated to him fully, as a part of the circumstances of the case, and his answer is worthy of your consideration

---

21   Copy of Richmond M. Pearson's ruling in Russell Papers. The whole affair is also treated in Memory F. Mitchell, *Legal Aspects of Conscription and Exemption in North Carolina, 1861–1865* (Chapel Hill: University of North Carolina Press, 1965), 83–86.

22   Russell's father to D. M. Carter, July 26, 1864, in the David Miller Carter Papers, Southern Historical Collection, University of North Carolina, Chapel Hill.

should you be disposed to judge him harshly hereafter. 'We can not afford,' he said, 'to remember such things now.'"[23]

Despite the magnanimity of Jefferson Davis, neither of the Russells was won over to the embattled Confederate president or to the swiftly dying cause of the Confederacy. The experiences of the war, in fact, when added to the lifelong aversion to Democrats felt by many old Whigs, made the Russells ripe for entry into the Republican party when that organization spread into North Carolina a few years after the Civil War. The evolution of Daniel L. Russell, Jr., from a proud, aristocratic young Whig to a zealous Confederate who quickly became a defiant southern dissident happened in a short span of time, but by 1865 he was well launched on a stormy career.

23 George Davis to Russell, October 20, 1864, in Russell Papers.

Chapter II

From Dissident Confederate to Radical Republican

The Reconstruction Era

WHEN WILMINGTON FELL to Federal troops in February, 1865, there were quite a number of sudden conversions to the Unionist cause.[1] In the case of the Russells, however, there certainly was no awkward turnabout or any need for apology or embarrassment. Their opposition to Jefferson Davis and his Confederate administration was rooted deeply in their antebellum Whig-Unionist views, which they had only temporarily laid aside.

Both father and son continued to live a portion of each year on the plantation in Brunswick County where they made their legal residence. But they also, as before the war, maintained a home in Wilmington, then North Carolina's largest town. Since "the prosperity of the Cape Fear country floated on turpentine," as one historian has put it, the quick recovery of the naval stores industry after the war, in contrast to the moribund rice industry, was advantageous for many people in the Cape Fear region.[2] Although presumably benefited by the postwar boom in naval stores, young Dan Russell had his eye on legal training and, since the law was the traditional pathway to service in government, probably on a political career also.

Shortly before the Civil War the editor of the *North Carolina University Magazine* had declared: "Law stands first in respectability in

1   W. McKee Evans, *Ballots and Fence Rails: Reconstruction on the Lower Cape Fear* (Chapel Hill: University of North Carolina Press, 1966), 47–48.
2   *Ibid.*, 59–60.

the eyes of the young man, and consequently the greater number must choose that."[3] Legal education in the nineteenth century typically consisted of reading law with and serving as an apprentice to an established member of the bar. Preparing for the oral bar examination administered by the justices of the North Carolina Supreme Court, many aspiring young lawyers read and reread numerous heavy volumes, with Blackstone's *Commentaries* usually heading the list.[4]

Daniel Russell, Jr., read law and served his apprenticeship in Wilmington, was examined by the judges of the supreme court, and was first admitted to practice in the state's county courts in 1867. After another examination a year later, he was admitted to practice in the superior courts.[5] Although he was only twenty-two years old when he became a full-fledged lawyer, Russell was about to become a judge of the superior court.

At the outset of his career as a lawyer and politician, Russell married his cousin, Sarah Amanda Sanders of Onslow County, on August 16, 1869. Daughter of Isaac Newton Sanders, who had so opposed secession and war that he had refused to fight, the young Mrs. Russell was herself a strong-minded, intelligent woman with a lively sense of humor, a quiet but deep religious belief, and a lifelong love of good literature, especially poetry. "Read poetry, child, memorize it," she urged her young kinfolk. "It feeds you like bread and meat."[6]

Although Daniel Russell, Jr., and his wife were destined to be childless, they belonged to a large, gregarious family, and various of their young nieces and nephews and great-nieces and great-nephews lived with them at different times. An independent-minded nonconformist like her husband, Mrs. Russell was a feminist in an era when North Carolina had few such bold women, and she gave strong support to the Women's Christian Temperance Union. Russell himself did not join the ranks of the "tee-total" abstainers though he apparently drank most moderately; he ate perhaps immoderately, since even the newspapers began to refer to his corpulence before he was thirty years old.

---

3   Quoted in Fannie Memory Farmer, "Legal Education in North Carolina, 1820–1860," *North Carolina Historical Review*, XXVIII (July, 1951), 271.

4   *Ibid.*, 292.

5   Wilmington *Daily Journal*, January 17, 1868. In light of subsequent developments, the fact that two of Russell's leading political adversaries in later life, Walter Clark and Samuel A. Ashe, were admitted to the bar at the same time is noteworthy.

6   Alice Sawyer Cooper, "Sarah Amanda Sanders Russell," (MS in the Daniel L. Russell Papers, Southern Historical Collection, University of North Carolina, Chapel Hill), 24.

Mrs. Russell possessed strong resources of her own. This is suggested by the fact that in the later years of her marriage when cash income was all too scarce despite the vast acreage Russell owned, she managed a dairy on their plantation at Belleville near Wilmington. From the back porch of her house in Wilmington, she even distributed a portion of the milk to various needy folk.[7]

Despite the prewar prominence and affluence of the Russell and Sanders families, Mrs. Russell, as the wife of a defiant and well-known Republican, encountered various types of social ostracism throughout her life. Although she was an Episcopalian (and her husband a Presbyterian), Mrs. Russell often meditated in the Roman Catholic church around the corner from her home in Wilmington. She could not feel comfortable in St. James Episcopal Church "because of the bitter political passions of the time."

Some fifteen years after the Russells had established their own home in Wilmington and after they had lived in Washington, D.C., during Russell's time in Congress, one of Wilmington's leading matrons finally called on her at a time when Daniel Russell, Jr., was temporarily out of the political limelight. After a pleasant interlude the visitor departed, saying, "And now, dear Mrs. Russell, I hope you will soon come to see me." Smiling gently, Mrs. Russell replied: "I believe the rules which govern calls in Washington are generally accepted in the rest of the country, and they prescribe that one wait before returning a call the same length of time as elapsed between one's arrival in town and the first call made. Therefore I regret that I will not be able to return your call for fifteen years."[8] Fortunately, the Russells both had ample resources of mind and character, as well as extensive family connections, for the controversial political career on which Daniel Russell, Jr., publicly embarked in 1868 was to last for forty turbulent years.

The Republican party made its official debut in North Carolina, as in most other former Confederate states, soon after the beginning of Congressional or Radical Reconstruction in 1867. The strong Republican majority in Congress, having gained the power to override the vetoes of President Andrew Johnson and proceed in defiant opposition to

---

7 *Ibid.*, 9.
8 Alice Sawyer Cooper, in collaboration with Louis Goodman, "Daniel Lindsay Russell: A Family and Friend's Memoir," (MS in the Daniel L. Russell Papers, Southern Historical Collection, University of North Carolina, Chapel Hill), 28, 46.

him, passed a series of acts that restored military rule in ten southern states and made their return to the Union contingent upon their ratification of the Fourteenth Amendment as well as upon their drafting new state constitutions embodying universal manhood suffrage.

Some newly enfranchised blacks in parts of the rural South may have been initially bewildered by their significant political roles and power in 1867. Such was certainly not the case in Wilmington, however, where blacks constituted a majority of the population that had numbered fewer than ten thousand before the war but had grown to an estimated fifteen thousand by 1867—and where a vigorous Negro political movement had begun as early as April, 1865, in connection with ceremonies marking the death of President Abraham Lincoln.[9] The importance of the black voters to the southern wing of the Republican party is indicated by one historian's recent estimate that white males cast only about 20 percent of the total Republican vote in the South as a whole. In North Carolina, however, as in other states of the upper South, white Republicans were more numerous and constituted closer to a third of the state's Republican membership.[10]

Wilmington, a seaport and North Carolina's liveliest commercial center at that time, had a significant number of northerners who had moved there both before and after the war and who became Republicans when that option opened to them in 1867. First labeled carpetbaggers by their political foes, and so known in history, the sample of the species in Wilmington and the surrounding area, as in the rest of the South, defied easy categorization. They ranged from Joseph C. Abbott, a former Union general from New Hampshire who helped conquer and command Wilmington in 1865 and stayed on to become a prominent capitalist and entrepreneur before going to the United States Senate from North Carolina, to none-too-scrupulous and petty opportunists who occasionally got caught with their hands in the public till.[11]

Among native white Tarheels who became Republicans—the scalawags so despised by the Democrats—none could boast of a more aristocratic background than Daniel L. Russell, Jr. This fact, plus his

9   Evans, *Ballots and Fence Rails*, 51–52, 86–90.
10 Carl N. Degler, *The Other South: Southern Dissenters in the Nineteenth Century* (New York: Harper & Row, 1974), 193.
11 Evans, *Ballots and Fence Rails*, 106 ff.

acknowledged mental prowess, was to give him a special role in the Republican party and make him a prize target for political potshots from the opposition.

Attacks on the scalawags by southern Democrats—or Conservatives as they were temporarily known—began early and remained vitriolic for many decades even after Reconstruction had ended. "There is one miracle neither God nor the Devil could work," declared one prominent southern Democrat at the outset of Radical Reconstruction, "viz: make anything but a traitor, a renegade, a coward and a scoundrel out of any Southern-born man who would desert his Southern mother in the hour of her agony and become a Republican."[12] A few years later, the Wilmington *Daily Journal*, one of the most influential Democratic newspapers in the state, made this pronouncement: "There has been no North Carolinian of prominence to ally himself with the Radical party who did not do so for the certainty or the hope of personal aggrandizement—ordinarily to be only obtained through practices at once dishonorable and criminal."[13]

Despite such attacks, the Russells, both father and son, became Republicans. They proudly and openly blended a number of distinctly Whiggish views with the newer reformist doctrines of the Republican party. Concerning property rights and the repudiation of debts by a state government, for example, both clung to orthodox Whig doctrine. The grand jurors of Brunswick County, with Daniel L. Russell, Sr., as their chairman and undoubted leading figure, declared in December, 1866, that they deemed it proper "to give expression to their unanimous opinion upon a question which vitally affects the interests and the honor of the State of North Carolina"—the question being that of repudiation. "The Grand Jury desire to promulgate as the sentiment of the County of Brunswick that every honest debt of the State as well as the citizens thereof should be honestly discharged. They are sensible that the terrible ravages of war and the loss and destruction of property resulting therefrom have greatly impaired their ability at present to meet promptly their obligations; but the war has left us our honor unimpaired, and this we cannot consent to surrender." The grand jurors concluded by declaring that "the public interest will be subserved and

---

12 Wilmington *Daily Journal*, July 26, 1867, quoting John Forsyth of the Mobile (Ala.) *Register*.
13 Wilmington *Daily Journal*, August 18, 1871.

the public credit to a great extent restored by a declaration by the honorable body [the general assembly] that under no circumstances will North Carolina repudiate her debts and that every obligation assumed by her shall be fully and faithfully performed."[14]

Despite such sturdy, Whiggish protestations about honor and the sanctity of contractual obligations, repudiation was much in the air during Reconstruction, with the victorious United States government first demanding and then securing the repudiation of all Confederate debts. Southern Democrats in many states were merely waiting until they could regain control of the state governments to repudiate all or part of the debts incurred by the Republican governments during Reconstruction. Such political tampering with public obligations was anathema to many, especially old-line Whigs; and though Daniel Russell, Sr., died in 1871, his son was to continue battling the repudiationist policy for the remainder of his life. In fact, the last spectacular episode in the career of Daniel Russell, Jr., involved certain North Carolina bonds that the state's Democrats had partially repudiated in the late 1870s. That, however, lay in the distant future. In 1868 young Russell was about to begin a political career in which he would ultimately become known as "the oracle of the Radical party" in the Cape Fear country.[15]

Although Russell was but twenty-two years old and only recently admitted to the bar, his background and brains obviously made him an important asset to the new Tarheel Republican party. He was, accordingly, nominated by it for the judgeship of the superior court in the new Fourth Judicial District that consisted of seven counties in the Cape Fear country—Bladen, Brunswick, Columbus, Duplin, New Hanover, Robeson, and Sampson. Democratic newspapers, which dominated the press of North Carolina, immediately ridiculed young Russell's nomination. The Wilmington *Morning Star* declared: "The idea of Dan. Russell being a *Judge* of anything except ground-peas or persimmon beer! We believe the whole thing is a wretched joke. Surely, Dan. has no serious intention of becoming Judge Russell? It

14   Wilmington *Daily Journal*, December 7, 1886; and Cooper, "Memoir," 88–89.
15   Just as Conservatives generally referred to Republicans as "Radicals," the Republicans preferred to call their Conservative opponents "Democrats" and thereby make it harder, or so the Republicans hoped, for the Democrats to appeal to the numerous former Whigs, former Know Nothings, Unionists, and other groups who had before the war bitterly fought the Democratic party.

would be doing him injustice to say he had no talent; for naturally, the boy has a good mind; but he has no more knowledge of Law than he has of Divinity."[16] The Raleigh *Sentinel*, launching an attack on the "mongrel judiciary ticket," conceded that Russell was "a tolerably piert [*sic*] youth" but insisted that he was "very innocent of law—almost as innocent as a child unborn."[17]

Unabashed, Daniel Russell, Jr., plunged into North Carolina's first struggle between Republicans and Conservatives. With characteristic candor he admitted publicly that he disapproved on principle of an elected judiciary, but, he contended, in incorporating that feature in the new state constitution the Republicans were merely carrying out "the old Democratic idea of free suffrage and popular elections in everything."[18]

Russell proceeded to take a prominent role in the Republican campaign, being flexible when necessary, even when it meant compromising certain of his Whiggish notions. Reporting on a "Radical Mongrel Gathering" in Wilmington, the *Daily Journal* made a pointed reference to Russell: "The whole of 'Afriky' in this part of the country was there—men, women and children, together with their white admirers, and some few respectable citizens attracted by mere motives of curiosity. Seated upon the stage was a curious compound of white and black. The *only* native white man we noticed in this conspicuous position, however, was that young Russell, from Brunswick, who aspires to be a judge."[19]

After he was elected chairman of the Republican congressional convention, Russell filled a number of joint speaking engagements with Republican nominee Oliver H. Dockery, a member of a politically prominent Richmond County family. The *Daily Journal*'s account of one "Grand Radical Hellabellow" had young Russell "rolling, rather than walking from the back of the stage to the footlights, and amid one long and prolonged yell from dusky throats" railing at the crowd "in no chaste or becoming language." Dockery, according to the Democratic reporter, spent his time "eulogizing Lincoln and villifying the old State which gave him birth and which he now attempts to dishonor."[20]

16 Wilmington *Morning Star*, March 22, 1868.
17 As quoted in the Wilmington *Daily Journal*, March 7, 1868.
18 Wilmington *Daily Post*, April 11, 1868.
19 Wilmington *Daily Journal*, March 24, 1868.
20 *Ibid.*, April 20, 1868.

Fortunately for Republicans in the Cape Fear country, as well as for better balance in the historical record, Wilmington for a few years during and after Reconstruction possessed something rare in the South—a Republican daily newspaper. Begun in 1867, the year of the Republican party's organization in North Carolina, the Wilmington *Post* naturally gave a different perspective from that of the *Daily Journal, Morning Star,* and other Democratic newspapers. The *Post's* account of what the *Daily Journal* had called the "Grand Radical Hellabellow," for example, included the information that the hall was decorated with a banner bearing the words: "WITH MALICE TOWARDS NONE, CHARITY TO ALL. A. LINCOLN. THE REPUBLICAN PARTY, THE PARTY OF THE PEOPLE." An all-black brass band from Engine Company No. 8 enlivened the occasion, and Russell, according to the *Post,* "held his audience's attention for an hour and a half" and was interrupted by frequent applause.

After defending the new Republican state constitution (save for the "great evil" of the elective judiciary), Russell had launched into an attack on the record of Democratic leaders. The *Post* reported him as saying: "How long, O! political madmen will you continue to abuse our patience! In 1860 they declared the South invincible and Cotton King —in 1861, that the men of the North would not fight—in 1862, that McClellan would seize the [United States] Government—in 1863, the Northwest would secede—in 1864, the Peace Democrats would sweep the country—in 1865, Johnson's policy would prevail (which it might have done but for their loathsome touch)—in 1866, the Congress would not dare force us under military rule—and lastly, they have been proposing to stop the wheels of the whole revolution by a *habeas corpus* and a bill in equity." Unlike the Democratic "architects of our ruin," the Republicans, Russell had concluded, would "oppress no man, but throw around all the protection of a free Constitution and equal laws."[21]

Russell's speech, when stripped of its partisan exaggeration, contained one central fact: equality before the law for all men, black as well as white, was indeed the rock on which the Republican party stood. That principle—so revolutionary in the South where a white majority had hoped to replace slavery with a permanent caste system

21　Wilmington *Daily Post*, April 10, 11, 1868.

—Daniel Russell not only genuinely accepted but acted upon as a judge and political leader. Certainly no liberal on racial matters by the standards of the late twentieth century, Russell, like so many of his fellow white Republicans in the North as well as the South, was himself tainted with racism. He was, however, free of hypocrisy to such a degree that he suffered politically from several of his statements that were easily distorted and misinterpreted by his foes; and he was sufficiently secure about his own identity not only to accept the emancipation of blacks but also their incorporation into the body politic as legal equals.

That equalitarianism—the glory and the burden of republicanism in Reconstruction—was the one unforgivable sin in the eyes of southern Democrats. In the same hall where Russell had excoriated Democrats and hailed equality before the law, "the beauty and intelligence of Wilmington," as the *Daily Journal* reported, had earlier gathered for a Conservative rally and heard the speaker insist that the "condition of servitude was one natural to the African race" and that "God and Nature's voice cannot be overcome by the Republican party."[22]

Certain Conservative newspapers were as frank as the obviously unreconstructed speaker in Wilmington had been, and the *Post* delighted in sharing with its readers some of the more extreme pronouncements. "No opportunities should be offered them [the blacks] to compete with the white man for anything, save as scavengers, stable boys or scullions," declared one editor in western North Carolina. Another, also from the west where blacks were scarce and white Republicans too numerous for Democratic comfort, asserted: "We have no hesitancy in stating that we are in favor of forming a white man's party. . . . We are not one of those who believe the negro was made out of the same dirt as ourself, and do not intend, willingly, to mix the Caucasian with the Ethiopian, as equals, in any sphere of life."[23]

By no means did all Conservatives take such a hard racial line, especially in the east where black political power was a factor to be reckoned with. When a black man deserted the Republicans, which happened so rarely that it was newsworthy, the Conservatives seized joyfully on the fact. In Onslow County, for example, a "Johnny Reb"

22   The Wilmington *Daily Journal*'s weekly edition of March 13, 1868.
23   Wilmington *Daily Post*, December 19, 1867, quoting the Lincolnton *Courier* and the Asheville *News*.

reported that a black man, "at the risk of his life," had defied his fellow blacks and voted with the Conservatives. "Now, for his heroism," the correspondent continued, "the people have taken steps to give him fifty acres of land, a good house on it, a good horse, and a year's provisions. Let the people do so everywhere that a case of the kind comes to their notice. Encourage the black men and show them who are really their friends, and in a little while the Radicals will be as scarce as the *'original secessionists'* are now."[24]

The Wilmington *Morning Star* announced before elections in the spring of 1868 that if "the colored people wish to live on good terms with the whites and advance their own interests, let them either vote the Conservative ticket or keep away from the polls." Soon after the elections, in which the Republicans triumphed at all levels and black voters demonstrated their loyalty to the party of Lincoln and Union, the *Star* began to call on Conservatives to recognize that they would never win unless they could succeed in some plan to *"divide the negro vote."* The *Star* next suggested, somewhat belatedly, that the time had come for Conservatives "to concede *qualified* suffrage to the colored man." While the majority of Conservatives were no doubt "unwilling to have negro suffrage in any form *forced* on them," they were "perfectly willing to concede it, as a lasting compromise, if guarded by the proper restrictions."[25]

Just as few blacks were lured away from the Republicans by appeals from "their real friends" in the Conservative party, neither were the newly enfranchised freedmen in the Cape Fear region intimidated by the Ku Klux Klan. The organization appeared in Wilmington on the eve of the 1868 spring elections, and Conservative newspapers attempted to play up "mysterious posters" purporting to be announcements from the Klan's headquarters. The head of the Klan in North Carolina was William L. Saunders of Wilmington, who at various times edited the *Daily Journal*. That paper solemnly announced: "Terrible was the phantom seen in the alley near the Post Office. . . . A skeleton, with a winding sheet drawn about his dry bones, seated upon a snow-white steed, whose nostrils emitted streams of flame with a strong odor of brimstone, was seen just before the heavy rain burst

24 Wilmington *Daily Journal*, November 30, 1867.
25 Wilmington *Morning Star*, March 27, May 7, 12, 1868.

upon the city."²⁶ Nonetheless, New Hanover County, and Wilmington in particular, saw the alleged power of the Klan quickly evaporate. On four successive nights, bands of blacks armed with guns, or even with fence rails, noisily patrolled the streets of Wilmington, making it clear that any attempt on the part of Klansmen or anybody else to intimidate them would be dangerous.

Not only did the blacks of Wilmington thus help keep out the terroristic arm of the Conservative party, but the Republicans soon had there a politically reliable state militia, something they clearly did not have in the Piedmont. Reconstruction in North Carolina, concluded a recent historian, "scarcely presents an antithesis more striking than the contrast between the Piedmont, with its political murders and skulduggery, and the lower Cape Fear . . . with its peaceful debates, orderly elections, and normally-functioning courts."²⁷

With the Conservatives unable—yet—either to intimidate or to cajole black voters, Tarheel Republicans elected William Woods Holden to the governorship in 1868, gained control of the legislature, and for the Fourth Judicial District easily elected Daniel L. Russell, Jr., judge of the superior court. If he knew little law at the outset of his six-year judicial term—and he much later declared that when he went on the bench he "didn't know any more law than a bull pup"—he learned quickly and soon commanded considerable respect, mixed perhaps with some fear, even from the Conservatives in the district.²⁸

In an era when there was neither television nor movies and, outside of a few metropolitan centers, little professional entertainment of any kind, judicial proceedings attracted great crowds. Courthouses were the main centers of activity in most towns, and judges and lawyers, most of whom emphasized oratory, became well-known figures.²⁹ "The position of superior court judgeship," one Tarheel scholar has written, "was in some respects the most important office in the state's judicial system." Having wide jurisdiction, superior courts tried practically all civil and criminal cases, and the people "regarded this court as their peculiar forum and attended its sittings in great numbers." Court week in each county was an important time when farmers from

26 Wilmington *Daily Journal*, March 24, April 18, 1868; Evans, *Ballots and Fence Rails*, 135.
27 Evans, *Ballots and Fence Rails*, 101–102, 134–38.
28 The quotation is from Cooper, "Memoir," 17.
29 Fannie Memory Farmer, "Legal Practice and Ethics in North Carolina, 1820–1860," *North Carolina Historical Review*, XXX (July, 1953), 336–40.

the countryside joined with townspeople to talk politics, exchange news, and "'swap horses and lies.'"[30]

Possibly because of the novelty of a Republican judge, and a twenty-three-year-old one at that, Russell's first court session in Wilmington attracted an unusual amount of attention. "The Court room is so thronged during the entire day," the *Journal* reported, "that it is with difficulty [that] a passage through the crowd can be effected." Russell's charge to the grand jury was described by the reporter as "neither pretentious nor brilliant," but it contained "the usual enumeration of offences known to the criminal law, and laid down the line of conduct which the jurors were to pursue under their oath."[31]

The "laborious session" of the superior court in Wilmington lasted two weeks, with a full criminal docket: of 108 cases tried, 48 were for larceny, 36 for assault and battery, 8 for affray, and so on down to 1 case for "malicious mischief." There were 47 convictions, 13 acquittals, 47 cases continued, and 1 case dismissed. The *Journal* noted that 44 of the 47 persons convicted were Negroes and proceeded to draw some dubious conclusions from that fact: "Thus, it is clearly evident that the effect of Radical rule and reconstruction has not tended to improve the state of society or the morals of the Negroes. Crime is confined almost exclusively to this class, and it cannot be charged that prejudice against the Negro influenced these convictions, as the Judge, the Sheriff, Deputies, and Clerk are all Radicals, and there was not a jury in the box but what contained at least four or five Negroes."[32]

Leaving aside the *Journal*'s biased notion that crime was confined to blacks and the probability that much law enforcement was so confined, even under Republican rule, one can see that Russell quickly earned a reputation as an efficient, fair judge. Conservative newspapers elsewhere in the state kept up a drumfire attack on their Republican judges, such as Albion Tourgée, the well-known Tarheel carpetbagger who presided over a superior court in eight turbulent Piedmont

30   Aubrey Lee Brooks, *Walter Clark: Fighting Judge* (Chapel Hill: University of North Carolina Press, 1944), 54.

31   Wilmington *Daily Journal*, October 20, 21, 1868.

32   *Ibid.*, November 1, 1868. A year later after another session of Russell's court in Wilmington, the *Daily Journal* (October 31, 1869) noted that "remarkable dispatch" had been used in trying a large number of cases. Through a special session, Russell was eventually able to clear the docket of many old cases, some of which had been continued from the war years.

counties.[33] Yet the *Journal, Morning Star,* and other Conservative papers in the Cape Fear region treated Russell with increasing respect—until election time. Some of his judicial rulings, however, not only challenged deeply rooted racial customs but also indicated the depth of his commitment to equality before the law.

As an aristocratic, Whiggish planter, Russell had never accepted the equalitarian dogmas for whites in which Jacksonian Democrats had specialized and by which they had won so many elections across antebellum America. Rather, he deeply believed and acted on the notion that men, like social classes, were unequal—in talents, opportunities, and attainments. Yet he lived in a time and place where political and civil equality had become realities for white men and, by 1868, were real possibilities for black ones. He might not personally like the facts, but events were to prove that he could accept them much more easily than the majority of his fellow white southerners.

From the outset of Radical Reconstruction in 1867, and even earlier, Conservatives had exploited the racial issue in the hope of scaring white voters away from the Republican party. Distorting the facts and raising issues that were not then before the voters, Conservative newspapers like the Wilmington *Journal* filled their pages before the 1868 elections with such queries as: "SHALL NEGRO GUARDIANS BE APPOINTED FOR WHITE WARDS? That is one of the issues. SHALL MARRIAGES BETWEEN NEGROES AND WHITES—amalgamation—be allowed? That is one of the issues."[34]

The Republican newspaper, the *Post,* responded as best it could to these racist appeals that pointed to the bugaboo of social equality. "In the good time coming," it overoptimistically prophesied, "the prejudices of to-day will be entirely obliterated" and people will "hardly be able to realize that a man in any enlightened community, was proscribed because of the color of his skin or the state wherein he happened to be born." More realistically, the *Post* concluded on a note that resembled Russell's position: "The cry raised about the equality of races is finally a political trick—a deception. Giving the right of franchise does not make the colored man socially the equal of the white,

33 Otto H. Olsen, *Carpetbagger's Crusade: The Life of Albion Winegar Tourgée* (Baltimore: Johns Hopkins University Press, 1965).
34 Wilmington *Daily Journal,* March 18, 1868.

[for] among the whites there is, there can be, no such thing as social equality."[35]

Republicans never succeeded in limiting the debate to the true issues. Still, as much as Conservatives cursed the blacks' right to vote, there were other areas where the questions became even trickier. In the first session of Russell's court in Wilmington one of the cases involved a white man accused of larceny. The counsel for defense objected to the testimony of one of Wilmington's black policemen, in light of a former state statute that permitted Negroes to testify only in cases where their rights of person or property were concerned. North Carolina's new Republican constitution, however, contained a section that read, "The laws of North Carolina, not repugnant to the Constitution and laws of the United States, shall be in force until lawfully altered." Acting on his own initiative and prior to the clarification that would soon come from the state's supreme court, Russell ruled that this section was sufficiently plain and that in inserting it the framers of the new constitution had had a special view to such a question as had been raised. He considered the old statute to be contrary to United States law and therefore nullified. Accordingly, he ruled the Negro's testimony admissible, and the white man was found guilty.[36]

More dramatic in popular impact than such legal matters were questions dealing with public accommodations for blacks, or the lack thereof. The so-called "Black Codes" the southern states had drawn up after the end of slavery had been struck down by the Republicans' Civil Rights Act of 1866 and then the Fourteenth Amendment. There remained a large gray area, however, and a bewildering pattern of race relations existed throughout the South.[37]

Regardless of ambiguities that may have characterized public accommodations for blacks in other parts of the South, white Wilmingtonians responded by indicating that they intended to discriminate against blacks and to segregate them wherever possible. As Republican rule approached in the spring of 1868, Conservative newspapers

35   Wilmington *Daily Post*, August 17, 1867. See also the *Daily Post* of April 12, 1868.
36   Wilmington *Daily Journal*, October 31, 1868. The state's supreme court, Chief Justice Richmond M. Pearson ruling, later declared that the North Carolina statute limiting Negroes to testifying only against each other had been repealed by the new state constitution. *Ibid.*, February 26, 1869.
37   The handiest introduction to the differing views of historians about this subject is found in Joel Williamson (ed.), *The Origins of Segregation* (Boston: D. C. Heath, 1968).

reported any incident that might suggest racial unrest. A black man who had carried a white lady's luggage up the stairs of a local hotel was told by the proprietor to remove his hat. When the black "impudently replied he would take it off for no man," the proprietor forcibly ejected him and, after the black threw a bottle, had him arrested. The same issue of the newspaper mentioned a "little difficulty" when a Negro demanded and was refused the right to buy a drink at Brock's Exchange.[38] Later five black men entered the Globe Saloon to buy drinks. When the clerk informed them that the saloon "did not sell liquor to colored people," the blacks left and obtained warrants against the proprietor on the ground of alleged violation of the Civil Rights Act. The resident United States commissioner ruled, however, that proprietors had a right to decline to sell to whom they wished, and the *Journal* concluded that the "action of the prosecutors [the five black men] meets endorsement only among the most ignorant and prejudiced of the colored people."[39]

Just as blacks were denied access to Wilmington saloons, so were they discriminated against in theaters and the opera house. They were forced to sit in a special gallery, and some refused to accept such an arrangement and protested the policy, to no avail, in the spring of 1870.[40] The matter was one that even the Republican paper, the *Post*, treated gingerly; but when a black Episcopal preacher was denied accommodations, either in a cabin or on the upper deck of a small steamer that plied the Cape Fear from Wilmington to Fayetteville, the *Post* mildly commented: "We think we need a small edition of the civil rights bill down here."[41]

Encouraged by the actions of such old-time abolitionist friends as Massachusetts' Senator Charles Sumner, who was strongly pushing for a new civil rights measure to guarantee Negroes equal access to public carriers, hotels, and other public places, the blacks of Wilmington persisted in seeking fairer treatment in the local opera house. On October 10, 1873, after a performance by a touring minstrel show, the *Post* reported: "Last evening three respectable colored men purchased first class tickets and took their seats in an orderly manner in some of

38 Wilmington *Daily Journal*, April 1, 1868.
39 *Ibid.*, October 10, 11, 1871.
40 *Ibid.*, March 20, 1870.
41 Wilmington *Daily Post*, May 28, 1873.

the orchestra chairs at the Opera House." The *Post* suggested that there was "but one reserved place for colored people, and this is a resort for prostitutes and other evil disposed persons, and no colored man who has proper respect for his wife will seat her there." The Republican newspaper claimed that "all the colored people ask is that certain seats be reserved for them in a respectable portion of the Opera House where they can be seated, free from molestation and annoyance." Concerning the same incident, the *Journal* asserted that it would be "well for the lessee of the Theatre and for managers of theatrical companies, to understand once for all, that the white people of Wilmington do not propose to illustrate the doctrine of social equality with negroes."[42]

The blacks, with their own active Equal Rights Club in Wilmington, were in no mood to heed the warnings of Conservative newspapers like the *Journal*. A writer identified only as a "Negro" submitted in the *Post* that the "time has happily long since passed when public rights are to be made the property of one portion of the community to the exclusion of the other."[43] When a group of blacks returned to the opera house a night or two after the initial seating incident, the manager threw them out. He was taken before a justice of the peace on a charge of assault and battery, was found guilty and fined $25.00 and costs—but he in turn made affidavits and obtained warrants against four of the black men for forcible trespass.[44]

This was the case that Judge Daniel Russell heard in the autumn of 1873. His ruling was sufficiently complex that he put it in writing, and the newspapers regarded it as important enough to publish verbatim. After a statement of the facts of the case, Russell declared: "No one is allowed to assert or enforce a mere civil right by resorting to violence. If one has my property and wrongfully withholds it, I have no right to take it from him forcibly." Coming closer to the issue at hand, he argued: "An inn-keeper or common carrier has no right arbitrarily or capriciously to refuse to entertain or carry a person. Yet if they do unlawfully so refuse, it is not for the injured party to take upon himself those powers which belong only to the officers of the law, and thus seek to enforce his rights according to his own construction of them, and by a resort to force not authorized by any legal process." Russell

42   Wilmington *Daily Journal*, October 7, 1873.
43   *Ibid.*, October 8, 1873.
44   *Ibid.*, October 10, 1873.

was saying, in other words, that the black defendants had adopted "unlawful means of asserting what they believe to be a right," and he ruled that the warrants against them should be dismissed at the cost of the defendants.

If he had let the matter go at that, no more might have been heard of Wilmington's "opera house case." But Russell hit white, Conservatives nerves as he pushed further: "The pretension that any person or class may be prevented from resorting to a public place whose doors are open to all but them and denied to them only on account of color or race, will not be tolerated by any Court honestly and sincerely desirous of expounding the constitution and laws according to their true meaning." Russell then added a comment that anticipated the separate-but-equal accommodations ruling that the Supreme Court of the United States would make a generation later in *Plessy* v. *Ferguson* (1896). He suggested that the manager of the theater might have "the right to separate different classes of persons whose close association is not agreeable to each other—always remembering that he must not discriminate against any; but that the accommodations given, the comfort, style, convenience and all other considerations for which parties pay their money, shall be the same as to all, or so nearly so as to furnish no substantial cause of complaint by any." Backing away from this larger question, Russell confessed that this "opens a wide field of argument into which I have not the time to enter."

Obviously aware that he was entering into areas where higher courts than his had thus far feared to tread, Russell concluded with a curious statement that was half-apology and half-defiance: "A Court is always sustained in giving expression to an *obiter dictum* when the purpose is simply to avoid a misconception of the extent or bearing of its decision. This opinion is formed almost without any opportunity for reflection, without any argument by counsel and without consulting a single authority. Hence I do not ask or expect for it any consideration greater than is usually given by the profession to the *dictum* of a *nisi prius* Court [one that tries a case before a single judge] rendered in the hours of business and without that deliberative and mature study always given to cases which are to be looked to as authority. I would not have put this opinion in writing but for the apprehension that the ruling would be misunderstood or misrepresented."[45]

45 *Ibid.*, October 24, 1873. The Wilmington *Daily Post* of the same date also carried the opinion.

The reaction of Wilmington's black community to Russell's ruling is not known, but many Conservatives were stunned. That was not because of the suggestion that separate-but-equal accommodations might be legally acceptable but because of Russell's assertion, so contrary to widespread practice and so shocking to many whites, that blacks could not legally be prevented from entering public places on account of their race. Strangely enough, the Conservative newspapers printed the full decision but refrained from commenting on it for several months. The editors of the *Journal* had already become embroiled in the courts on a charge of libel for calling one of North Carolina's federal judges "a scoundrel," and that fact may have encouraged the silence that initially greeted the court decision. Within a few months, however, when Russell had to stand for reelection, the voters would hear of little else but his open invitation to "full social equality" for blacks.[46]

As bold as some of Russell's rulings proved to be, once elected to his judgeship in 1868 for a six-year term, he moved carefully to the background in politics. "If any man ever did try to keep out of politics when he held a Judicial office," the *Post* insisted, "that man is Daniel L. Russell."[47] Yet in fact he belonged to a group of some fifteen or twenty Republicans in Wilmington that the Conservative press usually referred to as the "Ring." Professor W. McKee Evans, a recent historian of Reconstruction in the Cape Fear country, describes Wilmington's Republican party of that era as consisting of some 2,000 blacks plus from 100 to 150 whites. The "Ring" involved about a half-dozen first and second generation New Englanders whose families had come to the Cape Fear before the Civil War, another group of carpetbaggers who had been connected with the Union Army, a few former Whigs from leading families such as the Russells, and the heads of a couple of well-to-do black families. Through their control of money and patronage, as well as through their obvious educational advantages, the members of the "Ring" kept what control they could over the raucous, quarrelsome Republican party.[48]

---

46   The manager of the opera house heeded Russell's decision, and on November 13, 1873, the Wilmington *Daily Post* commended the "tardy act of justice" that had been done for "respectable colored people" through the orchestra seats for blacks that had been "boxed off to themselves, and a separate entrance provided."
47   Wilmington *Daily Post*, July 26, 1872.
48   Evans, *Ballots and Fence Rails*, 162–65.

By 1874 when Russell had to run for reelection, that party was in trouble. Not only had the Conservatives, through various means including the Klan's terrorism, regained control of the state legislature in 1870, but in Wilmington the faction-ridden Republicans had fallen into great disarray. One Republican leader warned, "Whoever disturbs, by word or deed, the equity of privileges of the three constituent elements of the [Republican] party, is an *enemy within the line*." He hailed the "royal oak of republicanism—of which the Negro is the protecting bark, the white native the heart, the immigrant the vivifying sap."[49] Russell had his private doubts about the composition of the "royal oak of republicanism." In a confidential letter to Thomas Settle, a prominent native Republican in the Piedmont, Russell diagnosed the Republican dilemma: "Not among the least of our difficulties is the fact that our Federal office holders, composed almost entirely of the carpet bag class, are utterly inefficient, politically worthless and intensely selfish. Their devotion to the party consists in their love of the salaries and fees incident to the holding of office. Take these away and they return North or go to the enemy. Deserving men, good speakers and first rate politicians of our own people are thrust aside to keep these men in power."[50]

Russell was probably too harsh in his judgment of the carpetbaggers who held federal office, but, regardless, his more serious reelection problems originated with the Conservatives. Through their control of the legislature the opposition could freely gerrymander electoral districts to help their cause. In Russell's case they added a couple of counties to the Fourth Judicial District and thereby changed it from one with a Republican majority of voters to one with a Conservative majority. Moreover, the Ku Klux Klan, which had been effectively checked along the lower Cape Fear, still rode in some of the inland counties of the district. Testifying in 1871 before a congressional committee that was investigating Klan activities, Russell had declared that in those counties in North Carolina where Klan outrages had gone unpunished "there is an absolute reign of terror, and there is no sort of

---

49   E. M. Rosafy of Brunswick County in the Wilmington *Daily Post*, December 29, 1873.
50   Russell to Thomas Settle, September 16, 1874, in Thomas Settle Papers, Southern Historical Collection, University of North Carolina, Chapel Hill.

security to either life, liberty, or property in favor of any man against whom there is reasonable suspicion that he is a Union man and favorable to the Government."[51] One of Russell's supporters warned him, "You are to be bitterly assailed for the stand you have taken against the Ku Klux."[52]

In view of the many obstacles Russell faced in seeking reelection to his judgeship, he followed a course that clearly better suited him personally: he ran as an independent candidate and confined his campaign to letter writing. Among a number who advised that course, Russell's half-brother, who lived in the interior county of Robeson, explained: "All young men who are Democrats . . . are Ku Kluxs and have taken an oath not to support any nominee of the Republican party and therefore can not support you if nominated in Convention."[53]

Russell faced an uphill fight, even though he hoped to add some Conservative votes to his Republican support and thereby survive. His opponent, Colonel Allmand A. McKay of Sampson County, opened the campaign by speaking at the Memorial Day services in Wilmington's Confederate cemetery. He closed with stanzas from Father Ryan's "Conquered Banner," and the Conservative newsreporter noted that "this beautiful and appropriate custom of honoring our brave martyrs of the 'Lost Cause' is increasing in favor."[54]

While McKay capitalized on the burgeoning "Lost Cause" cult, another Conservative speaker nailed Russell as "the first advocate of civil rights in the state" who deserved to be "the first martyr." With debate on Senator Sumner's civil rights bill prominently featured in each day's news from Washington, the Wilmington *Morning Star* assailed the bill as "the crowning infamy of the spawn of Radicalism" which would "rouse the dormant energies of the white men of North Carolina, firing their hearts and nerving their arms for the great struggle."[55]

As for Russell's posture as a nonpartisan candidate, the *Morning Star* insisted that he was "the representative man of the Radical party in the Cape Fear section; he is the oracle of that party." According to

51 *Senate Reports*, 42nd Cong., 1st Sess., and the Special Session of the Senate, 1871, No. 1468, p. 181.
52 James Sinclair to Russell, May 11, 1874, in Russell Papers. Russell's judicial reputation as a friend of the Negro and Indian is mentioned in W. McKee Evans, *To Die Game: The Story of the Lowry Band, Indian Guerrillas of Reconstruction* (Baton Rouge: Louisiana State University Press, 1971), 147–48.
53 T. B. Russell to Daniel Russell, May 26, 1874, in Russell Papers.
54 Wilmington *Morning Star*, May 12, 1874.
55 *Ibid.*, May 12, June 3, 1874.

the Conservative editor, who concentrated more fire against Russell than against any other Republican, "All the little Radical whippersnappers from Columbus, and Brunswick, and Bladen, and other counties of this region come to Wilmington to consult their oracle, and they would really have no influence if they did not have Russell to supply them with political ammunition and show them how to use it." In a left-handed tribute to Russell's ethics, the *Star* conceded that it had "never heard him accused of any unusual degree of recklessness in the distribution of currency for party purposes." But "he does supply the party with brains."[56] Russell, therefore, was a prime target for the Conservatives, who proceeded to capitalize on his decision in the opera house case.

Although Republicans in North Carolina did their best to dissociate themselves from Sumner's civil rights bill, the Conservatives pulled out all the stops in using Russell's decision in the opera house case against him. The full decision was carried in almost every issue of the leading Conservative newspaper in Wilmington from June until the election in August, 1874; it was also printed as a circular and made available in bulk orders for a minimum price. Quoting key passages from the decision, the *Morning Star* warned: "Let the white men of this District ponder these words. They mean equality in places of amusement. After this and equality in the schools [is] granted comes social equality as a sequel." Russell's decision could only "lead inevitably to full social equality." Conservatives should regard Russell as "the eager Judge rushing with pliant *obiter dicta* to the embraces of his negro supporters, the first to sound in North Carolina . . . the Civil Rights, Social Equality slogan."[57]

Under the circumstances, Russell could not have been too surprised that he was beaten. The *Morning Star* led the Conservative exultation over the defeat of "the most able and popular Radical leader in Eastern Carolina."[58] Not only had the Republican party of Wilmington split and the number of Negro voters declined sharply, but in the interior counties many black and white Republican voters had been frightened into political quiescence by Conservative tactics.

Russell received a number of letters during the campaign which

56   *Ibid.*, August 6, 1874.
57   *Ibid.*, July 4, August 2, 1874.
58   *Ibid.*, August 8, 1874.

suggested what was happening. One man wrote that he was for Russell but did not want "to let it be known." Another advised, "Seal your communications to me carefully," and another reported: "We had a Hell of a time in Clinton [in Sampson County]. Spoke at the peril of our lives. Were followed out of Town by a band of armed Horsemen but nevertheless [we] were not subdued, but come off victorious—and believe we done good." One ally declared that the mail service was so unreliable he preferred to get his Republican newspaper, the Wilmington *Post*, from a post office just across the border in South Carolina.[59]

From Kenansville, North Carolina, a friend sent a striking confession: "I will not deceive you. I did not vote in the Judge's election. I knew you would not require me to make myself and family amenable to the overbearing and proscriptive disposition of my surroundings." This correspondent added that he had acted as registrar and had done his best to prevent fraud. He believed, however, that the "only chance for protecting the Ballot box is for Congress to carry out the Constitutional provisions" of the Fifteenth Amendment, which prohibited the states from denying the right to vote on account of race, and to "enact that in all the states at every Election only one box and one ballot shall be used." If Congress would only pass "more stringent laws on the subject of intimidation and bribery" and let the United States courts have jurisdiction over all such matters, this correspondent avowed that the "Democracy will hide its turbulent head."[60]

No such legislation forcing southern Democrats to hide their "turbulent heads" was forthcoming. The whole experiment of Reconstruction, in fact, was fast ending by 1874, not only in North Carolina but throughout the South. In those few southern states where Republicans still managed a shaky hold on power, particularly South Carolina and Louisiana, the end would come in 1876–1877 and be part of the compromise whereby the Republicans kept their grip on the presidency and handed over to the Democrats those last Republican states in the South.

For Russell, the end of Reconstruction began to be foreshadowed after his own defeat in 1874. Writing to his fellow Republican in Raleigh, Governor Curtis H. Brogden, he tried to put on a brave front and

59   W. J. Sutton to Russell, July 1, 1874, H. R. Kornegay to Russell, July 1, 1874, T. H. Sutton to Russell, July 7, 1874, and D. K. Bennett to Russell, July 7, 1874, in Russell Papers.
60   W. D. Pearsall to Russell, August 11, 1874, *ibid*.

suggest that the federal Congress and President Ulysses S. Grant would yet act to protect the rights of black and white Republicans in the South. "The last man and the last dollar to enforce political and legal, not social, equality," Russell declared. *"In hoc signo vinces!"* [61] Yet to Thomas Settle, Russell made a more candid assessment of the situation: "We [Republicans] are badly hacked in the East, have lost about all our counties except two or three and these though saved at the polls are about to be lost by our party, officers elect failing to give bonds, our men intimidated and the whole of us threatened with unparalled persecution." Seeking an historical analogy Russell concluded: "As things now look we are about where free soilers were in the South before the war and an attempt to save the State in 1876 will be about as futile as it would have been to attempt to carry the State for Fremont in 1856 or Lincoln in 1860. The Conflict seems to be deepening." [62]

Despite his temporary gloom Daniel Russell was not down to stay. The Tarheel Democrats would hear more of him, sooner than they could have imagined in 1874. He would again and again find ways to champion his nonconforming views and, in the process, make life as miserable as he could for Democrats.

61   Russell to Curtis H. Brogden, September 23, 1874, in the Curtis H. Brogden Papers, North Carolina Division of Archives and History, Raleigh. The authors wish to thank Eric Anderson for bringing this letter to their attention.
62   Russell to Settle, September 16, 1874, in Settle Papers.

Chapter III

"The Knight of the Lordly Strut"
Fighting the Bourbon Democracy

NEITHER THE PRACTICE of law in Wilmington nor the management of his extensive plantations in Brunswick and Onslow counties could long suffice as occupations for the politically ambitious and astute Daniel L. Russell. Turning thirty in August, 1875, he was already a veteran of political battles that had been as fiercely fought and rancorous as any in the nation. As a native white Republican, a scalawag, Russell was a sworn enemy of Bourbon Democrats and a wily proponent of strategies to defeat them. His next opportunity was not long in coming.

The nationwide economic depression that followed the panic of 1873 included farmers among its foremost victims. Since the South continued to be overwhelmingly agrarian, hard times for the great majority of people, white as well as black, accompanied the end of Reconstruction. Long inhibited by the processes of Reconstruction from participating in national debates about currency, banking, and other pressing economic issues, the South after 1877 saw a sharply rising interest among its poverty-stricken voters in just such matters. *Greenbacks* and *free silver* became in the late 1870s what they would remain for two decades: emotion-laden fighting words and symbols of dissent in southern political life.

The Democrats had whipped the Republicans, but one-party domination of such a heterogeneous, long-memoried people was no easy feat, even with assistance from the flourishing cult of the Lost Cause, the romantic myth of the Old South, and the highly biased version of Reconstruction that became a staple item of the southern Democratic creed. Various groups of southern voters were breaking away from the "solid South" even as that Democratic ideal and goal began to be discussed nationally.[1]

A group of reformers representing eastern laborers and western and southern agrarians met in Toledo, Ohio, early in 1878 and organized the National Greenback Labor party. Denouncing both major parties, the Greenbackers blamed the continuing hard times on money lenders, bankers, and bondholders; they demanded, among other things, that the federal government scrap the national banking system started by the Republicans during the Civil War and assume exclusive responsibility for issuing legal tender notes, that is, money.[2]

By the summer of 1878, Greenback clubs were cropping up over much of the South, including North Carolina, and Democratic political observers and editors nervously eyed the development. Southern Democratic hegemony depended significantly on racist appeals and avoidance of concrete economic issues that would divide the "white man's party." Thus the Wilmington *Morning Star* initially assailed the Greenbackers as wild reformers who "would destroy capitalism through regulation of railroads, income tax, and the direct election of United States Senators."[3] Yet when popular sentiment in North Carolina and across the South grew increasingly sympathetic to currency and banking reform, Democratic newspapers and politicians were quick to embrace the cause, or at least some portions of it, and to insist that any change must come through the Democratic party. "That is the political ark in which [the people] must ride over the tempestuous financial sea," argued the *Morning Star*.[4]

---

1   The classic treatment of this period in southern history is C. Vann Woodward, *The Origins of the New South, 1877–1913* (Baton Rouge: Louisiana State University Press, 1951), esp. Chaps. 3 and 4.
2   Theodore Saloutos, *Farmer Movements in the South, 1865–1933* (Berkeley: University of California Press, 1960), 52.
3   Wilmington *Morning Star*, August 3, 1878. Some Republicans in the South were as hostile to the Greenbackers as Democrats were initially. The Wilmington *Weekly Post*, March 1, 1878, for example, declared that the currency question was not a sufficient basis for any new political combination, that there were "but two classes in the nation—those who saved it, and those who attempted to destroy it."
4   Wilmington *Morning Star*, October 3, 1878.

As the two old parties and the new Greenbackers prepared to make their congressional nominations in the early autumn of 1878, Democratic leaders were worried not only by the introduction of the Greenback element but also by widespread apathy among Democrats as a nonpresidential election approached. Indeed, in North Carolina's Third Congressional District, consisting of twelve counties in the southeastern corner of the state, the Greenbackers were preparing a large surprise.

The Greenbackers' nominee for Congress in the Third District was none other than Daniel L. Russell. Mrs. Russell probably exaggerated in later years when she confided to a family friend that she and her husband were "both really Socialists."[5] They were interested in and read about the Fabian socialism that appeared in England in the late nineteenth century; they frankly recognized, according to Mrs. Russell, that the wealth of the antebellum planter class, to which their families had belonged, had rested on the exploitation of slave labor. But despite those unorthodox sympathies, Daniel Russell was too much the old Whig, who believed in property rights and the sanctity of contract, ever to become a genuine Socialist. He did, nevertheless, genuinely embrace a number of reform causes, particularly those having to do with currency and the regulation of corporate enterprise. Furthermore, it bothered him not at all to become a Greenbacker— especially if doing so meant a better chance to beat a Democrat. The "former Napoleon of Eastern Radicalism" had mastered the intricacies of the currency question, one Democratic writer conceded, and that he was "an able exponent of this new party" could not be denied by those who knew his "well known mental powers as a speaker."[6]

Russell's Democratic opponent in the congressional race was the incumbent, Alfred Moore Waddell of Wilmington. A former Whig who had championed racial moderation and qualified suffrage for blacks immediately after the war, Waddell had become a staunch Democrat during the course of Reconstruction and would remain one of Russell's bitterest political enemies. In this congressional contest, however, Waddell became ill during the campaign and announced midway that he could no longer canvass the district.[7]

5 Alice Sawyer Cooper, in collaboration with Louis Goodman, "Daniel Lindsay Russell: A Family and Friend's Memoir" (MS in the Daniel L. Russell Papers, Southern Historical Collection, University of North Carolina, Chapel Hill), 19.

6 Wilmington *Morning Star*, October 8, 1878.

7 *Ibid.*, October 18, 31, 1878.

Waddell's illness may have helped Russell, but the Democratic newspapers did what they could to ridicule the former Republican judge. Quips about Russell as a "horny-handed son of the soil"–and an oversized "ton of soil"—filled the Wilmington *Morning Star*, as did references to "the Duke of Brunswick" and the "the Knight of the Lordly Strut."[8]

Whereas the Republicans attacked Russell for leaving his old party, the Democrats accused him of having remained in the Republican party "as long as there was a pea in the pot or a sop in the pan." On the other hand, the Democrats insisted that his conversion to greenbackism was spurious and that "every time his back is scratched it is a Radical that feels good."[9] Ignoring these attacks Russell issued a broadside calling on the voters to ignore "all the issues of the past, which grew out of the Negro question." He called for the substitution of legal tender greenbacks for the notes issued by the privately owned national banks and for the greenbacks to be the "absolute money" of the land, "a full legal tender in the payment of all debts, public and private and not convertible into coin except at the option of the Government." The nation's existing policy had hurt businessmen as well as farmers through the "dearness and scarcity of currency," and unless the monetary policies were changed the "few who hold money, bonds, mortgages, and other forms of credits must eventually become the owners and masters of the country."[10]

Russell's bold advocacy of financial reform undoubtedly appealed to many poor voters. A few days before the election the Republican congressional candidate declared that Russell, compared to Waddell, was the lesser of two evils and still had the confidence of Republicans "upon all measures not connected with financial conditions." The Republican candidate, thereupon, quietly withdrew from the contest, and the worst fears of the Democrats in the Third Congressional District began to materialize. Appeals to the memory of Reconstruction had constituted a major Democratic theme from the beginning. Russell urged the voters to forget, but Waddell responded: "If I know the people of this District, that is just exactly what they do *not* propose to do. They have a very retentive memory as to the 'issues of the past,'

---

8   *Ibid.*, October 18 to November 5, 1878.
9   *Ibid.*, October 22, 23, 1878.
10 Russell, "To the Voters of the Third Congressional District of North Carolina," 1878, in the North Carolina Collection, University of North Carolina, Chapel Hill.

which *he* (Russell) has been so instrumental in making and sustaining for many years."[11] *"Remember the Past!"* the Democrats urged on the eve of the election. "Remember 'the *Reconstruction Era of Plunder!'* Remember those *dark days of humiliation and oppression!* Remember that then Daniel L. Russell was a Radical—*hand in glove with your oppressors!*"[12]

All such exhortations were in vain, for the "Knight of the Lordly Strut" won the election, with 11,611 votes against Waddell's 10,730. Several thousand Democrats who had helped send Waddell to Congress in the presidential election year of 1876 chose to stay home in 1878, and with a majority of some 1,300 votes in New Hanover County alone, Russell had Republican ballots and Democratic voter apathy to thank for his victory.[13]

The only Greenbacker elected to Congress in North Carolina and one of only thirteen from the nation, Russell went into a Democratically controlled legislature. Of the South's 106 congressional districts, Democrats had won all save four, "the few survivors in a contest waged for the extermination of the Republican party in the South," as one veteran leader of the Grand Old Party put it.[14] A first-term congressman belonging to a small third party had little chance to accomplish much. The controlling Democrats, moveover, spent much of their time during the closing phase of Rutherford B. Hayes's term in a sterile struggle with the president that echoed many old sectional themes of the North, the South, and blacks. When the Democrats attached riders to army appropriation bills—riders prohibiting the use of federal soldiers or marshals at the polls—Hayes vetoed the measures and, after considerable political acrimony, won his point.[15]

Daniel Russell took great pleasure in helping to pour hot coals on the heads of Democrats, especially those from the South. In a speech on the apportionment of representation in the House, delivered in

11 Wilmington *Weekly Post*, October 27, 1878, for the Republican candidate's withdrawal and Wilmington *Morning Star*, October 31, 1878, for Waddell's statement.
12 Wilmington *Morning Star*, November 2, 1878.
13 The Wilmington *Morning Star*, November 17, 1878, carried the official returns and on November 19 a card from Waddell stating that he would not contest the election which he believed to have been a fair one.
14 James G. Blaine, *Twenty Years of Congress* (2 vols.; Norwich, Conn.: Henry Bill, 1886), II, 639.
15 H. Wayne Morgan, *From Hayes to McKinley: National Party Politics, 1877–1896* (Syracuse: University of Rochester Press, 1969), 52–54.

1881, Russell defended the Fourteenth and Fifteenth amendments and what he termed "free suffrage." He probably caused some discomfort to northern Republicans, too, when he attacked the use by certain northern states of voting qualifications such as the poll tax and literacy test. Prophesying quite accurately, as later events in the South would reveal, Russell contended: "If Massachusetts and Rhode Island can disfranchise the poor and the humble citizens of foreign birth within their limits, then South Carolina and Mississippi may easily avoid what they regard as the danger of universal negro suffrage." Russell noted that some Democratic newspapers in South Carolina and elsewhere in the South were beginning to call for a legal method of limiting suffrage rather than the fraud and violence that had long been used to thwart black voters. If South Carolina should imitate the literacy test of Massachusetts and include a "grandfather clause" allowing anyone who had the right to vote before 1868 to keep it, Russell suggested that "the government of the old slaveholding oligarchy" would be restored, and nine-tenths of South Carolina's black voters plus a small proportion of poor white ones would be disfranchised.

Reiterating his Greenback principles, Russell pointed to "lawless capital" and "monopolists" as the forces which sought the overthrow of free suffrage. The power of money was being translated into political power, and "Vanderbilt and Gould are our masters." In language that would become much more familiar during the Populist revolt in the 1890s, Russell declared that eastern capital saw universal suffrage as its "cheapest enemy." He believed that the political alliances of the future, therefore, would have to be between the West and the South, especially the upper South, as opposed to the existing coalition between "eastern millionaires and southern Bourbons." As for free suffrage in the meantime, he concluded, "Execute the Constitution or change it." [16]

Russell's speech to the House of Representatives is striking even if it did not change anything. It accurately forecast the moves to disfranchise blacks that southern Democrats would adopt toward the end of the century, and its Greenbacker orientation also neatly foreshadowed issues and alignments that became familiar realities in the 1890s.

Russell was happy to excoriate both major political parties. In a

16 "Apportionment of Representatives," speech by Russell on February 26, 1881, in Russell Papers.

speech to the House in 1879, he argued that the country regarded "as settled the issues of the war on which both the old parties are still living and seek to live—living for no honest purpose, so far as reasonable men can see, unless it be to save funeral expenses." His hardest blows, however, were against southern Democrats, for he asserted that the "ascendancy of Bourbon democracy" menaced free institutions and meant retrogression and reaction. In an incisive even if partisan analysis of Bourbon Democratic rule, Russell explained: "It means the minimum of liberty to the many and the maximum of power to the few. It means the denial of education to the masses and the active propagation of ignorance among them. It means a return in some form to those manners and customs under which humble birth was a calamity which nothing but the grave could conquer, and honest toil a disgrace for which nothing but wealth could atone."

In stern words that Congress seldom heard from native white southerners, Russell called for "unqualified loyalty to the flag, universal obedience to and absolute equality before the law, complete toleration, entire freedom of speech, of thought, and of action." None of those things could be achieved, he concluded, "until the last vestige of Bourbonism is trampled out; until the white South shall cease to whine and weep over the lost cause, and shall frankly and sincerely confess that the God of battles was right and we were wrong."[17]

Russell did not direct all of his efforts in Congress toward protesting Democratic rule in the South; he also undertook to serve various interests of his constituents in the Third Congressional District. He succeeded, for example, in making Fayetteville on the upper reaches of the Cape Fear River a port of entry. This made the Cape Fear "free and open to all the steamboats or other vessels" that wished to ply the river to Fayetteville. Put another way, it was no longer lawful for any corporation or person to exact tolls on any portion of the river. One constituent wrote to congratulate Russell on the measure and, after citing cases where boats and barges had been required to pay steep tolls on the upper Cape Fear, declared: "We feel proud that the time has come that we have a statesman in Congress who take[s] pride in looking out for the interest of the Cape Fear district."[18]

17 Russell's speech in the House of Representatives, April 21, 1879, *ibid.*
18 *Congressional Record*, 46th Cong., 2nd Sess., 4298; Alfred Lazell to Russell, January 2, 1880, in Russell Papers.

Russell chose not to run for Congress in 1880. Not only was that a presidential election year, when Tarheel Democrats could be expected to rally their forces more effectively than in 1878, but he well knew that his victory over Alfred M. Waddell had been made possible through a special set of circumstances. Even so, the post-Reconstruction South was by no means "solid" in the 1880s, and though Russell had temporarily retired to the sidelines, he was never far from the political arena.

Southern politics after Reconstruction, despite Democratic claims to the contrary, was in a state of flux, and various insurgents often challenged Democratic solidarity. In 1881 a strong prohibition movement swept North Carolina and led to a temporary alliance of "wet" Democrats and "wet" Republicans. When the whiskey forces defeated prohibition in a statewide election, John J. Mott of Statesville, the GOP state chairman, seized the opportunity to erect a new political coalition. In 1882 he attempted to combine wet Democrats with Republicans and old Greenbackers under the aegis of the Liberal Anti-Prohibition party.[19]

Russell, perhaps swayed by his wife's temperance views, had favored prohibition. But the Liberal movement of 1882 won his endorsement. He had watched with interest the Readjusters in Virginia— essentially a coalition of black and white farmers, workers, and small businessmen who wished to repudiate part of the state's large debt— as they gained control of both the legislature and governorship in 1881, much to the chagrin of Bourbon Democrats. As one Virginian wrote him: "We must build up a Liberal party in the South, & then join that party at the North which will do the most to materially advance our section."[20] Russell took an active part in the Liberal campaign of 1882, and though the Liberals lost, they came within four hundred votes of electing a Republican congressman-at-large in a statewide race. The lessons of that election were lost neither on Russell nor on Mott. Coalition politics—a "new line"—had nearly succeeded, and as Mott warned one Republican stalwart, "I will not go back to the old ruts."[21]

---

19   See Daniel J. Whitener, "North Carolina Prohibition Election of 1881 and Its Aftermath," *North Carolina Historical Review*, XI (1934).

20   William Lamb to Russell, November 25, 1881, in Russell Papers.

21   J. J. Mott to Settle, December 10, 1882, in Thomas Settle Papers, Southern Historical Collection, University of North Carolina, Chapel Hill.

Russell's maverick tendencies, as a Greenbacker and then anti-Prohibitionist, hardly endeared him to the Republican Old Guard in North Carolina or in Washington. He had an active desire to be appointed to the federal bench and in 1882 sought a judgeship in the United States Eastern District Court in North Carolina. Various Tarheel Republicans pledged support and insisted that President Chester Arthur would name him to the post. When it went instead to another Republican, Russell's supporters blamed his defeat on the carpetbaggers in North Carolina who had supposedly betrayed him. Another rumor held that he had been passed over because he came from a rich, slaveholding family and thus was of the "Bourbon stock" who had "no sympathy with the Masses & Co."[22] That ironic charge must have piqued the old Russell temper.

Again in 1890 Russell sought an appointment to the federal bench. This time he enlisted the help of an old political ally, Albion W. Tourgée, who had left North Carolina more than a decade earlier. Writing Tourgée in New York, Russell sardonically stated his Republican credentials. "If you want to know who will be applicants [for the judgeship] you can ascertain by making a list of all the nominal, actual and *quasi* Republicans who claim to be lawyers in the Virginias and North Carolina. You would have to exclude me from the list because when the party surrendered to triumphant nullification I left it and joined the Radical party of which I am Chairman, Secretary, Treasurer, Executive Committee and only surviving charter member."[23] Russell again failed to get the appointment.

Defining southern republicanism simply as belief "in the Union of the States and the Declaration of 1776," Russell proved a cantankerous critic of the party when it failed to live up to its principles or ignored his recommendations on strategy—a fact not unnoticed by party stalwarts.[24] Indeed, in the late 1880s and early 1890s he emerged as one of the chief leaders, along with John J. Mott, of a strong minority faction in the Tarheel GOP, though he held no political office or official position.

22 See S. H. Manning to Russell, January 24, 25, February 9, 10, 12, 14, 1882, A. W. Tourgée to Russell, February 6, 1882, Ike J. Young to Russell, March 7, 1882, all in Russell Papers.
23 Russell to Tourgée, April 19, 1890, in Albion W. Tourgée Papers, Chatauqua County Historical Society, Westfield, New York.
24 Russell to Tourgée, October, 1879, *ibid*.

Russell set the stage for his political reemergence with a typically blunt public letter to the citizens of North Carolina in July, 1888. In the election of 1884 Russell had been the Republican nominee for the state supreme court. When offered the opportunity to run again in 1888, however, he declined. Ostensibly he feared that the Democrats would once more attack his Wilmington opera house decision of 1873, but what he really objected to was a statewide Republican ticket which opened the GOP to the Democrats' use of the "color line." Faced with discriminatory election laws and the opposition's racist rhetoric, Russell believed that the Republicans should nominate only congressional and senatorial candidates since state and county GOP candidates faced nearly certain defeat. Above all, the faction that Russell represented opposed and was fearful of black aspirations toward local party leadership.[25]

In his public letter Russell assailed the Democratic solid South that had come in his eyes to stand for states' rights, low tariffs, and the nullification of the Constitution. He particularly chided the Bourbons or "Southern gentlemen" who refused to educate the masses, white and black, who paid "pauper wages," and who considered themselves "the natural and only rightful rulers of this Republic."[26]

Defending southern republicanism, Russell revealed toward Afro-Americans a distinctly paternalistic attitude. He admitted that no white men in the South, even Republicans, would ever "submit to negro rule. . . . The negroes of the South," he averred, "are largely savages. We with Northern aid and sanction kidnapped them, enslaved them, and by most monstrous wrong degraded them so that they are no more fit to govern than are their brethren in African swamps." Denying that he opposed black suffrage but insisting that he was merely speaking the "truth" about "many of our colored voters," Russell urged blacks to seek racial uplift through avenues other than politics, and he affirmed his belief that a compulsory education system should be established in North Carolina. He concluded that "negro rule" was an impossibility, for any "misrule" in the localities with black

---

25 Wilmington *Messenger*, July 14, 1888, in Russell Scrapbooks, North Carolina Collection, University of North Carolina, Chapel Hill. Also see Joseph F. Steelman, "Vicissitudes of Republican Party Politics: The Campaign of 1892 in North Carolina," *North Carolina Historical Review*, XLIII (1966).

26 Wilmington *Messenger*, July 14, 1888, in Russell Scrapbooks.

majorities would inevitably be "corrected by the law making power . . . by a Republican as well as a Democratic legislature."[27]

Russell's outspoken stand on Negro citizenship lent itself to easy distortion. His views were doubtless shaped by his aristocratic background and were strongly tinged with racism, but the Whiggish planter also recognized the injustice and prejudice of the Bourbon South and believed that all men—white and black—should have the equal opportunity in life that education could provide. Concentrated power—whether economic or political—as exercised by the Bourbon Democrats frustrated equal opportunity and led to an uninformed and basically unqualified electorate. Thus, until such time as men like Russell could correct that condition, the Negro's role in politics must be a limited one in which "natural" leaders—men of property, wealth, and education to whom power inexorably flowed—held office and directed affairs of state. The old antebellum system of deference and paternalism, particularly that of the Whiggish stamp, ultimately underpinned Russell's thinking.

Through education, property ownership, and hard work the majority of Afro-Americans might eventually play a larger role in politics; in the meantime the Russell-Mott wing of the Tarheel GOP preferred to obscure the association of Negroes with Republicanism. For that reason the Russell faction regarded the strategy of the statewide and full Republican slate as counterproductive since the Democrats could then more easily raise the race issue. The eastern counties of North Carolina included sixteen with black majorities that tended to vote Republican when their ballots were counted. Although the Republicans obviously needed black support, they were unwilling to give the Negro more than a token share of the offices.

When not berating the GOP for being the party of Radical Reconstruction and the Negro, the Democrats thwarted Republican chances for victory by bribing black electors, challenging black voters, stealing elections, and urging several blacks to run for the same office in order to split the Republican vote.[28] Partly because of such tactics and possibly through honest conviction, an estimated 17 to 20 percent of Negro

27   *Ibid.*
28   Helen G. Edmonds, *The Negro and Fusion Politics in North Carolina, 1894–1901* (Chapel Hill: University of North Carolina Press, 1951), 15; Frenise A. Logan, *The Negro in North Carolina, 1876–1894* (Chapel Hill: University of North Carolina Press, 1964), 13–24.

male adults consistently voted Democratic in North Carolina during the 1880s, even though the Democrats still portrayed themselves as the party of Redemption and of the white man.[29]

Russell did not regard himself as a lily-white Republican, but many of his supporters in the Tarheel GOP probably made no distinction between his paternalism and their desire to remove the "color line" from politics. In 1889 Russell declared: "The allegations of Democratic leaders in our State, as to danger to property under the elective system in counties where colored people largely predominate are not without a basis of truth." Since the Democrats had regained power during Reconstruction, the general assembly had appointed county commissioners and justices of the peace thereby eliminating local self-government and depriving Republican strongholds of Republican officials. Russell proposed that "home rule" could be reinstituted if one provision were included: a majority of the property-owning taxpayers in a county or township could petition the governor to stop elections if property were endangered by the election of incompetent or dishonest officials. In that extreme case, the governor would then appoint county officers. Russell frankly admitted that such a system would only be used in those counties with large black majorities, but he did not believe that it would curtail blacks' present political privileges. "Besides," argued Russell, "the intelligent African leaders ought to stand up and recognize the actual condition of their race and so act as to show the white people of the State that negro rule is not wanted by the Republican party."[30]

Wearied and frustrated by the race issue, the Russell faction found new hope with the emergence of the Farmers' Alliance, which appeared in North Carolina in 1887. The Alliance quickly became a strong political lobby for the farmer by advocating state regulation of railroads, a uniform interest rate, and other reforms designed to relieve the farmer of his mounting debts in a period of shrinking prices for his crops.[31] As early as 1889 an anonymous Wilmington correspondent of the Raleigh

---

29 J. Morgan Kousser, *The Shaping of Southern Politics: Suffrage Restriction and the Establishment of the One-Party South, 1880–1910* (New Haven: Yale University Press, 1974), Table 7.1, p. 183.

30 Raleigh *Signal*, January 24, 1889. The *Signal*, edited by J. C. L. Harris, was the organ of the Russell-Mott faction of the Tarheel Republican party.

31 See Stuart Noblin, *Leonidas LaFayette Polk: Agrarian Crusader* (Chapel Hill: University of North Carolina Press, 1949).

Signal, who styled himself "Progress" and who sounded suspiciously like Russell, called for a political coalition of Republicans and Alliancemen against the Bourbon Democrats who catered to "corporate interests" and the "Aristocratic element." Prominent Republicans like Russell and Mott had already joined the Alliance in demanding a railroad commission whereas leading Democrats had resisted the innovation. "In North Carolina," asserted the correspondent, "the Republican party is the party of the common and middle classes as against the aristocrats and corporate influence." A new political alignment would allow blacks to gravitate to whatever party they wished. "Disband and join the Farmers' Alliance," he urged white Republicans, "and force issues between that organization and the Democratic party."[32]

By 1892 the radical wing of the Alliance had bolted from the Democrats to form the Populist party. The entrance of the Populists into North Carolina politics presented the Russell–Mott wing of the Republican party with an opportunity, in Russell's words, to readjust party lines on "issues other than race and color." That was also the aim of the Populists. Russell and Mott, as in 1888, opposed placing a statewide Republican ticket in the field. Early in the campaign of 1892 Russell called simply for a policy of nonaction so as to permit the People's party to draw votes from the Democrats.[33]

As the campaign heated up, however, it became clear that the wing of the party led by state chairman John B. Eaves, who favored a full Republican slate, would prevail. Russell's attacks became more vituperative and his position more extreme. He charged that Henry Plummer Cheatham, black congressman of the Second District, was the "actual leader of the party . . . whose only qualification for leadership is the color of his skin." In Russell's opinion, the Eaves faction wanted to "drive all white men out of the party in the negro belt" in order to "turn over the negro counties to negro government." But though white Republicans would never settle for Negro rule, Afro-Americans should be "treated with liberality and justice." Russell asserted, however, that "the attainment of this great end is remote so long as the negro indicates by his political conduct that he only wants power to enact in the

32   Raleigh *Signal*, November 21, 1889, and October, 15, 1891.
33   *Ibid.*, April 5, 1892.

South the scenes which have demonstrated his incapacity for self-government in Hayti, Jamaica, and San Domingo."[34]

Privately, Russell decried the "bummer negroes" who were drawing the "color line" on white Republicans and driving them out of the party. "The blacks are more aggressive and proscriptive and ungrateful and treacherous than you would suppose it possible," he complained to Albion Tourgée's wife. Even so, he was not unmindful of the effects of racial prejudice. "Of course there are good people among them," he wrote, "and *their* condition is pitiful because they are persecuted by the whites and betrayed by their own race."[35]

But more revealing than his racial views in the 1892 election were his political and economic stands. Russell called for a coalition ticket of Populists and Republicans to "redeem" the state from the Bourbon Democrats. According to this former Greenbacker congressman, there was nothing in the Populist platform objectionable to southern Republicans. "Almost everybody in the South is in favor of Free Silver. The graduated income tax is nothing but common justice. . . . And who would be hurt by government control of railroads except the people whose money is invested in railroad securities?" Russell argued that government ownership of railroads was a workable scheme that would mean lower rates for everyone. "True it is that the People's party are hitting States Rights doctrines some heavy licks," he admitted, "but why should Republicans take the 'conniptions' about that? After all, the most important mission of the Republican party is to enforce the principles of broad Nationality, as taught by John Marshall and Washington and Hamilton." The Populist platform, he concluded, was a good one.[36]

If Russell's sympathetic views of Populism were not enough to infuriate stalwart Republicans, he confounded them further by urging Republican support of Populists at all levels except presidential electors and congressmen. He even vowed to "down" the Eaves faction if it

---

34 *Ibid.*, August 5, 1892. The *Signal* waged a vitriolic campaign against Eaves throughout 1892: "The Republicans for who[m] The *Signal* speaks are as much opposed to putting the negroes in control of the affairs of North Carolina as it is possible for them or the Democrats to be, and they do not intend by their votes to contribute to any such infamous result." *Ibid.*, July 21, 1892.
35 Russell to Mrs. Tourgée, June 13, 1892, in Tourgée Papers.
36 Interview with Russell, Raleigh *Signal*, August 5, 1892.

meant voting for the "Democratic state tickets . . . to smash their schemes."[37]

Russell's estimate of the potential in Republican–Populist cooperation proved correct, for the combined vote of the two parties would have defeated the Democrats. In the gubernatorial race the Democrats received only 48.3 percent of the ballots. More dramatically, Negro voting in North Carolina dropped to a post-Reconstruction low with an estimated 36 percent of black adult males not voting and an estimated 34 percent voting Democratic. The Republicans, no doubt suffering from Russell's bitter campaign, received only 27 percent of the Negro vote.[38] Shrewdly surveying the results of the 1892 election, astute politicians in the Republican and Populist parties began mapping a strategy for 1894.

The Democratic legislature of 1893 helped fuel cooperation between the agrarian radicals and the Republicans by placing severe strictures on the Alliance's charter. By 1894 talk of a Republican– Populist coalition—or "fusion" as the Democrats termed it—was a dominant note in political discussion. The question of fusion merely underscored the old rift in the Tarheel GOP between the Russell–Mott wing and the Eaves wing. As one Republican complained, "Eaves hates the Populists so bitterly that he is not even willing for them to take off votes from the Democrats in counties hopelessly Democratic."[39] To such attacks Eaves retorted: "I am still of the opinion that there is nothing for the Rep. party to gain in a Joint State ticket, and very likely much to lose."[40] As GOP state chairman, Eaves believed that local Democratic squabbles and the unpopularity of President Grover Cleveland's national administration, especially in view of the panic of 1893, insured the success of a straight Republican ticket. Fusion-minded Republicans, on the other hand, took a straightforward view of cooperation with the Populists: "We think it the only way to wrench the State from the hands of the Democrats."[41]

The Populists—under the leadership of Marion Butler, a Sampson

37 *Ibid.*, September 15, 29, 1892.
38 Kousser, *Shaping of Southern Politics*, Table 7.1, p. 183.
39 See A. E. Holton to Settle, January 24, 1894; and Richmond Pearson to Settle, January 31, 1894, in Thomas Settle Papers.
40 John B. Eaves to Richmond Pearson, March 3, April 10, May 28, 1894, in Richmond Pearson Papers, Southern Historical Collection, University of North Carolina, Chapel Hill.
41 D. W. Patrick to Schuyler S. Olds, April 19, 1894, in Settle Papers.

County legislator and editor of the Clinton (later Raleigh) *Caucasian*
—and the Republicans had much to gain by cooperating on the state
and local levels. Both parties favored electoral reforms. Since 1876 the
Democratic legislatures had ruthlessly maintained partisan election
laws that enabled Democratic registrars to disfranchise voters on the
flimsiest pretext. The election law of 1889 was particularly obnoxious,
and it had been upheld by the state supreme court in *Harris v. Scar-
borough* (1893). The court ruled that persons who gave indefinite information to registrars concerning their places of birth could be denied
the right to vote. As noted earlier, the Democrats had also centralized
the county governments in the hands of the legislature thereby nullify-
ing home rule. Other issues that the Populists and Republicans could
agree upon included larger appropriations for public schools and a
nonpartisan supreme court.[42] Marion Butler told one Republican
bluntly: "If those who are opposed to the election methods of the Democratic hypocrisy & incompetency at Washington do not concentrate
their strength to redeem North Carolina . . . this year they will be
guilty of [a] folly that will be little less than a crime. . . . Ballot reform
should be made the rallying cry for the present fight." After electoral
reform, Butler argued, "other measures & methods of reform & relief"
could be enacted.[43]

The Republican and Populist fusionists in 1894 overcame the
straight-ticket wings of their respective parties, combined their state
and county tickets, and won a resounding victory over the Democrats.
State issues were emphasized and sharp differences on national economic policies and currency reform were shunted aside. With an
impregnable majority in the legislature, the fusionists set about dis-
mantling many of the laws that had been enacted by the Bourbon
Democrats. The fusionists sent Populist Marion Butler to the United
States Senate for a full six-year term and Republican Jeter C. Pritchard
was named to complete the two-year term left vacant by the death of
Zebulon Vance. In a sweeping reform program, the fusionist-controlled
legislature returned home rule to the counties, set the legal rate of in-

42 Joseph F. Steelman, "Republican Party Strategists and the Issue of Fusion with Populists in
    North Carolina, 1893–1894," *North Carolina Historical Review*, XLVII (1970), 254–55;
    Edmonds, *Negro and Fusion*, 35–36.
43 Marion Butler to Richmond Pearson, January 22, February 19, May 17, June 12, 18, 25,
    1894, in Pearson Papers.

terest per annum at 6 percent, substantially increased state appropriations for public schools from the elementary to the college level, augu-
mented expenditures for state charitable and penal institutions, and
showed a willingness to raise taxes on railroads and businesses. Most
importantly, the fusionists adopted a new election law, described by one
recent historian as "probably the fairest and most democratic election
law in the post-Reconstruction South." The statute permitted one election judge from each party to be present when the ballots were counted,
limited the registrars' powers to disqualify voters capriciously, made
partisan challenges against voters more difficult, and helped illiterates
by allowing colored ballots and party insignia on the ballots.[44]

The fusionists had engineered a virtual revolution in North Carolina politics. Buoyed by the reforms, Daniel Russell cast an ambitious
eye toward the coming elections of 1896. Not since Reconstruction
had North Carolina elected a Republican governor. Now there was
hope for permanently ending the Bourbon Democratic hegemony with
the election of a fusionist governor who could work effectively with the
fusionist legislature. Fusion "on the State ticket and on the County
tickets in the counties where the Pops show strength," in Russell's
words, would insure the defeat of the Democrats.[45]

But not every Republican agreed with Russell. The breach in the
Tarheel GOP between straight-ticket advocates and fusionists remained deep. "I am sorry to see," one Old Guard Republican wrote
Congressman Thomas Settle, "that some good men are joining hands
with those of our party [Russell and Mott] who in the past have been
our ruin to try & lead us squarely into the populist camp & . . . by a
path that would lead to ruin in the long run."[46] Even Alfred Eugene
Holton, the state chairman who had replaced John B. Eaves in 1894
and who had originally supported fusion, feared renewed cooperation
with the Populists in 1896: "We have to make the fight to the finish
[for a straight ticket] or give up to Butler."[47] The fusion movement was
strongest in the East and West and weakest in the Piedmont. Western
Republicans, steeped in a heritage of Whiggery and Unionism, had
scant sympathy for the Negro Republicans of the East whom they

---

44 Kousser, *Shaping of Southern Politics*, 185–87; Edmonds, *Negro and Fusion*, 37–39.
45 Russell to Settle, October 15, 1895, in Settle Papers.
46 Charles A. Reynolds to Settle, September 19, 1895, *ibid*.
47 Holton to Settle, October 17, 1895, *ibid*.

blamed for saddling the party with the race issue. Like eastern white Republicans, they wished to escape the race question, and the fusion strategy apparently solved that problem while providing home rule.

With all their talk of local self-government and a free ballot and fair count, however, the fusionists could not hide the fact that their reforms expanded the Negro's potential role in the political process, as both a voter and officeholder. After the fusion victory of 1894, Russell had addressed that issue: "We do not say that the colored men shall not hold office, but we do say that office holding must be confined to those who are fit for it and who are friendly to the whites and to such limits as to show [that] our local affairs will not be controlled by the colored vote." Although he had boasted that the fusionists could "sweep North Carolina . . . without a single Negro vote," he knew that no fusionist—Republican or Populist—could afford to take that gamble.[48]

Thus, with the approach of the 1896 election a number of tantalizing questions confronted the fusionists. What direction would the Democratic party take, since it was badly split between the conservative goldbug and the free-silver factions? Would the Populists, who saw themselves as the party that would supplant the Democrats nationally, be willing to cooperate once more? With the election of a president in the offing, could Populists and Republicans ignore national differences and simply focus on state issues? And what of the Negro electorate in North Carolina? Having shunned both the Republicans and Populists in 1892, would it contribute essential support to the fusionists despite the lily-white rhetoric of leaders like Russell and Butler? To all these questions Daniel Russell believed he held the answers.

---

48 Raleigh *National Outlook*, April 10, 1896. The *Outlook* was a black newspaper edited by R. H. W. Leak.

Chapter IV

"Free Thought, Free Speech, and Free Ballots"
North Carolina's Election of 1896

THE NORTH CAROLINA election of 1896 stands out as one of the most important in the post-Reconstruction South. Because of electoral reforms achieved by the fusionists and the high degree of interest in the election, an astonishing 85.4 percent of the electorate turned out to vote.[1] Although the multiplicity of state and national issues no doubt confounded many North Carolinians as three different parties vied for their support, there was no uncertainty about the fusion experiment. The voters returned an overwhelmingly fusionist legislature to the statehouse and elected Daniel L. Russell governor. The election proved the appeal and viability of coalition politics. The Democrats, so long accustomed to winning, would not soon forget—and never forgive—Daniel Russell and the fusionists. But their revenge lay several years in the future.

The road to the governor's mansion was an arduous one for Russell. At the outset of the campaign the Republican party remained badly divided over policies, principles, and candidates. Radical fusionists, led by Russell, favored cooperation at all levels with the Populists, including the presidential electoral ticket. They were also unabashed advocates of free silver, the popular agrarian panacea for curing the nation's economic ills with the unlimited coinage of silver in order to

---

1 J. Morgan Kousser, *The Shaping of Southern Politics: Suffrage Restriction and the Establishment of the One-Party South, 1880–1910* (New Haven: Yale University Press, 1974), Table 1.5, p. 41. Voting rose seven points over the turnout in the 1892 election.

increase the money supply. The Republican Old Guard, on the other hand, demanded a straight ticket, and while recognizing the gains accomplished by fusion at the state level, abhorred the idea of cooperating with Populists on an electoral ticket or endorsing such a radical notion as free silver. John C. Dancy, a leading Negro Republican, had warned Congressman Thomas Settle as early as 1895: "You may rest assured that while we [Negroes] like co-operation, which means in North Carolina home rule and fair elections, that we can never surrender our party faith at the behest of any man or set of men in order to strengthen some party plank [free silver] that is not yet a test of party fealty."[2]

Opposed to Russell stood a trio of Piedmont Republicans—Oliver H. Dockery, Alfred Eugene Holton, and Thomas Settle. Dockery was an old-line Republican from Richmond County who had helped organize the Tarheel GOP and had served in Congress from 1867 to 1871; he had been the party's nominee for governor in 1888. Holton was the Greensboro attorney who had succeeded John B. Eaves as party chairman in 1894. Thomas Settle, elected to Congress from the Fifth Congressional District in 1892 and 1894, came from a proud old Whig–Republican family. His father, Thomas Settle, Sr., had run against Zeb Vance in the memorable gubernatorial campaign of 1876. Although the younger Settle was often approached about running for governor in 1896, it was Oliver Dockery who carried the fight against Russell for the Old Guard.

The battle between Russell and Dockery for the Republican gubernatorial nomination in the early months of 1896 shaped itself around the black electorate. Russell, who had the support of Senator Jeter C. Pritchard, expected strong backing from the western counties where Pritchard was organizing for a fusionist fight. Dockery could depend on carrying the Piedmont counties where business and industry were taking root and where Republicanism did not necessarily carry the stigma of Reconstruction. Thus the eastern counties, especially the black ones, were pivotal, and that presaged trouble for Russell. His blunt calls for limitations on officeholding by Negroes since 1888 had alienated some powerful leaders in the black community, though he had potent black allies as well.

2   J. C. Dancy to Settle, October 31, 1895, in Thomas Settle Papers, Southern Historical Collection, University of North Carolina, Chapel Hill.

The schism in the Afro-American community reflected both the rifts among white Republicans and the philosophical differences among Negro leaders. In general these leaders were professional men or tradesmen who belonged to the black middle class and took an active role in black social organizations. In varying degrees they displayed a sense of race pride. During the campaign of 1892, Maurice N. Corbett, a black politician from Caswell County, explained to Thomas Settle that the Negro community could no longer afford to support candidates opposed to "Afro American *political* equality." Blacks could not quietly follow the GOP when their "brethren" were being lynched with "no howl against it. . . . We have followed blindly the leadership of Mott and Judge Russell," complained Corbett, "and now we find them the worst enemies the negro has had in the state, having used their utmost influence against the appointment of any colored men . . . to positions in the state."[3]

Acutely sensitive to the charges of GOP leaders like Russell, yet wary of the Democrats, Negro Republicans sought a secure status in the community with protection from violence and prejudice. They looked to certain white leaders for that security and to politics for the cues and symbols that would inform both blacks and whites of the Negro's status. Populism challenged the status quo in the Negro community no less than in the white, and schisms developed among black leaders as they argued about which political strategy could most effectively safeguard the Negro's interests.[4]

Conservative black leaders such as former congressman Henry P. Cheatham and John C. Dancy distrusted the Populists and opposed fusion in 1896. They preferred traditional Republicanism, a straight ticket, and friendly bonds with the white upper classes. Dancy, editor of several black periodicals in the 1880s and 1890s and customs collector at Wilmington under President Benjamin Harrison from 1889 to 1893, argued that the Negro's interests were best served when the black community aligned with plutocrats and aristocrats rather than with poor whites and hayseeds. Upper-class whites remained "for the

3   Maurice Corbett to Settle, July 22, 1892, *ibid.*
4   See William H. Chafe, "The Negro and Populism: A Kansas Case Study," *Journal of Southern History*, XXXIV (1968); and Dorothy A. Gay, "Crisis of Identity: The Negro Community in Raleigh, 1890–1900," *North Carolina Historical Review*, L (1973).

most part defenders and respecters of the law, and the reign of the law, rather than of the mob," whereas lynchers and mobs were "made up chiefly of the class who were once the overseers and patrols of lowly birth and lowlier instincts."[5] Essentially accommodationists, these conservatives feared that fusion would undercut their status within the Republican party and the status of blacks in society at large. They perceived a danger to interracial cooperation if a coalition should be forged between Negro Republicans and embattled agrarian radicals. If the Democrats resurrected the racial antipathies of Reconstruction to break such an alliance, the Negro community, they reasoned, stood to lose most. Above all they resented Daniel Russell's racial insults.

Arrayed against the conservatives were the black fusionists, for whom Negro political rights were a principal concern. The leader of the fusionist faction, James H. Young, was a radical free-silver Republican, a state assemblyman from Wake County, and editor of the Raleigh *Gazette*. Another, George H. White of Edgecombe County, though indifferent toward free silver eagerly wished to challenge Cheatham for the congressional nomination in the Second District. For men such as Young and White (who was to leave North Carolina in 1901 and attempt to build an all-Negro town in New Jersey), politics was more than a means of protecting the Negro from prejudice and violence. It was a means of racial uplift, and thus played an active, not a passive, role. Indeed, Young, the most articulate spokesman for the black fusionists, associated the electoral and county government reforms of the fusionists with what he termed black liberation. Black fusionists thus tended to disregard the lily-white rhetoric of Republicans like Russell. For the pragmatic Young, political alternatives in North Carolina were stark, for although he admitted that blacks had grievances against certain Republicans, the GOP at least permitted Negroes "to vote and scuffle" for office. The Democratic party, Young warned prophetically, "not only denies our right to hold office but wants to take away . . . the privilege of voting."[6] Terming the Populists friends, an-

---

5   John C. Dancy (ed.), *African Methodist Episcopal Zion Church Quarterly Review* (April, 1894), North Carolina Collection, University of North Carolina, Chapel Hill.
6   Raleigh *Gazette*, January 2, November 20, 1897.

other black fusionist contended: "The colored people desire a free vote and fair count in every county and especially in all the eastern counties where there are no white Republicans to stand up and aid the colored men in enforcing their rights at the ballot box."[7] Fusion, then, had a strong appeal to a significant portion of the Negro community.

By the early months of 1896, Negro Republicans were sedulously combing the eastern counties to organize the black electorate for their respective candidates. John C. Dancy and Reverend R. H. W. Leak of St. Paul's African Methodist Episcopal Church in Raleigh, launched the Dockery campaign in the black counties, while James H. Young led the Russell forces. At the annual meeting of the Emancipation Association in January, 1896, Young and Leak, who had been feuding since the election of 1894, called for "harmony and good feeling among the leaders of the negro race." But the breach among black leaders remained deep, dividing the Negro community, according to one account, between black Methodists and the professors at Shaw and St. Augustine colleges led by Leak, and on the other side the Negro Baptists led by Young.[8]

White Republicans depended heavily on the canvassing efforts of their black colleagues and supplied necessary travel expenses. A. E. Holton admitted privately that Leak had to be financially "taken care of if all else stops," for he and John Dancy were good "husters." Henry Cheatham confidently reported to Thomas Settle that "Russell & James H. Young have put three candidates in the field against me—but my friends say I am stronger than all of their forces." He promised to "capture the 'East'" for Dockery and a straight electoral ticket and to thwart Russell and fusion.[9]

In Raleigh the energetic Leak organized the North Carolina Negro Press Association, and at a convention attended by some thirty-five black editors representing twenty newspapers, the Dockery forces were in full evidence. Holton and several members of the Dockery family were present to hear Leak assert that all but two of the black

7 Raleigh *Signal*, September 22, 1892.
8 R. H. W. Leak to Settle, January 8, 1896, Dancy to Settle, January 16, 1896, in Settle Papers; Raleigh *News and Observer*, January 3, 1896.
9 Holton to Settle, January 17, March 8, 1896, Cheatham to Settle, February 6, 1896, Dancy to Settle, February 3, 1896, in Settle Papers.

newspapers "are with us & indorse our course." Young's support, he believed, was evaporating daily.[10]

Despite glowing reports from Dancy, Cheatham, Leak, and others that they were sweeping the East for Dockery and no fusion, other Negro Republicans were more cautious in their assessment and cited the treacherous influence of Young. James E. Shepard, a Durham druggist and future president of North Carolina College in Durham, warned that "negro democrats & disgruntled white republicans" were effectively organizing for Russell. A black politician from Edgecombe County confirmed Shepard's fear. William Lee Person declared, "Every white man I have met in the East that takes any part in Politics is for Russell."[11] Russell's record on Negro officeholding obviously helped him among some white voters in the eastern counties.

The tactics used by the Russell forces in the black districts capitalized upon painful memories of slavery and sometimes generated racial tensions. One dramatic device was a "negro sale." At a political meeting a white Republican, resurrecting memories of slavery and secession, "took a big black fellow set him on a block and auctioned him off @ $1500." The gimmick worked, for the Negroes reportedly "went wild and swore they would lynch any negro that voted the Democratic ticket."[12]

Within the Republican party racial tensions also intensified. When Russell supporters charged that Leak and Dancy were holding bogus county conventions in the East to which white Republicans were not invited, pro-Dockery blacks responded bitterly. Declaring themselves to be "the rank and file of the party in this section," they argued that

10 Leak to Settle, February 10, 1896, *ibid.*; Raleigh *News and Observer*, February 6, 7, 1896; Charlotte *Observer*, February 8, 1896. The two dissident papers were probably Young's *Gazette* and the Laurinburg *Post*, edited by N. F. McEachin, who declared to Russell that his journal was "one of the colored newspapers that stood firmly by you when many others were strong in their efforts to divide the colored population in the state." N. F. McEachin to Russell, April 26, 1897, in Executive Papers of Daniel L. Russell, North Carolina Division of Archives and History, Raleigh, hereinafter cited as Governor's Papers. Among those Negro journals opposing Russell were Leak's Raleigh *Outlook*; the Maxton *Blade*, edited by Robert B. Russell; the Wilmington *Sentinel*, edited by Armond W. Scott; and the Durham *Safe Guard*, edited by James E. Shepard.
11 W. L. Person to Settle, February 15, March 28, 1896, Shepard to Settle, March 10, 1896, Dancy to Settle, February 3, March 2, March 11, 1896, in Settle Papers.
12 J. R. Henderson to Russell, May 21, 1896, in the Daniel L. Russell Papers, Southern Historical Collection, University of North Carolina, Chapel Hill.

those white Republicans who did not attend had "deserted the Republican party and joined the Populist party at its first advent . . . to get rid of the 'niggers'." According to one black spokesman, "There are many colored Republicans who have some following in this part of the State who would not support Russell if he should get the nomination."[13]

Despite his former pronouncements on the essentially unfit character of many Negro voters, Russell himself found it politically expedient to woo the black electorate. Speaking in Raleigh, he defended fusion and emphasized the electoral reforms enacted by the fusionist legislature. He vowed that he supported the Populists not because they "stood for our financial views, but for our liberties," and he asserted: "We [Republicans] were disfranchised. I was as much disfranchised as any negro on my rice plantation, and I am as much under obligation to [the Populists] for my liberty as the negroes in slavery were to the Grand Army of the Republic."[14] Russell continued: "The Populists and Republicans stand together on State issues and the law of self-preservation demands co-operation between them. . . . Free thought, free speech, and free ballots are worth more than free silver." He even tried to excuse his previous attacks on Negro citizenship by explaining that he had not called all Negroes savages, but had asserted that "there were black savages and white savages."[15]

At the Dockery rallies Shepard insisted that "no self-respecting negro" could ever vote for Russell, and in one instance he cunningly engaged in some political skullduggery by packing a Russell rally in Durham with Leak's "gang" and capturing it completely for Dockery.[16] The Reverend C. H. King of Greensboro, at another meeting, denounced fusion and stated that he liked even Democrats better than "that little runt Populist party . . . because he could always tell where to find the Democrats, but you never know where to find a Populist."[17] But Dr. Lawson A. Scruggs, a Negro physician from Southern Pines, spoke most plainly for conservative blacks who wished to protect the Negroes' status. He protested the effort being made to "array the black man against the white man" in an "unwise and damnable" attempt to

13   Winston *Union-Republican*, March 19, April 2, 1896.
14   Raleigh *News and Observer*, April 17, 1896.
15   Charlotte *Observer*, April 29, 1896; Raleigh *News and Observer*, April 30, 1896.
16   Shepard to Settle, March 23, March 26, 1896, J. M. Hornaday to W. C. Hornaday, April 1, 1896, in Settle Papers; Raleigh *News and Observer*, March 28, 1896.
17   Raleigh *News and Observer*, May 1, 1896.

nominate Russell. Such "inflammatory political harangues" as those delivered by Russell only prejudiced one race against the other and endangered the Negro's interests. Interracial harmony, in Scruggs' opinion, meant stability and security.[18]

The internecine warfare raging in the Republican party tended to obscure the question of whether the Populists would even be willing to cooperate with the GOP. They were cannily biding their time, and Populist Senator Marion Butler was not convinced that cooperation was either necessary or desirable. He feared the GOP was trying to force cooperation on terms that would demoralize and disrupt the People's party. After 1894, Butler and many other Populists had viewed theirs as a growing national party, dedicated to financial reforms, and prepared to supplant the Democrats. They hoped the Democrats of the 1890s were doomed to disintegrate as the Whigs had in the 1850s. Consequently, in the 1896 elections Butler wanted to make the fight along lines of principle in order to attract reformers from the old parties. Since free silver was to be the bridge to the Populists' first national victory, the sharpest line had to be drawn on this money question. In other words, national issues could not be divorced from state issues during a presidential election.[19]

Butler maintained that the Republicans posed a greater threat to the Populist party than did the Democrats, for the former—led by Russell—proposed to split the electoral ticket. The effect of such a division might result in a ticket containing gold standard advocates as well as free silver partisans. Rather than accept that risk, Butler favored putting up an "Independent Electoral ticket, pledged not to vote for any gold man for President." Any other course might destroy the People's party. "There has been a general understanding that we should co-operate," confessed Butler, "but there has been no understanding that we should co-operate on whatever terms the Republicans might name without consulting us." In his opinion, there would be no fusion until a "full and frank conference" had been held by Populists and Republicans.[20]

---

18   *Ibid.*
19   Marion Butler to John A. Sims, February 17, 1896, in Marion Butler Papers, Southern Historical Collection, University of North Carolina, Chapel Hill; Robert F. Durden, *The Climax of Populism: The Election of 1896* (Lexington: University of Kentucky Press, 1965), 8–13.
20   Marion Butler to Sims, February 17, 1896, in Butler Papers.

Such a conference met in Raleigh on April 16 and 17, 1896, and representatives from the Populist and Republican state committees negotiated at great length. Reportedly neither side would surrender the governorship; each wanted to name the governor on a fusion ticket. In addition the Republicans apparently received no guarantee that the Populists would support the reelection of Senator Pritchard in 1897. The Populists, moreover, insisted that the GOP nominate only free silver candidates and agree to an independent electoral ticket. Hopelessly deadlocked, the conference disbanded.[21]

The failure of the conference disheartened the Russell faction, but Dockery forces were pleased if not jubilant. Russell, who had taken part in the negotiations, issued a statement to the Republican faithful: "I want to say to all Republican friends of fusion, be not discouraged. Do not listen to the false clamor of enemies of fusion in our own party nor to the big brag of the Democratic press. Presidential fusion is not important. State and county fusion we can get, and will have it, if its real friends in our party will keep cool, control their tempers and hold level heads." He urged the rank and file to send "the real friends of cooperation" to the state convention.[22]

Meanwhile, the Populists, who believed that the "fight going on between Russell & Dockery and the general scramble" among Republicans helped to unite free silver forces, also speculated about possible support from the black electorate.[23] In Dockery's home county, Richmond, the blacks were reportedly "split all to pieces and 4 to 1 say they will vote for silver and they say they will go in to the P. P. [People's party] convention that they are dun with the old Rep. party."[24] But other Populists, especially in the black belt, were less certain. Abram J. Moye, a Populist from Pitt County, desperately urged Senator Butler to cooperate with the Republicans, on the grounds that fusion was a necessity east of Raleigh to prevent massive Negro officeholding. "We can't even afford to cooperate with the so called Silver Democrats," Moye cautioned, "for if we do we will loose [sic] all of our negro allies

---

21 Charlotte *Observer*, April 19, 1896.
22 *Ibid.*
23 W. A. Guthrie to Marion Butler, April 30, 1896, in Butler Papers.
24 Y. C. Morton to Marion Butler, April 30, 1896, *ibid.* For rumors of a black defection to the Populist party, see the Raleigh *Caucasian*, March 19, 26, April 30, May 14, June 18, and July 9, 1896. Also see Shepard to Settle, April 7, 1896, W. E. Clarke to Settle, June 26, 1896, in Settle Papers.

and the Republicans will carry the state." Without fusion his township would vote Republican and elect a Negro constable and three magistrates, at least two Negro county commissioners, and a Negro or a Democratic state assemblyman.[25]

Fusion, then, appealed to different factions for different reasons. If it restored home rule to the counties and provided a fairer election law, it also increased Negro political activity. Black and white perceptions of self-interest in supporting fusion contrasted sharply. For the Negro, it presented a new, expanded political role. For the white Populist and Republican in the East, it was a route to power which utilized the Negro vote without risking Negro rule.

Still the Republican Old Guard resisted. When Russell declared that "everybody is for free silver," A. E. Holton demurred and asserted that the GOP would never adopt such a position. He hinted that the "extreme fusion element in the party" really contained Populists in sheep's clothing. Perhaps Russell wanted to be classed as a Populist because of his frank espousal of fusion and free silver. If so, Holton hoped the Populists would nominate him for governor.[26]

Battle-scarred but emotionally charged by the Dockery-Russell struggle, the Republican state convention assembled in Raleigh on May 14, 1896. Clearly neither the Dockery nor the Russell faction had achieved a commanding lead, and the decisions of the credentials committee promised to decide the nomination. Ten counties had each sent two delegations, and the committee had to judge which delegates would be seated. After deliberating the entire night, the credentials committee offered majority and minority reports. The majority called for eighteen delegates pledged to Dockery and sixteen pledged to Russell. The minority report recommended seating thirty Russell delegates and only four Dockery designates. When delegates backing several minor candidates combined forces with Russell's supporters to adopt the minority report, Dockery's chances for nomination on the first ballot dissipated. The bitterness generated by that decision set the tone for the entire convention.[27]

---

25 A. J. Moye to Marion Butler, April 30, 1896, in Butler Papers.
26 Charlotte *Observer*, May 3, 1896.
27 The account of the GOP state convention is taken from the Raleigh *Caucasian*, May 21, 1896; the Raleigh *News and Observer*, May 16, 17, 1896; and the Charlotte *Observer*, May 16, 1896.

With tempers at a fever pitch the nominations began. Shepard and Dancy made seconding speeches for Dockery, while one Russell supporter declared, "I want Russell because the Democrats don't want him. The negroes want him." James Young made a passionate appeal for Russell and quoted the renowned Negro churchman, Bishop Henry M. Turner of Georgia, as saying, "I wish we could get nine Russells on the Supreme Court bench. He is the only judge who ever sat upon the bench who had the courage and audacity (I take back the word audacity) to say that the Constitution doesn't know the difference between the colored man or white man. If you nominate Russell, fusion is assured." Russell won the nomination on the seventh ballot. Senator Pritchard, supposedly the absolute master of the convention, had kept the fusionist forces in line for Russell as Dockery's strength eroded.

Russell's acceptance speech was a studied attempt to conciliate Negro Republicans. Although he made appropriate references to his desire for fusion, a protective tariff, and a stronger central government, his main thrust appeared to be aimed at embittered blacks who had supported Dockery. By now a man of nearly 300 pounds, Russell humbly announced: "I entertain a sentiment of deep gratitude to the negroes. . . . I stand for the negroes' rights and liberties. I sucked at the breast of a negro woman. I judge from the adult development, that the milk must have been nutritious and plentiful. The negroes do not want control. They only demand, and they ought to have it, every right a white man has." A spirit of old Republican principle and Whiggish paternalism marked his words, but his pleas for conciliation fell on many deaf ears.

Among white Republicans displeased by the nomination, Oliver Dockery merely stated that he was not bitter. But one disgruntled delegate slyly observed: "Russell is so fond of minority reports that we intend to give him one from Halifax in November." An obscure group of lily-white Republicans were said to be "annoyed at the result of the convention, as they hoped to see the campaign made on protection, sound money and white supremacy."[28] But Judge Hamilton G. Ewart, who had supported Dockery, defended Russell. He scoffed at rumors of a Negro bolt from the party and promised, "Russell will poll as many negro votes as is generally given the Republican ticket."[29]

28   Charlotte *Observer*, May 17, 1896.
29   Raleigh *Times*, n.d., in Russell Scrapbooks, North Carolina Collection, University of North Carolina, Chapel Hill.

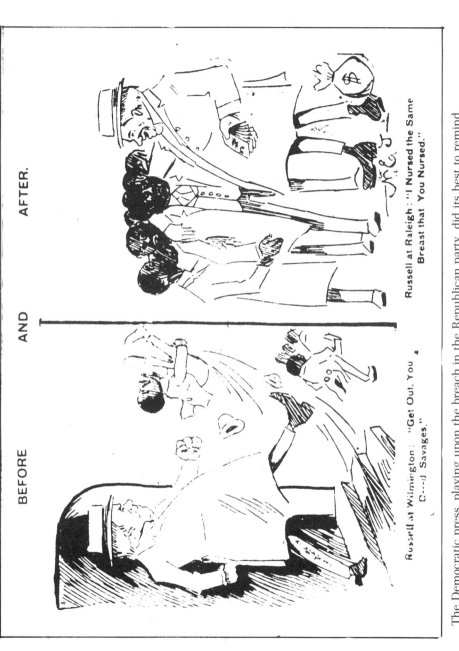

BEFORE

AND

AFTER.

Russell at Wilmington: "Get Out, You
C---d Savages."

Russell at Raleigh: "I Nursed the Same
Breast that You Nursed."

The Democratic press, playing upon the breach in the Republican party, did its best to remind Afro-Americans that in past campaigns Russell had questioned the blacks' fitness for office-holding. This cartoon by N. E. Jennett appeared May 17, 1896, in the Raleigh *News and Observer*.

THE BAD BOY MUST COME DOWN.

Rev. Leak Thinks Stealing a Nomination as Bad as Stealing Apples.

An old man found a rude boy up one of his trees stealing apples, and desired him to come down; but the young sauce-box told him plainly he would not. "Won't you?" said the old man; "then I will fetch you down," so he pulled up some turf of grass and threw at him; but this only made the youngster laugh to think the old man should pretend to beat him down from the tree with grass only.

"Well, well," said the old man, "if neither words nor grass will do I must try what virtue there is in stones;" so the old man pelted him heartily with stones.—From Webster's Blue Back Spelling Book.

Russell moved rapidly to heal the wounds of his party by defending his record. As one Populist warned him, his election and the fusionist cause were jeopardized unless he reconciled the factions in the Republican ranks.[30] Russell insisted that he had always supported the Republican ticket despite differences in policy and strategy in 1888 and 1892, but many stalwarts questioned his claim.[31] From Senator Butler he privately received assurances that the Populists would make no final decision on fusion in the state until after the national party conventions in June and July when the political atmosphere had cleared.[32] More significantly, he published a letter designed to placate black opposition. Arguing that he had never demeaned Afro-Americans —"all that is false and baseless"—Russell asserted that his famous "Savage letter" of 1888 had contained "a truth which no intelligent person will deny, and was accompanied with expressions of friendship for that race."[33] Russell's newest paternalistic declaration no doubt merely added insult to injury, for certain Negro Republicans were already in open revolt against his candidacy.

These dissident blacks warned that the Afro-American community would work for Russell's defeat by cutting his name off the ticket. The "silent vote" of the black electorate that had "some sense of race pride and integrity" would defeat him. The Wilmington *Sentinel*, edited by a black, Armond Scott, predicted that Russell would lose by thirty thousand black votes. "Thirty years of educational facilities should have taught the negroes a degree of self-respect. We shall see how it is."[34]

Immediately after the Republican convention, a coterie of pro-Dockery blacks formulated plans to defeat Russell or force him from the ticket. "There seems to be a great deal of dissatisfaction over the nomination of Judge Russell," James Shepard confided to Thomas Settle, "and we have decided to call an independent Convention next month to consider the advisability of supporting Judge Russell or endorsing the populist nominee."[35] Maurice Corbett, another anti-Russell black, intimated to Settle that most of the pro-Dockery black leaders had joined the anti-Russell movement. "We have an organization on

30 Sims to Russell, May 26, 1896, in Russell Papers.
31 Russell to J. M. Moody, May 23, 1896, *ibid.*
32 Harry Skinner to Russell, May 29, 1896, *ibid.*
33 Winston *Union-Republican*, June 25, 1896.
34 Wilmington *Sentinel* as quoted in the Raleigh *News and Observer*, May 19, 1896. Also see *ibid.*, May 17, 1896.
35 Shepard to Settle, May 19, 1896, in Settle Papers.

foot to defeat Russell for governor," Corbett declared, "and all the leading colored men[,] with the exception of J. C. Dancy[,] who opposed his nomination are in the movement." The dissidents expected to deprive Russell of fifty thousand black votes.[36]

A June broadside by the anti-Russell blacks invited both whites and blacks to attend their convention slated for July 2 in Raleigh. It recounted Russell's former statements about Afro-Americans and added that "he foments racial strife and thereby jeopardizes our educational progress by subordinating all to corrupt politics and politicians." The convention proposed to protect the status and security of the Negro community by defeating Russell and promoting friendly relations between the races.[37]

Although they opposed fusion the pro-Dockery blacks were willing to support the Populist nominee for governor, who, it was assumed, would be the Durham attorney and former Republican, William A. Guthrie. If nothing else they expected to "put the quietus on D. L. Russell," for the "colored voters" were "determined that he shall never be governor of the state."[38] Essentially the anti-Russell movement based its campaign on race pride and appealed to the average Negro to affirm his manhood and reject Russell's insults.[39] By so doing, conservative black leaders hoped to demonstrate to "better-class" whites that the black community would not be seduced by the fusionists whose political and economic policies divided the white electorate, increased the potential power of the black electorate, and left the Negro's status perilously vulnerable to racial demagoguery.

The anti-Russell meeting of Republicans convened in Raleigh on July 2, with some forty Negroes representing sixty-five counties attending. Denying charges that the convention would join the Democrats, R. H. W. Leak censured his critics as those who "have gone further into the Democratic party than we have" and praised the assembly for speaking its sentiments without reserve.[40] Black leaders denounced

36   Corbett to Settle, May 27, 1896, *ibid.*
37   Broadside, June 6, 1896, in Butler Papers. Also see Raleigh *News and Observer*, June 17, 1896.
38   Guthrie to Marion Butler, June 7, 1896, Shepard to Marion Butler, June 22, 1896, in Butler Papers; Corbett to Settle, June 11, 1896, in Settle Papers.
39   See the Raleigh *Outlook* as quoted in Raleigh *News and Observer*, June 3, 13, 1896.
40   The account of this convention is taken from the Raleigh *News and Observer*, July 3, 1896, and Raleigh *Caucasian*, July 9, 1896.

Russell for insulting "every self-respecting colored man in the State," and William Myers, from Wilmington, bitterly assailed the nominee and other "white Republicans [who] say, 'Let the nigger talk and gas; his protestations don't amount to anything; we can buy him back again for a few dollars.'"

The convention adopted a platform and resolutions that upheld the national Republican ticket and platform. Blacks were urged to work for Russell's defeat since he was an "enemy to the public school system" and "inimical to the educational progress of the negro race." And Populist William Guthrie received the assembly's endorsement for governor despite some heated opposition from old-liners who merely wanted "to teach the machine politicians a lesson."

This movement of dissident Negro Republicans reached its apogee at the July convention; in the next few months it waned as other campaign developments weakened black opposition. But the potential mass defection of blacks from the GOP was not the only problem plaguing Russell's candidacy. Persistent reports circulated that he would withdraw from the race. Fusion remained an open question, for the Republicans had nominated a skeleton state ticket and left the path clear for the Populists to fill positions for lieutenant governor, secretary of state, state treasurer, and superintendent of public instruction. One rumor held that Guthrie would become the fusion candidate for governor, Senator Pritchard would go into William McKinley's cabinet, and Russell, "a free-silver Republican," would become the new fusion senator from North Carolina.[41]

At Russell's behest a conference of the Populist and Republican state committees met in Raleigh on July 18 to consider fusion. Russell now believed that the Populists should cooperate with the Democrats on the electoral ticket in support of free-silver candidate, William Jennings Bryan, but fuse with the Republicans at the state and local levels. The two parties continued to bicker over the governorship. One Republican complained that the Populists were "too exorbitant in their demands, insisting that we [Republicans] vote for a silver electoral ticket and in addition give them the Governor as the price of their cooper-

---

41 For rumors of Russell's withdrawal, see Charlotte *Observer*, June, 14, 28, 1896; Wheeler Martin to Russell, June 12, 1896, J. B. Fortune to Russell, July 2, 1896, in Russell Papers; Corbett to Settle, July 22, 1896, in Settle Papers.

ation."[42] Thus the conference failed to effect fusion, but when rumors again cropped up about Russell's imminent withdrawal, a Russell Republican scotched the notion by stating: "Russell is a 16 to 1 Republican, a free-silver man out and out, an enemy of trusts and monopolies and a true friend to the Populists."[43]

After a series of complicated maneuvers, including the nomination of Oliver Dockery for lieutenant governor by the Populists, a fusion agreement was hammered out in a September meeting. Guthrie had received the Populist nod for governor, and according to Hal Ayer, Populist state chairman, he was to remain on the fusion slate because of a purported "tacit understanding that Russell will come off the ticket in a short time." In return Dockery would withdraw in favor of a Republican nominee for lieutenant governor, Charles A. Reynolds. On the congressional ticket the fusionists put up four Republicans and five Populists, and most importantly the two parties combined their county tickets in order to win control of the legislature.[44]

The Populists, who distrusted the large Negro element of the Republican party, decided to cooperate in order to defeat "the arrogant and hypocritical Democracy" while checking "any wild or reckless plan that might be advocated by the Republican party." The fusionists, as Ayer explained to the Populist party, quite simply wanted to beat the Democrats in order to "preserve the present election law, the county government system, the present school system, the six per cent law and other reforms which the people demanded and secured two years ago."[45] One crucial question remained: how soon, if at all, would Russell withdraw?

Republicans admitted that Russell did not want to come off the ticket, but at least one thought that "when properly pressed he will yield."[46] The Populist nominee, William Guthrie, doubted that Russell would ever withdraw. Guthrie opposed fusion and felt the Republicans had been "trifling with us all along and [that] Russell and his crowd never had any real serious idea of supporting me on the State ticket."[47]

42   J. C. Pritchard to Russell, July 12, 1896, Richmond Pearson to Russell, July 22, 1896, in Russell Papers.
43   Charlotte *Observer*, July 18, 19, 1896.
44   Hal Ayer to Marion Butler, September 11, 1896, in Butler Papers; Raleigh *Caucasian*, September 10, 1896; Raleigh *News and Observer*, September 11, 1896.
45   Circular letter by Ayer, n.d., (*circa* September, 1896), in Butler Papers.
46   J. W. Shook to Marion Butler, September 3, 4, 13, 1896, *ibid.*
47   Guthrie to Marion Butler, September 4, 13, 1896, *ibid.*

Then, in a dramatic private meeting between Guthrie and Russell, the Republican nominee assured his Populist counterpart that he would not withdraw under any circumstances—that he would "run the race to its finish." When pressured about the purported terms of cooperation, namely his withdrawal, the cagey old judge replied that "he had *heard* of such a thing himself before but . . . nothing of that kind met his own approval."[48]

The governorship thus became a three-cornered race involving Russell, Guthrie, and Cyrus Watson, the Democratic nominee. Guthrie and Watson made a joint canvass that soon turned into a sweetheart campaign for William Jennings Bryan—presidential candidate of both the Populist and Democratic parties—and free silver; state issues were ignored. Guthrie's behavior quickly alarmed and disgusted Populists and Republicans alike.[49] Russell refused to participate in any debates. According to Oliver Dockery, who was still running for lieutenant governor on the Populist ticket, the "Russell plan" was to avoid joint discussions in order to prevent the "Democrats from reaching the crowds & thereby holding the negroes solid." Russell, however, explained that he had not consented to joint debates because in the past Democrats had been known to howl down Republican speakers. Furthermore, he cautioned, in the eastern counties there continued the danger of stirring up race trouble.[50]

Nevertheless, Russell vigorously took to the stump. The old Whig delighted in calling the Democratic party the "war party" that had stood for slavery, nullification, secession, and Jeff Davis. Terming the Tarheel Democrats a "fraudulent, disfranchising Democratic machine," Russell blamed President Grover Cleveland for the depression and accused the Democrats of trying to swallow the Populists by stealing their platform and endorsing free silver. On national issues, he candidly favored free silver but a Republican protective tariff. On state matters, he stressed the accomplishments of fusion and urged cooperation between Republicans and Populists.[51]

Russell also sought to defuse the race issue. In Charlotte he observed: "The Democrats are now cursing out McKinleyism, Russellism

48 Guthrie to Marion Butler, September 26, 1896, *ibid.*
49 Ayer to Marion Butler, October 6, 1896, Shook to Marion Butler, September 18, 1896, *ibid.*
50 Charlotte *Observer*, October 14, 1896.
51 *Ibid.*; A. C. Lehman to Russell, October 5, 1896, in Russell Scrapbooks.

and negroism. Years ago they . . . said that Russell was a Republican hating negroes and now they are trying to prove that he is in favor of negro supremacy." Denying that he supported "anything like we had in reconstruction days," Russell discounted any "negro problem" in North Carolina. "The negro does not want on top," he asserted. "All he wants is his rights and his just protection." Fusionists stood for the Negro's political rights, the Democrats for disfranchisement. If elected, Russell pledged to "protect men and their property" in contrast to other southern states that "quit raising cotton and corn . . . and went to raising hell."[52]

By October, 1896, nervous Populists and Democrats conceded that Russell was the frontrunner. The Republican party had largely united behind him. Republican stalwarts who had "little use for a Democrat & possibly less for a populist" had forgotten "the mistakes at Raleigh & wheel[ed] into line . . . [to] vote a good, solid Republican ticket." Many agrarian radicals frankly declared that they, too, would vote for the Republican nominee. "There are many Pops," reported one Populist leader, "that say they do not want to take any chances about letting the Dems get back so they will vote for Russell." Even some silver Democrats found Russell's candidacy "a blessed alternative."[53]

More importantly, Republican organization at the grassroots level, especially in the black community, had insured a large turnout at the polls. One stalwart reported that white Republicans had worked "hard and heavy . . . drilling the negroes . . . in your [Russell's] favor." In Rockingham where the Negroes "to a man" and most of the white Republican leaders supported Russell, a large white McKinley and Russell Club was formed. Populist tacticians despaired that the Negro vote would go solidly for Russell.[54]

The Republicans had taken full advantage of the new election statute. The Democrats charged that Populists in the black counties were appointing black registrars and judges who were really Republicans. But Populists were equally displeased with Republican utilization of

---

52   Charlotte *Observer*, October 16, 1896.
53   Reynolds to Russell, July 16, 1896, in Russell Papers; W. H. Worth to Marion Butler, October 8, 1896, O. H. Dockery to Marion Butler, October 22, 1896, W. S. Pearson to Marion Butler, June 20, 1896, in Butler Papers.
54   F. M. McDuffie to Russell, September 1, 1896, W. R. Terry to Russell, July 11, 1896, in Russell Papers; Ayer to Marion Butler, October 6, 1896, B. F. Keith to Marion Butler, October 13, 1896, in Butler Papers.

the new law. A Populist leader in Halifax County, heart of the black belt, detected a plan by the GOP managers to use "local fusion . . . to influence our people in getting out a full Republican registration & thereby secure a full & solid vote for State & National ticket[s]." Republican operatives were circulating throughout the eastern counties "instructing their voters & watching registration closely." When Russell had canvassed the county, he "was very particular in urging a full registration & asked many questions regarding it." Moreover, Republican registrars reported weekly to state chairman A. E. Holton on the prospects of polling a full vote. Alarmed by such aggressive activity, eastern Populists believed that the GOP was "playing a sharp game through local fusion," designed to "deceive many of our people."[55]

William Hodge Kitchin, a Halifax Democrat who had briefly flirted with Populism, concluded, "hell has broke loose in this state." He insisted that because of the "infamous election laws" as many as eight thousand unqualified Negroes had registered, although they were underage, residents of other states, or criminals. A "conservative populist like Guthrie," fulminated Kitchin, did not stand a chance since even the Populists would vote for Russell to defeat the Democrats.[56]

The Winston *Union-Republican*, organ of the Tarheel GOP, happily confirmed the Populist and Democratic allegations. It reported that the "negro vote registered so far, under the arrangement between the Populist and Republican election officers, has swollen the Republican strength enormously." The newly registered Negro vote promised to bury the Democrats in the November election[57]

Another important component of Republican organization was the role played by black fusionists under the generalship of James Young. An effective organizer and propagandist, Young ardently advanced the cause of free silver and fusion in the black community. "I am without condition or equivocation for free silver," he maintained, "and believe that if I was to go out in Wake county to talk to a crowd, all colored men, and was to begin advocating the gold standard that I would be driven from the stump." Young compared the current election to the

---

55 W. E. Fountain to Marion Butler, October 6, 1896, J. B. Lloyd to Marion Butler, October 10, 1896, in Butler Papers.
56 W. H. Kitchin to Marion Butler, n.d. (*circa* October, 1896), *ibid*. For an able analysis of Kitchin's politics, see H. Larry Ingle, "A Southern Democrat at Large: William Hodge Kitchen and the Populist Party," *North Carolina Historical Review*, XLV (1968).
57 Winston *Union-Republican*, October 15, 1896.

state campaign of 1835, remembering that the Democrats had then pledged to protect suffrage of free Negroes only to renege on the promise in the constitutional convention of the same year. A Democratic victory in 1896 would mean disfranchisement of the black electorate once again. Young's analogy no doubt struck a responsive chord inasmuch as Democrats in Mississippi and South Carolina had already disfranchised Negroes. As Young put it, the South Carolina constitution made for interesting reading in the Afro-American community of North Carolina.[58]

Even in Dockery's backyard, Richmond County, black fusionists had assumed control despite the efforts of anti-Russell blacks to sow disaffection. In late August a convention of "the most influential and leading colored men in the county" met in Rockingham to endorse candidates. Attorney W. H. Quick, an original member of the anti-Russell movement, delivered a venomous speech against the Republican nominee, but the convention nonetheless pledged its support to Russell with only a few dissenting votes.[59]

Such developments demoralized conservative black leaders. Maurice Corbett conceded to Thomas Settle that the allure of fusion and free silver, compounded with the popularity of Jim Young, had effectively quashed the anti-Russell movement. The "silverites" would carry Durham County with "seven out of ten colored voters." Indeed, dissident Negro Republicans such as James Shepard had dejectedly given up and were "simply drifting with the current." Opportunists like Young, in Corbett's view, had betrayed Republican principles and the national party in order "to capture some state plumb [*sic*]."[60]

Confronted with the prospect of a four-year reign by "Russell & his negro rulers," the panic-stricken Democratic party turned to the Populists in early October to seek cooperation. The Democrats hoped to splinter the Republican–Populist coalition on the local level and play upon the breach in the black electorate. Neither of these strategies succeeded, since the Populists refused any deal on the state level that did not include the governorship. As "bad as they hate[d] Russell," the Democrats balked and declined to remove their gubernatorial candi-

58   Raleigh *News and Observer*, July 23, 1896; Raleigh *Caucasian*, August 13, 1896.
59   Enclosure of Laurinburg *Post*, August 26, 1896, McEachin to Russell, April 26, 1897, in Governor's Papers.
60   Corbett to Settle, August 2, 1896, in Settle Papers.

date, Cyrus Watson. However, the two parties did agree on electoral fusion for the presidential ticket—just as Russell had suggested two months earlier—with the Democrats naming six electors and the Populists five.[61]

All hopes of cooperation with the Populists on the state level having evaporated, the Raleigh *News and Observer*, edited by Josephus Daniels, launched a virulently racist campaign against the Republicans and Russell in an attempt to draw Populists back into the Democratic fold. Daniels and Furnifold M. Simmons, future strategist of the Democratic white-supremacy campaigns of 1898 and 1900, revived the spectre of Reconstruction, warning that Russell's election would mean Negro domination in the eastern counties. Determined to save the state from "Russellism and its attendant evils," Daniels claimed that the Republican managers had silenced "the negro leaders who were talking for silver and against Russell." (Actually, anti-Russell blacks had consistently opposed both free silver and fusion.) "Those who six months ago confidently predicted that the nomination of Russell would split the negro vote half in two," Daniels contended, "have cause to realize that all their prophecies were false. If the negro will vote for Russell, he will do anything that Republican politicians order him to do." The black community, Simmons suggested, would vote more solidly Republican than anytime since 1868, and in that case the only defense against black solidarity was white solidarity. Otherwise, with Russell in the governor's mansion, North Carolina would suffer a traumatic return to the "negro rule" of Reconstruction.[62]

Russell well understood such Democratic tactics, and in fact early in the campaign had predicted the strategies that would be used against him. Writing a Republican colleague, he had mused: "The Democrats will try the old dodge of trying the 'Color Line' but it worries them to discover just how to do it. They have been preaching to the white people that Russell is dead against the negroes, that he favors white supremacy and that he is opposed to even the mildest form of negro government. Now they will proceed to prove that he is in favor of compelling every white woman to marry a negro, and that he, himself,

---

61 Keith to Marion Butler, October 13, 20, 1896, Ayer to Marion Butler, October 6, and n.d. (*circa* October, 1896), in Butler Papers; Raleigh *News and Observer*, October 13, 1896.
62 Raleigh *News and Observer*, October 14, 15, 17, 18, 1896.

is a mulatto. This is a rather heavy job for them, but not too big for them to attempt."[63]

Black fusionists responded sharply to the Democratic barrage. Characterizing Daniels' newspaper as a "malicious and vindictive negro-hating organ," James Young excoriated the Democratic attempt to "intimidate and bulldoze honest voters and law-abiding" citizens. No self-respecting Negro, in Young's opinion, could afford to vote against the fusionists. "If the Democrats get control of the legislature they will pass an election law that will virtually and practically disfranchise a large majority of the voters."[64]

More dramatic proof of the coalescence of the black electorate was the reversal of the Wilmington *Sentinel.* Disquieted by Democratic claims that "civilization" was at stake in North Carolina and by the Democratic press's racist campaign, the black journal endorsed Russell and declared: "Just such political stuff as this should put us all in line, and from now on we shall fight as hard for Judge Russell as we ever fought against him."[65]

The racist strategy of the Democrats in the final weeks of the campaign doubtless brought many wavering Negro Republicans back into fusionist ranks and converted some of the recalcitrant ones. Organized black opposition to Russell was no longer visible or vocal. Although black fusionists could not conceal Russell's paternalistic view of Negro citizenship, they could point to Mississippi and South Carolina—the first two southern states to disfranchise Afro-Americans—as indices of Democratic perfidy and the future direction for North Carolina if the Republican–Populist coalition collapsed. Given the narrow range of options open to black North Carolinians in 1896, a vote for fusion represented a pragmatic attempt to protect black interests. Russell, to be sure, had trod a strange path during the campaign. He illustrated the ambivalence of southern Republicans caught in the dilemma of needing black votes to win, believing in equality before the law for all races and classes, yet resenting Negro officeholding and activity in party circles. The Negro's political role, in Russell's opinion, must be limited and subject to white direction. In the end, therefore, Republican orga-

63   Russell to James H. Ramsay, May 27, 1896, in James G. Ramsay Papers, Southern Historical Collection, University of North Carolina, Chapel Hill.
64   Raleigh *Gazette*, October 31, 1896. For reaction of white fusionists, see Raleigh *Caucasian*, October 29, 1896, and Winston *Union-Republican*, October 29, 1896.
65   Wilmington *Sentinel*, October 24, 1896, as quoted in Charlotte *Observer*, October 27, 1896.

nization, Democratic demagoguery, and the popularity of fusion reforms, more than Russell himself, probably secured traditional black
votes for the GOP.

The fusionists carried North Carolina in a stunning manner. Russell received 153,787 votes to 145,266 for Democrat Cyrus Watson and
31,143 for Populist William A. Guthrie, who on the eve of the election
voluntarily withdrew from the campaign and urged white voters to
unite behind the Democrats. Russell's vote represented an increase of
57,103 over the Republican total of 1892. Black counties which had
cast 18,643 votes in 1892 delivered 33,900 in 1896, and every one of
the sixteen counties in the black belt voted Republican. Eleven black
legislators, including James Young, were elected, and George White
would represent the Second District in the next Congress. Most impressively, an estimated 59 percent of the black electorate voted for
Russell, while 20 percent cast ballots for the Democratic candidate
and 8 percent for the Populist. In other words, 87 percent of the eligible black voters had gone to the polls under the liberal election law
adopted by the fusionists. The black vote for Russell marked a thirty-
two point increase over the 1892 results and represented the highest
Negro vote for the GOP in North Carolina since 1884 when the Republicans received 74 percent of the black votes.[66]

In no other post-Reconstruction election in North Carolina had a
campaign been so freely conducted and ballots so freely cast. The general assembly in 1897 would contain seventy-two Republicans, sixty-
four Populists, one Silverite, and only thirty-three Democrats. Deci-
sively beaten, the Democrats wildly charged that 120,000 Negroes had
voted, although according to the census only 109,000 black males
were eligible. No matter; the Democrats had learned the implications
of a free electorate and free elections, and they were determined not to
allow that mistake to be repeated.

The fusionist victory seemed to signal a new day in Tarheel politics
if the tenuous coalition of Republicans and Populists could be maintained. No man understood the importance of continued cooperation
better than Daniel Russell, and perhaps no one was better suited to
conduct a fusionist administration than this old Whig-Greenbacker-

66 Helen G. Edmonds, *The Negro and Fusion Politics in North Carolina, 1894–1901* (Chapel
Hill: University of North Carolina Press, 1951), 56–60; Appendix, Table 3; p. 230–32.
Kousser, *Shaping of Southern Politics*, Table 7.1, p. 183.

Republican. Russell plainly shared as many views with the Populists as he did with the Republicans, and for his governorship to succeed, he would have to become a broker for both groups. After the muddled election Russell's ability to mold a working coalition in the general assembly would be severely tested. As one Democratic observer ominously predicted, "Chaos seems to reign in N.C. politics. It is likely to continue, for there are too many demagogues and envious persons in command of the machinery in each party."[67]

67 W. W. Fuller to A. W. Graham, November 5, 1896, in Augustus W. Graham Papers, Southern Historical Collection, University of North Carolina, Chapel Hill.

Chapter V

Russell's Shaky Base
of Power
The Collapse of
Fusion

DANIEL RUSSELL HAD not even taken the oath of office when fissures in the fusionist alliance began to appear; interparty squabbling, factional jealousies, and the fierce struggle over the reelection of Republican Senator Jeter C. Pritchard had shattered the coalition's unity. Troubled by this disintegration Russell nevertheless boldly plotted a progressive course that he hoped would cement the Republican-Populist alliance.

In the days before the general assembly of 1897 met, the governor-elect worked hard to lay the groundwork for continued cooperation. He approached key Populist leaders for their support. S. Otho Wilson, Populist member of the state railroad commission, responded to Russell's overtures: "Yes, I know your position as to the maintenance of present relations between the Pop & Rep. organizations." Wilson promised to fight any attempt at "co-operation between Pops & Dems in the Gen'l Assembly on any matters."[1]

A Republican intermediary attempted to arrange a conference between Russell and Populist Senator Marion Butler. Butler was reportedly anxious to have such a meeting, but believed it would be bad policy for the two fusion leaders to get together at that time. Nevertheless, Butler appeared "exceedingly anxious to unite with you [Russell] in all

1 Wilson to Russell, November 30, 1896, in the Daniel L. Russell Papers, Southern Historical Collection, University of North Carolina, Chapel Hill.

matters touching State Legislation." Russell "wanted it so arranged & understood that the Pops & Republicans stood together and that nothing must be done that required Democratic aid," and the Populist chieftain agreed, not wishing to hamper the new governor in any way.[2]

But even as Russell was making such proposals and receiving positive assurances, other forces were disrupting the fusionist alliance. Since early 1896, Butler's *Caucasian* had been attacking Senator Pritchard as no true friend of free silver. Aside from the silver question, the reasons for the attack were not altogether clear. In the Senate Pritchard and Butler had similar voting records, and Pritchard had never denounced free silver to espouse unequivocally a single gold standard. The pressures of presidential politics had compelled him to support the national Republican platform which ambiguously called for an international bimetallic monetary system, but he had also lent his name in the spring of 1896 to the Teller resolution, an unsuccessful attempt to tie a free-silver amendment to the Dingley tariff.[3]

But Marion Butler had been elected national chairman of the Populists in 1896, and needed to protect the independent identity and character of his party. If the Tarheel Populists were to help send a Republican to the Senate, where the gold and silver forces were closely matched, the state's party and the national chairman would certainly be embarrassed. There was also tension between Populists and Republicans in North Carolina for leadership of the fusion movement. The Republicans had won the governorship despite the Populists' assertion that there had been a "tacit understanding" to withdraw Russell; now the Populists were determined to name their own candidate for the United States Senate.

Immediately after the November election, Butler had been pressured by Democrats and Populists alike to eschew further cooperation with the Republicans and steer a middle-of-the-road course. Speaking for rural Democrats, John H. Pearson admonished: "Alliance with extreme Republican politicians like Judge Russell means giving lease to the white line [*i.e.* racism] in public discussions and distracting the

2   Marshall L. Mott to Russell, December 3, 1896, *ibid.*; Mott to Marion Butler, November 8, 1896, in Marion Butler Papers, Southern Historical Collection, University of North Carolina, Chapel Hill.
3   Carroll Leslie Pegler, "The Feasibility of Populist-Republican Fusion Re-Evaluated: Marion Butler Versus Jeter Pritchard" (M.A. thesis, George Washington University, 1966), 63–142.

people from the things which most concern them."[4] A chorus of Democrats, Populists, and even Republicans urged the Populist senator to abandon Pritchard in favor of a rock-ribbed silver candidate. John J. Mott, Russell's former ally, told Butler that the 1896 election had demonstrated the "utter worthlessness of the Republican party in the State as a distinct organization." The defeat of Pritchard and election of a true free-silver senator would forge a new party of reformers. The senatorship, in Mott's view, was the "disintegrating power, and the party to mainly disintegrate here in this State is the Republican party."[5]

The Populists themselves were divided. The "mid-roaders" wanted to keep the party's *"organization distinct."* Demanding the election of a Populist senator, they believed that the party should get "into the-middle-of-the-road . . . with a barbed wire fence on both sides of it."[6] Another faction supported cooperation with the Democrats, and the third urged continued cooperation with the Republicans. "As we fused with the Reps and got control of the legislature," reasoned J. F. Click, editor of the Hickory *Mercury*, "it seems we should work together in selecting the Senator."[7]

Faced with a party very much confused by the senatorial question, Butler quickly publicized his opposition to the election of a "gold Senator" from North Carolina. He threatened to deadlock the general assembly if a "straight silver-man" were not nominated. Butler declared that Pritchard no longer represented the "sentiments and interests of the people of North Carolina," since William Jennings Bryan, the apostle of free silver, had carried the state over William McKinley.[8]

The Republicans were outraged by the "basest ingratitude" of the Populists. "Whether the Populists," asserted the Winston *Union-Republican*, "will regard 'principle,' which now means free silver, above honor remains to be seen." The Republicans pointed to the apparent pledge Butler had made when he received the long Senate term

4 John H. Pearson to Marion Butler, November 23, 1896, in Butler Papers.
5 J. J. Mott to Marion Butler, November 10, 24, 1896, *ibid.*
6 R. L. Stroud to Marion Butler, November 7, 1896, J. B. Schulken to Marion Butler, December 2, 1896, *ibid.*; Richard B. Davis to Cyrus Thompson, in Cyrus Thompson Papers, Southern Historical Collection, University of North Carolina, Chapel Hill.
7 John Graham to Marion Butler, December 2, 1896, J. F. Click to Marion Butler, November 18, 19, 1896, in Butler Papers.
8 Raleigh *Caucasian*, November 12, 1896; Raleigh *News and Observer*, November 17, 1896.

in 1895 and Pritchard the short. Then he had "favored continuing this co-operative fight in order to show the Republicans that the Populists were not acting selfishly when they claimed the long term in this fight, for the next time we will give it to a Republican." Butler denied any such commitment by the party and explained that he had merely stated his personal opinion, not party policy.[9]

The mounting hostility between the two fusionist parties left Russell in an awkward position. While some silver Republicans believed that the new governor would stand by Butler, the Populist leader knew better. Even if he were so inclined, Russell owed too great a political debt to Pritchard to oppose his reelection. Butler admitted privately that "he had expected nothing else" from Russell.[10]

Pritchard and A. E. Holton had placed the Republicans on the defensive. The senator's plan was to secure "at least 16 true and tried Populists" in the legislature to support his reelection. Coupled with a solid Republican vote, those sixteen Populists would give him the majority he needed.[11] Even so, some Republicans believed that unless an ardent free-silver candidate like Russell, who "was really a Populist many years before the Populist party was organized," supplanted Pritchard, fusion was doomed. "For populists to elect a gold bug to the Senate from this state," insisted one Republican to Russell, "is to absolutely kill the populist party[;] if the republicans wish to do this let them succeed in forcing enough pops to vote for Pritchard, and the thing is done." Russell's senatorial candidacy might save cooperation in North Carolina, since his "sympathies . . . [were] with the people and against the plutocrats."[12]

Russell, however, would have no part in such schemes. Instead he tried to conciliate the feuding parties and sought grounds for cooperation. In a widely publicized interview, he announced his unyielding support for Pritchard but denied any rancor toward Senator Butler since the Populist leader was a strident opponent of the "Democratic

---

9   Winston *Union-Republican*, December 3, 1896; Raleigh *Caucasian*, December 24, 1896.

10   J. J. Mott to Marion Butler, November 10, 1896, in Butler Papers; M. L. Mott to Russell, December 3, 1896, in Russell Papers.

11   T. E. McCrary to James H. Ramsay, November 24, 1896, in James G. Ramsay Papers, Southern Historical Collection, University of North Carolina, Chapel Hill; Pritchard to George Z. French, November 28, 1896, in Russell Papers.

12   Raleigh *News and Observer*, November 26, 1896; A. H. Paddason to Russell, November 30, 1896, in Russell Papers.

machine." Adroitly playing upon Republican and Populist themes, Russell expressed his dissatisfaction with the gold standard but suggested that an international bimetallic system—the Republican proposal—might prove salutary if given the chance. He employed the Populist rhetoric that would characterize his administration, saying, "The money kings of the world do not want silver as standard money even on a parity with gold." A silver standard, however, might become mandatory if the present gold system continued to foster the decline of "property and labor." [13]

So far the governor-elect had spoken as a Republican with some progressive views on the money question. But Russell soon demonstrated his Populist mettle and the crusading direction he intended to take, by attacking the Southern Railway. In August, 1895, Governor Elias Carr had leased the North Carolina Railroad (NCRR) to the Southern Railway for ninety-nine years without consulting the adjourned fusionist legislature. Carr's action infuriated the Populists and other antirailroad forces who argued that the North Carolina Railroad had in effect been sold to J. Pierpont Morgan's Southern Railway without the consent of the people.

The history of the NCRR and the lease to the Southern Railway was complex. [14] The state owned three million of the four million dollars of capital stock in the NCRR. To raise that sum, the state had issued its own 6 percent bonds with the railroad stock as collateral. In 1871 the NCRR was leased to the Richmond and Danville Railroad for thirty years at the rate of 6 percent of its value. During the 1890s, however, the Richmond and Danville was racked by sensational disclosures of poor management that had led to the deterioration of the road and its value. Unable to meet its financial obligations during the panic of 1893, this line, already in receivership since 1892, appeared ready to collapse. Frantic security holders entreated J. P. Morgan of Drexel, Morgan and Company to reorganize the Richmond and Danville, Richmond Terminal, and the dozens of other associated lines that were on the verge of dissolution. Morgan accepted the assignment, thereby

---

13 Raleigh *News and Observer*, December 1, 1896.
14 Jeffrey J. Crow, "'Populism to Progressivism' in North Carolina: Governor Daniel Russell and His War on the Southern Railway Company," *The Historian*, XXXVII (August, 1975), 651–52, hereinafter cited as Crow, "Russell's War on the Southern Railway."

bringing the southern roads under the aegis of the House of Morgan and the control of northern capital and management.

The Richmond and Danville became the stem of the newly consolidated Southern Railway Company. Almost immediately, the Southern Railway undertook a program of road improvements and expansion to restore profits. Since the NCRR was the most direct route to the lower South, it figured prominently in the Southern's plans, but the lease of the road by the Richmond and Danville was due to expire in 1901. Obviously needing some assurance that it could use the road beyond that date, the Southern Railway in 1895 proposed a ninety-nine-year lease. The new rail leviathan hinted that if it did not get the lease it would build its own line to parallel the NCRR.

The directors of the NCRR had reason to fear this not-so-subtle threat. The Southern owned the roads from Greensboro to Mocksville and from Mooresville to Charlotte. By building a thirty-mile link it could parallel the NCRR from Norfolk through Danville and Greensboro to Charlotte. The North Carolina road would then lose all through traffic and much of the local as well. Under the 1871 lease, moreover, the NCRR only had to be returned in the same condition in which it had been leased. Consequently, the state stood to lose twenty-five years of improvements. So Governor Carr, the directors, and the private stockholders authorized the lease. Besides the ninety-nine-year provision, the Southern agreed to pay all taxes on the property while renting the line at 6.5 percent for the first six years and 7 percent thereafter.

In a preinauguration interview, Russell challenged the propriety and legality of the ninety-nine-year lease as well as its wisdom. He pointed out that since 1871 the state had made virtually no profit on the NCRR to help defray expenses. The money earned from the 6 percent lease to the Richmond and Danville merely paid the interest on the bonds. Now the NCRR had become a "golden link," for it tied the Southern's main stem in Virginia to thousands of miles of track to the south. Russell demanded that the state receive a larger return on its property. Addressing himself to the Southern's threat to parallel the NCRR, he declared: "They have not paralleled it and if our Legislature is equal to its duties, they will not be allowed to do it." Pledging to do all in his power to protect the state's property, the governor-elect appealed to the Populists, who had decried the lease in their 1896 platform, to support his cause. In bold fashion he urged the general assembly to cancel the ninety-nine-year lease.[15]

Russell's interview showed unmistakably his Populist temperament and earned him the agrarian radicals' respect. But it also made him suspect to many Republicans. And despite his attempts to conciliate the two parties, the breach remained as wide as ever because of the senatorial question. Commenting on Butler, Jeter Pritchard complained, "I can't understand the man. He certainly acts like he would prefer to be a democrat in the future."[16] But as one trenchant Populist observed: "There is a great deal more than simply Jeter Pritchard back of all this matter—more even than a Senatorship. Involved in this fight is the perpetuation of fusion."[17] Amid rumors that as many as twelve Populists were committed to Pritchard's reelection, the general assembly convened on January 6, 1897. In a startling move Pritchard published a letter on the same day in which he declared himself a "staunch friend of all reforms contemplated in the Populist movement" and a firm proponent of free silver. When Marion Butler demanded that all Populists in the legislature abide by the decision of the party's caucus, nineteen "Pritchard Populists" bolted and charged Butler with "gag rule."[18]

With the fusion alliance crumbling, Daniel L. Russell took the oath of office as governor of North Carolina on January 12, 1897. Relishing the irony of the moment, he began his inaugural speech by echoing Zebulon Vance's words of twenty years earlier: "There is a retribution in history." Russell called his election a victory for the "weak and oppressed" over the "entrenched battlements of prevailing privilege and lawless power," and he set forth a progressive and ambitious program of reform, declaring that his administration marked a new era of "freedom of thought, of speech and of action" in North Carolina.[19]

The new Republican governor called for a higher tax rate for support of the common schools, larger appropriations for the state university, reformatories for youthful criminals, protection of lawful public meetings, and a more efficient court system. Commending the election law of 1895 for rescuing the state from the "disgrace, degradation

15 Raleigh *News and Observer*, December 1, 1896.
16 Pritchard to Thompson, December 26, 1896, in Thompson Papers.
17 Raleigh *News and Observer*, December 22, 23, 1896.
18 *Ibid.*, January 6, 7, 1896.
19 *Public Documents of the State of North Carolina*, 1897, Doc. A., p. 3–15.

and shame of a debauched ballot," he recommended an amendment that would extend the jurisdiction of the judiciary over election officers to insure compliance with the law. In his opinion, the judiciary needed unquestioned authority over elections to prevent fraud.

In regard to Afro-Americans, Russell displayed a cautious conservatism. To combat lynching that had risen dramatically in the 1890s, he vowed to "remove the excuse for it" by expediting judicial processes. He failed to address himself to lynching as a means of extralegal social control to terrorize a black minority, asserting: "Scarcely a case of mob murder of a guilty culprit has occurred wherein he would not have been convicted by judge or jury." Futhermore, he pledged that taxpayers in municipalities would be protected from "the danger of misrule by propertyless and ignorant elements," clearly intending to limit Negro officeholding in the black counties.

The truly progressive thrust of Russell's inaugural speech came on the question of government "regulation of State and inter-state commerce by common carriers." Attesting that railroads had benefited capitalists and North Carolina alike, and with a bitter memory of the large-scale Democratic repudiation of much of the state's debt in 1879, the governor declared that his administration would "not encourage, sanction or countenance financial repudiation in any form." But railroads were also "servants of the public" and subject to governmental control. Asserting a cardinal Populist principle, Russell predicted the conversion of railroads into "public highways, owned and controlled by the nation." As governor, he promised to work closely with the railroad commission, and he urged the reduction of freight rates because of the enormous decline in the value of commodities being transported. Farmers and merchants alike would thus obtain relief.

Russell again attacked the NCRR lease to a Yankee-dominated, "foreign or non-resident corporation." Terming the lease an attempted sale, the governor urged the legislators "to adopt every and all measures within your competency, looking toward the recovery of this property for the benefit of the people and the taxpayers of the state." The reform-minded governor proposed a comprehensive law that would forbid a nonresident corporation to hold or operate a railroad in North Carolina without a license. He warned further that any charter permitting the paralleling of the North Carolina roads should be repealed. Manifesting a distinct hostility toward monopolistic practices, he also asked the lawmakers to outlaw the absorption of one railroad by another if both lines ran through the state. Competition, observed Governor Russell, engendered lower rates. Claiming that North Carolina had "broken the Solid South" to return to the "Union in fact as well as in form," the first Republican governor in more than two decades assumed his office.

That Russell enjoyed the distinction was evident. He invited Washington Duke, patriarch of the American Tobacco Company and a steadfast Republican, to stroll around the grounds of the governor's mansion with him, showing the Bourbon Democrats that a new day had arrived. The aristocratic old Whig declared to Duke: "We admit their [Bourbons'] partnership but decline to acknowledge their superiority or mastery."[20] Despite Russell's social class, his economic and political views hardly stamped him as a Bourbon.

Russell's inaugural speech was generally applauded for its "conservative" tenor and progressive stand on railroads, education, and legal reforms. Not everyone, however, would have agreed with Charles A. Cook, a close Republican ally, who declared: "He is a grand man. His address was patriotism embellished with statemanship. Today has been the grandest for North Carolina . . . in over thirty years."[21] The Wilmington *Messenger*, a longtime opponent, criticized the "old Russell ring" and "genuine partisan stamp" of the speech and called it "a sort of echo of reconstruction times." But the Democratic journal admitted that Russell, whom it had never underrated, was "the very foremost man in ability in the republican party in North Carolina."[22]

Despite the Populist hue of his inaugural address, Russell could still not rally the fusionist forces or overcome the bitter rift over the senatorship. One well-known opponent of the railroad lease anonymously chided the new governor for continuing to support Pritchard's reelection. The Farmers' Alliance and Populists were prepared to join Russell in his railroad fight, for it would "require the whole power of the Governor's friends in the Legislature, and every other resource he can bring to bear to defeat the lease." But if Pritchard were reelected

20 Russell to B. N. Duke, November 30, 1896, in Benjamin Newton Duke Papers, Duke University.

21 C. A. Cook to his wife, January 12, 1897, in Charles A. Cook Papers, Southern Historical Collection, University of North Carolina, Chapel Hill.

22 Wilmington *Messenger*, January 13, 1897.

"the lease will stand, and the Governor's pet measure will sink into nothingness."[23]

With Republican ranks holding fast and those of the Populists splintered, the general assembly reelected Jeter Pritchard to the United States Senate on January 20, 1897. Seventeen Populists had voted for the Republican and forever smashed fusionist harmony in North Carolina. Pritchard's defeat, however, might well have had the same effect. Ushering Pritchard into the legislative chambers, Russell plainly felt aggrieved to be associated with the pyrrhic victory. He voiced the hope that the silver issue would in no way impinge on state policy. Pritchard, meanwhile, promised the Populists that he would always support free silver.[24]

The deed was done. The majority Populists who had refused to vote for Pritchard held a caucus and denounced fusion as "suicidal" to the "organic existence of the People's party." The Raleigh *Tribune*, a new Republican daily newspaper, exultantly declared: "Butler and Butlerism are dead in North Carolina." Responding to the Asheville *Register*'s suggestion that with the reelection of Senator Pritchard the "time is drawing near for final amalgamation" and the absorption of the Populists into the GOP by 1900, the Raleigh *Caucasian* fulminated: "We'll be——if Populists and niggers can ever amalgamate in this State and Country. Do you hear?"[25]

Russell's whole program, which hinged inescapably on continued cooperation between Populists and Republicans, had now been seriously jeopardized. His support for Pritchard had doubtless cost him valuable Populist strength in the legislature, yet he and the agrarian radicals had much in common; both desired stricter regulation of railroads and annulment of the ninety-nine-year lease. The troubled governor set about rebuilding a viable coalition.

Soon after Pritchard's reelection, Russell met with the Populist bolters and urged them to return to the majority Populist caucus. The Republican press warily eyed his intrusion into Populist politics. The Raleigh *Tribune* suggested that he held the key to the situation in regard to continued cooperation, but noted that stalwart Republicans

23   Raleigh *News and Observer*, January 19, 1897.
24   *Ibid.*, January 21, 1897.
25   *Ibid.*; Raleigh *Tribune*, January 21, 22, 1897; Raleigh *Caucasian*, January 28, 1897.

were alarmed because "Russell is inherently a fighter . . . [who] throws prudence, politics and religion to the dogs when fighting for minority rights." The GOP preferred him to act more like a Republican and less like a fusionist. With Butler politically dead, according to the *Tribune*, the "enemy's country is not a propitious field for executive missionary work." If Russell persisted in his efforts to save the Populist party, then "his friends . . . are at a loss to know what he will do in the premises."[26]

Russell, however, could not placate the embittered Populists led by Senator Butler. Determined in his own words to quash "Mark Hanna, the World, the Flesh, and the Devil," Butler declared an end to fusion and blamed Russell for not pressuring the Republicans to uphold the terms of cooperation. He claimed the governor had pledged to "throw the whole weight of his influence and administration" behind continued cooperation to "insure the enactment of such legislation as would set aside the lease of the North Carolina railroad and effect other remedial legislation." Instead Russell had yielded to the demands of Old Guard Republicans who wanted patronage spoils distributed only to Republicans. Butler accused the Populists who had supported Pritchard of doing so in order to share the spoils from the reorganization of state institutions, that is, the appointment of Republicans and Populists to posts previously held by Democrats. And Russell was circumventing fusion to "build up a 'Russell administration party' in the State" by rewarding his friends and punishing his enemies. Butler thus vowed that Russell's course would henceforth be "in one direction and ours . . . in another."[27]

The Populist senator, however, underestimated Russell's resolve to annul the NCRR lease, an effort that obviously needed sturdy Populist support. Since early December, Russell had been personally researching the case to be made against the Southern Railway. Because he saw this war as a nonpartisan effort, he enlisted the best legal minds in the state to aid him, including Republican Charles A. Cook; Populist John Graham, president of the North Carolina Farmers' Alliance; and Democrat Alphonso C. Avery, former justice of the state supreme court. This legal brain trust drafted an omnibus bill that embodied the

26   Raleigh *Tribune*, January 26, 1897.
27   Marion Butler to his wife, January 25, 1897, Marion Butler to George Washburn, February 5, 1897, in Butler Letterbook, both in Butler Papers; Raleigh *Caucasian*, February 4, 1897.

salient points and proposals concerning the lease outlined in Russell's inaugural address.[28]

Charles Cook, as a member of the general assembly, introduced on January 29, 1897, the bill that would have fateful consequences for the 1897 legislative session and for the governor himself. As designed by Russell and his advisers, the Cook bill forbade any foreign corporation from owning or operating a railroad in North Carolina or building a parallel line without a license. Under the terms of the license, the railroad was subject to state sovereignty and barred from removing any litigation from state to federal courts; the license was also revocable at the governor's discretion—an immense power. Moreover, any nonresident railroad currently operating a line in the state had to apply for a license by May 1, 1897, or become liable to a fine of one to three thousand dollars per day. All previous charters permitting the extension or construction of track in certain specified areas were repealed. The Cook bill declared the NCRR lease to the Southern Railway Company null and void and further stipulated that open, competitive bidding for a new lease, limited to twenty years, should take place.[29]

As a sweeping reform of relations between corporations and state governments, the Cook bill rivaled similar legislation adopted elsewhere in the nation during the Populist-Progressive era. Conservative business forces were quick to recognize that threat. The Raleigh *Tribune*—which Democrats regarded as the organ of the railroads and "the tobacco trust" (the American Tobacco Company)—charged that Russell's scheme would "compel railroad companies to surrender their constitutional rights and pay for the privilege." The bill concentrated too much power in the governor's hands, declared the Republican journal, for the Southern Railway would have to "lease the road upon such terms as the Governor may impose." The more cautious Winston *Union-Republican* stated that the question of the lease should be treated solely as a "business proposition, and without party bias." But, it warned, to rescind the contract with the Southern might "check the flow of capital toward North Carolina."[30]

28 John Graham to Russell, December 9, 21, 1896, in Russell Papers; Graham to Marion Butler, (*circa* January 29, 1897), in Butler Papers.
29 Raleigh *News and Observer*, January 30, 1897.
30 Raleigh *Tribune*, January 31, 1897; Winston *Union-Republican*, January 28, February 4, 1897.

In an astounding reversal of roles, the Democratic *News and Observer* of Josephus Daniels welcomed "Governor Russell as a laborer in the contest against powerful agencies that are seeking to give away the heritage of the people to a rich syndicate." The Raleigh *Tribune*, on the other hand, became Russell's sternest critic. Believing that "a Republican Governor and a Republican newspaper may differ without in any wise compromising their devotion to the party," the Republican daily warned that capital was being frightened away from North Carolina by Russell's "revolutionary State legislation."[31] The two Raleigh newspapers continued to quarrel for the remainder of the legislature, with Daniels defending the governor's railroad bill and the *Tribune* attacking it.

Before battle lines in the general assembly could even take shape, Governor Russell, in a message to the lawmakers on February 4, revealed his exchange of letters with R. C. Hoffman, president of the Seaboard Air Line Railroad. Hoffman had written the governor on January 20 to express an interest in leasing the NCRR if the contract with the Southern Railway were annulled. Hoffman intimated that he had tried to submit a higher bid than the Southern in 1895 but that Governor Carr and the directors of the North Carolina Railroad had ignored the Seaboard's bid. Eagerly seizing upon this damning allegation, Russell had requested more specific information from Hoffman about a possible twenty-year lease.

Hoffman had replied that Russell's letter constituted the first opportunity for the Seaboard to bid for the state's property on an "equal footing" with competing lines. Noting that the NCRR had been leased at a rate he believed to be inconsistent with its true value to stockholders and taxpayers alike, Hoffman had proposed to lease the road under the terms of the Cook bill for $400,000, the equivalent of 10 percent of the railroad's capital stock.[32]

Armed with this counter offer and the hint of scandal, Russell pressed his attack on the lease. He called the lack of competitive bidding "startling," and charged that the president and directors of the NCRR might be guilty of fraud for virtually selling the state's property

---

31 Raleigh *News and Observer*, January 30, 1897; Raleigh *Tribune*, February 6, 7, 1897.
32 Raleigh *News and Observer*, February 4, 6, 1897. The Hoffman–Russell correspondence is in the Executive Papers of Daniel L. Russell, North Carolina Division of Archives and History, Raleigh, hereinafter cited as Governor's Papers.

in a ninety-nine-year lease "at a price less than was offered by responsible bidders." The governor raged: "Any Director or other Trustee who would sell or lease property belonging to his fiduciaries, when he knew that he could get a better price, would be rebuked and removed and the transaction itself vitiated by the Equity Courts." Russell did not go so far as to recommend to the lawmakers an endorsement of the Seaboard's offer, for other lines were likely to bid on a railroad that traversed such an "indispensable" route. But he did note that the increased income from such a contract could lessen taxation and augment the school fund. The proper course for the legislature, he reasoned, was to pass the Cook bill.[33]

Russell's shocking message stirred the house to hold committee hearings on the NCRR lease. Charles Cook served as committee chairman, and Alphonso Avery as the governor's counsel. For three days a parade of business, legal, and political figures appeared to state what they knew about the lease and the circumstances under which it had been negotiated. Attorneys for the Southern Railway and NCRR denied any collusion in executing it, and cast some doubt on whether Hoffman had ever genuinely bid for the NCRR. They reported that in August, 1895, two days after Southern Vice-president Alexander B. Andrews had submitted a bid, Hoffman had said that he would not bid since the Southern would probably remove the NCRR's "betterments" if it lost control of the line. Russell's lawyers argued that the lease was illegal, unconstitutional, and fraudulent. Consequently, although the hearings were sensational, they really threw little new light on the matter.[34]

They did, however, produce a final break between the governor and the Raleigh *Tribune*, which declared: "The Governor is not the whole State. . . . He stands almost alone in the matter, so far as his party is concerned—white and black." Suspiciously questioning Russell's newfound Democratic allies, notably Josephus Daniels and Alphonso Avery, the *Tribune* thundered: "There is no party principle involved in this matter, and no Republican is under obligation to support the Governor because he is a Republican Governor." Russell was playing a dangerous game, concluded one Old Guard Republican, when he consorted "with such Ishmaelites as Avery, Daniels & Co." Republican

33 *Ibid.*
34 *Ibid.*, February 7, 8, 9, 1897.

Congressman Richmond Pearson put it more bluntly: "Apparently the Populists are not wavering, but it is plain enough, in talking to them, that they see in the present agitation a movement to Russellize the Populist party in the State."[35]

The deepening rift in the Republican party, moreover, was developing a sectional dimension. The Wilmington *Messenger* perceptively reported: "The republican fight over the matter of the lease of the North Carolina railway is assuming a sort of sectional character; in other words, the Russell men in the east are against the Pritchard men in the west. Governor Russell is wrapped up in the idea of annulling the lease, while Lieutenant Governor [Charles A.] Reynolds [of Winston] is bent on having the lease stand; and so it goes all through the party."[36] This analysis gained more credence because the Seaboard Air Line Railroad controlled a number of roads in the eastern section of the state, whereas the Southern Railway owned lines cutting through the Piedmont to the west. Whichever line leased the NCRR could expect to monopolize the through traffic to the detriment of competing roads. Interestingly, Piedmont businessmen who were already chafing at the high rates charged by Yankee-dominated railroads were yet unwilling to rally to the cause of regulation—at least while the Populists and the reform-minded Republican governor espoused the cause.[37]

Few Republicans publicly stood by Russell as he assaulted the lease. One faithful ally, however, was John J. Mott, who urged the free-silver members of the legislature to annul the lease because the "chief owners of this great system, the Southern Railway, are single gold standard men."[38]

The Cook bill came before the house on February 16. Charles Cook explained that the proposed law was intended to test the validity of the lease in court, subject foreign corporations to the same conditions as state corporations, and prevent monopolies in the state. In support of the bill one Populist assemblyman defined the issue as "whether the railroads should control the people, or the people the railroads." Both Republicans and Democrats attacked the bill as "poppy-cock legisla-

---

35 Raleigh *Tribune*, February 5, 6, 7, 11, 1897.
36 Wilmington *Messenger*, February 13, 1897.
37 Crow, "Russell's War on the Southern Railway," 666–67; Joseph F. Steelman, "Edward J. Justice: Profile of a Progressive Legislator, 1899–1913," *North Carolina Historical Review*, XLVIII (1971), 148–60.
38 Raleigh *News and Observer*, February 16, 1897.

tion which slapped capitalism in the face" and arrayed "workers against capital." In the end, however, the measure narrowly passed by a vote of sixty to fifty-four. Twenty Republicans, eight Democrats, and thirty-two Populists had voted in favor, but thirty-four Republicans had resisted, since, as the Raleigh *Tribune* asserted, the bill was "populistic in theory and practice." [39]

The Cook bill's passage revealed Russell's arm-bending techniques in lobbying the legislature, as well as his famous temper. Shortly before the assembly convened, the governor met with John T. Howe, a Negro Republican legislator from New Hanover County. Howe gave this version of what happened: "Governor Russell asked me my views on the lease bill. I told him I sympathized with the Southern Railway. He walked aside and then came back at me and said, 'I don't want to talk to this G——d d——d scoundrel. He has sold out to the Southern!'" Later on the floor of the house, Howe spoke to a point of personal privilege and denounced the governor's "tyrannical" conduct. Democratic newspapers gleefully saluted the "Republican opponents of the Governor" who were determined to frustrate "the one-man power that the Governor was striking for." [40]

In less than six weeks the general assembly had ruptured into at least five factions. The thirty-three Democrats were divided on the railroad issue; the Populists were still quarreling among themselves, but with few exceptions remained united. The Republicans were bitterly split by Russell's war on the lease, and of the seventy-two in the assembly, Russell could count on the support of no more than a third. As one Republican despaired, "Old man Russell has raised Cain and split up things terribly." [41]

The fractious political situation in the legislature doubtless prevented the adoption of many progressive measures. The Populists introduced bills to lower railway, telegraph, and telephone rates and to provide for the popular election of railroad commissioners, but none of the bills passed. Two laws were enacted, however, that brought the railroads under closer government supervision. The Fellow-Servant Act made railroad companies liable for damages in the injury or death

39   Raleigh *Tribune*, February 17, 1897; Raleigh *News and Observer*, February 17, 1897.
40   Charlotte *Observer*, February 17, 1897; Wilmington *Messenger*, February 17, 1897.
41   B. C. Sharpe to Settle, February 24, 1897, in Thomas Settle Papers, Southern Historical Collection, University of North Carolina, Chapel Hill.

of an employee through a co-worker's negligence or a defect in the machinery. The lawmakers also prohibited the widespread practice of giving free railroad passes to public officials.[42]

Perhaps the most progressive new law was one promoting educational reform. In an attempt to encourage local taxation for public schools, the legislators appropriated fifty thousand dollars to be divided among those school districts that levied a special tax to support their schools. The state promised to provide a sum equal to the tax raised by any school district that voted for local taxation in a state referendum set for August. Any district that failed to approve the tax in 1897 was enjoined to hold an election every two years until the tax passed. The fusionists' achievement has often been overshadowed by the educational program of the Democratic administration that followed.

The fusionists, of course, were not opposed to a little spoilsmanship during a depression decade that followed twenty years of Democratic control. The Republicans could unite on that issue, and the Pritchard Populists obviously expected certain favors for reelecting a Republican senator. But Russell, though wishing to reform the public institutions, was not eager to turn them into political sinecures. "We found these institutions in politics," the governor contended. "They were run by one party. No consideration or recognition was given to Republicans or Populists, who constitute the majority of the people in this State."[43] As Russell explained to his good friend, Benjamin Newton Duke, his administration would prevent the public institutions "from being controlled entirely by one party and the patronage given to their pets as it has been and is."[44] The fusionists passed a number of acts altering the names of the institutions and the number of directors of each. North Carolina's mental hospitals, penitentiary, and various agricultural boards thus came under the control of the new governor.[45] How Russell used his patronage powers would say much about his perception of reform and coalition politics.

The fusionists—particularly the Republicans—also wanted to overturn Democratic "courthouse rings" in a number of eastern cities. Es-

---

42   *Private Laws of North Carolina*, 1897, Chap. 56, p. 83; *Public Laws of North Carolina*, 1897, Chap. 206, p. 347.
43   Russell to E. B. Borden, March 13, 1897, in Governor's Papers.
44   Russell to Duke, June 10, 1897, in B. N. Duke Papers.
45   *Public Laws of North Carolina*, 1897, Chap. 265, pp. 450–52; Chap. 219, pp. 361–65; Chap. 85, pp. 130–31.

pecially targeted were New Bern and Wilmington. Since Russell had promised the taxpayers of municipalities protection from misrule by the propertyless and ignorant, he sought the extraordinary executive power to appoint city aldermen. The Republicans introduced bills altering city charters to allow each municipal ward to elect one alderman and the governor to appoint one. The Democrats protested with justification that the Republicans had reneged on their own campaign slogan of home rule. They claimed further that the Republicans planned to "foist negro rule and domination" on the state. But the Republicans clearly were not interested in turning any cities over to Negro rule; quite the contrary. Negro Republicans in Wilmington denounced the plan, saying, the "negro is left out in the cold by this bill." Nevertheless, the New Bern and Wilmington municipal charters were revamped. The New Bern charter increased the number of city aldermen from five to eleven, with the voters electing one alderman in each of six wards, and the governor appointing the additional five. The Wilmington charter empowered the governor to appoint just as many aldermen as the electorate chose. The Raleigh *Tribune*, which now opposed Russell on every issue, declared: "News of the passage of the bill making the Governor literally czar of Wilmington was received with joy by administration Republicans and those termed Russell Democrats."[46]

The passage of such bills had required a solid Republican vote and help from Pritchard Populists, but it had done little to patch up the cracks in the fusionist alliance or mounting opposition to Russell in the GOP. The Cook bill, stalled in the senate, remained a source of controversy, but Russell, by all accounts, was standing firm on the bill.[47] Then on February 25, Hiram L. Grant—an old carpetbagger from Goldsboro and leader of the railroad forces in the senate—introduced a measure to supplant the Cook bill. The Grant substitute reduced the length of the 1895 lease to thirty-six years but validated the Southern's claims in all other major respects, including the 7 percent interest rate. Russell was outraged. "It simply gives the North Carolina Railroad to the Southern on its own terms," the governor argued. Not only did the Grant proposal place the Southern Railway in a more profitable posi-

---

46 Wilmington *Messenger*, February 25, 26, 1897; Raleigh *Tribune*, March 3, 1897; *Private Laws of North Carolina*, 1897, Chap. 149, pp. 280–89; Chap. 150, p. 282.

47 S. Otho Wilson to Marion Butler, February 23, 1897, in Butler Papers.

tion, but it legalized the "larceny of the people's property" while depriving them of a "voice to protest against the spoliation of their State." Calling for the bill's defeat, Russell concluded, "I suppose they [the people] are expected to be thankful and duly grateful to the money kings for allowing them to keep the old capitol and an empty treasury."[48]

In an extremely close vote of twenty-six to twenty-four, the senate adopted the Grant substitute on February 26 and returned the bill to the house for consideration. Twenty-one Populists and three Republicans had voted against the measure; all seven Democrats, fifteen Republicans, and four Populists had supported it. Two of the Populists who had voted for the bill had reportedly been seen during a recess emerging from the office of the vice-president of the Southern Railway. A switch of two votes would have changed the outcome, and Russell's mercurial temper exploded. "I would go into the penitentiary," the governor declared, "and pick out the worst criminal there, issue him a pardon, and then appoint him on the Board of Penitentiary Directors before I would appoint ... [those] scoundrel[s] ... to anything."[49] The Raleigh *Tribune*, however, applauded the apparent defeat of Russell's "populistic, communistic ... tendency to fight railroads."[50]

Russell had never stopped trying to court the majority Populists, and by the last week of the legislature he had come to realize that his disagreements with the Republicans on the railroad question were too deep and too acrimonious for him to hope to regain their confidence. In desperation the governor, who under the state constitution lacked the power to veto legislation, turned to the Butler Populists to save the Cook bill and block the Grant substitute. George Butler, a state senator, wrote his brother Marion that Russell was "now virtually a populist." The governor had approached Hal Ayer, editor of the *Caucasian*, with the urgent plea that Senator Marion Butler come immediately to Raleigh. "Russell is disgusted with his crowd," George Butler intimated, "and can control [only] three or four of his folks and he is inclined to go with us & protect us, in all future legislation."[51] Another Populist informant told Marion Butler that Russell had become a gov-

48   Raleigh *News and Observer*, February 26, 1897.
49   *Ibid.*, February 27, 28, 1897.
50   Raleigh *Tribune*, February 26, 27, 1897.
51   George Butler to Marion Butler, February 28, March 1, 1897, in Butler Papers.

crnor without a party. He had "locked horns with his people & the [Populist] bolters & wanted you . . . to arrange a new combination which Ayer thinks is of greatest importance to you & the party at this moment." But, the Populist admonished, "I believe Gov. Russell is scheming to get in [the] lead & build up a Russell party & may possibly fool our people at this critical moment."[52]

To form the nucleus of a new party that would include Butler Populists, Russell Republicans, and reform-minded Democrats, the governor had agreed to oppose the new election law endorsed by the Republican caucus, and reportedly had pledged to obtain enough Republican votes to defeat the measure.[53] The election bill, drafted by Hiram Grant, contained a number of significant changes from the statute of 1895, but one clause in particular aroused dissenting views. The 1897 proposal removed the power to appoint judges and registrars from the chairman of the state executive committee of each party to place it in the hands of a county board of elections. The new "election commission" consisted of each county's clerk of the superior court, register of deeds, and chairman of the county commissioners. In other words, the power to appoint election officers would be truly decentralized and placed at the local level.[54] In the black belt, the election machinery could conceivably fall into the hands of Afro-Americans, since home rule in the counties had meant in some instances the election of Negroes to those local offices that would constitute the election commission.

Russell announced his opposition to the Grant election bill in an interview with Daniels' *News and Observer*. The governor expressed his belief, first stated in his inaugural address, that the election law should be placed under the impartial eye of the superior and supreme courts, not under the partisan purview of party chairmen and appointed election officers. Terming the Grant plan an "unfair and dangerous" tool, Russell contended that the Populist party would be deprived "of any representation in . . . [the] election law or machinery." Thousands of "white men"—Populists—had enabled "Republicans to recover their constitutional rights and franchises." If fusion were not reinvigorated

---

52   Fountain to Marion Butler, March 2, 5, 1897, *ibid.*
53   George Butler to Marion Butler, March 1, 1897, Fountain to Marion Butler, March 2, 1897, *ibid.*
54   *Public Laws of North Carolina*, 1897, Chap. 185, pp. 311–19.

the agrarian radicals might return to the Democrats, thereby precipitating a new era of "violence and lawlessness."[55]

Russell's opposition merely reinforced Republican suspicions. The Old Guard chastised him for being a "stumbling-block to his party or a majority of it in the legislature." Grant, now feuding with the governor on two major issues, charged that Russell "was or would be the head of the populist party." Declared another Republican, "The republican prophecy that the majority populists would become the governor's supporters now comes true."[56]

The Russell and Butler men were unable to stop the adoption of the Grant election law, but their new alliance promised to produce a ferocious fight in the house over the Grant substitute. On March 5, "Hell broke loose in the House," Josephus Daniels reported. Shortly before noon, Charles Cook, who conveniently served as speaker of the day, recognized a Russell Republican who took the floor and refused to yield it. The special order for twelve o'clock was a vote on the Grant bill; the Russell forces, however, had a filibuster in mind. Prorailroad legislators yelled for recognition, but Cook refused to grant it. The session ended in complete pandemonium.[57]

The railroad forces rightfully blamed the filibuster on Governor Russell and his men, especially Charles Cook. The following day when the house met in a marathon session from early morning until midnight, the Russell forces continued their filibuster with increased vigor. In desperation one frustrated Republican accused Cook of "gag rule," to which Russell's ally boldly replied: "This is a struggle for what we believe are the interests of the people. We are going to do all we can under our parliamentary rights to represent the people."[58] The Raleigh *Tribune* scored Russell and the "revolutionists of North Carolina" for their "disgraceful" tactics and attack on the railroads.[59]

The Grant measure was tabled on March 8, both sides claiming victory. The *Tribune* pointed out that the Cook bill had been killed by Republicans; even though it was the governor's "pet measure," only twenty-three Republicans had supported it, whereas forty-nine had been opposed. Russell expressed his disappointment that the school

55 Raleigh *News and Observer*, March 3, 1897.
56 *Ibid.*, March 3, 4, 1897; Wilmington *Messenger*, March 2–5, 1897.
57 Raleigh *News and Observer*, March 6, 1897.
58 *Ibid.*, March 7, 1897.
59 Raleigh *Tribune*, March 9, 1897.

fund would not receive additional monies from a new lease, but he was also pleased that "combined capital" had failed to debauch the legislature and deliver the state to the "myrmidons of the money kings." With Populistic fervor, Russell predicted that the "assault of combined capital against popular rights" would cause North Carolinians to "settle with these alien money nabobs in 1898." Marion Butler, meanwhile, complimented the governor on his "splendid work for the People" and also vowed that the election of 1898 would settle the lease issue.[60] Russell and Butler had clearly struck a political alliance.

The general assembly of 1897 adjourned on March 9. Fusion, according to the Democratic Charlotte *Observer*, had been "put to the test and the test had proven disastrous."[61] The fight over the senatorship and Russell's stubborn attack on the Southern Railway's ninety-nine-year lease had ruptured the Populist-Republican alliance, and having lost the backing of the GOP, Russell had become a governor without a party. The overriding political issue in North Carolina, however, remained the ninety-nine-year lease, and on that question the governor, Senator Butler, and the radical Populists stood together.

Russell's overtures to Butler during the last days of the legislature had met the Populist senator's approval, and a new political coalition was in the making. Two days after the legislature adjourned, Butler's *Caucasian* discounted the "vagrant suggestions and pugnacious hints that the Populists and Democrats would form a coalition for the next election. . . . If there ever was a possibility of such a thing it has been knocked into froth and fog by the Democrats by their record on this ninety-nine-year lease question."[62] Building a new party, however, would prove no simple matter.

60 Raleigh *News and Observer*, March 9, 1897.
61 Charlotte *Observer*, as quoted in Raleigh *News and Observer*, March 15, 1897.
62 Raleigh *Caucasian*, March 11, 1897.

Chapter VI

"Running Things on Purely Populistic Lines"
The Russell Administration at High Tide

HAVING TIED HIS political fortunes to those of Marion Butler and the radical Populists, Russell intensified his attack on corporate power in the months following the 1897 legislative session and ambitiously plotted the restructuring of party politics in North Carolina. One of the first questions facing the governor was the distribution of patronage. True to his word, he attempted a nonpartisan policy by appointing Republicans, Populists, and even Democrats to positions in state institutions.[1] When he appointed two Populists to the board of agriculture, the Raleigh *Tribune* exploded: "Great God, what a travesty upon the loyalty of Republicanism!" Even Russell's appointment of James Young to the same board stirred the GOP journal's wrath. "Jim Young," the *Tribune* asserted, "is a reputed colored Republican, but if he was a white man, [he] would be a Populist. His Republicanism is not the kind that benefits his race."[2]

A court ruling limited Russell's appointive powers in the state institutions, but his new authority over certain eastern municipalities remained unimpaired. After the municipal election in Wilmington in March, 1897, Russell appointed five aldermen—four Republicans and one silver Democrat—to serve with the five elected aldermen who included two Negro Republicans and three Democrats. One of Russell's

1 Richard Lewis to Patrick Murphy, March 10, 16, 1897, in Patrick L. Murphy Papers, Southern Historical Collection, University of North Carolina, Chapel Hill.
2 Raleigh *Tribune*, March 24, 1897.

appointees was a Negro Republican—John G. Norwood. When the three newly elected Democratic aldermen refused to meet with the governor's appointees, the Russell aldermen and the two popularly elected black aldermen chose a Republican as mayor. At the same time, the incumbent Democratic mayor and board of aldermen declared that they would not "surrender the city government until ordered by the courts." To confound matters further, the eight Democratic candidates who had run for alderman in the five city wards proclaimed themselves the "legal board" and elected a third mayor.[3]

In New Bern a similar situation developed after Russell appointed five aldermen—all white Republicans—to serve with the three Democrats and the three Negro Republicans who had been elected. The Wilmington and New Bern "muddle" resulted in a suit to determine whether the new charters were constitutional, whether the elections were valid, and which of the aldermanic boards and mayors were entitled to hold office. Democrats charged Russell with "Czarism," whereas black Republicans denounced him for appointing white men "where negroes predominate fifty to one."[4] The governor's extraordinary power notwithstanding, the crux of the problem was whether white Democrats or white Republicans would have home rule.

The state supreme court upheld the constitutionality of the New Bern and Wilmington charters in November, 1897, and declared the GOP mayors and Republican-dominated aldermanic boards to be the rightful officeholders. Republican Chief Justice William T. Faircloth ironically noted in his decision that prior to 1875, "the principle of local self government was absolutely safe and secure." But the Democratic-controlled constitutional convention of that year had determined "to give the legislature full power by statute to modify, change or abrogate any and all provisions" relating to charters, ordinances, and municipal corporations. Thus the legislature of 1897 had legally empowered the governor to appoint city aldermen.[5]

This confusion of city charters and aldermen would be a more amusing footnote to the fusion period if it did not illustrate so graphically the Democrats' assault on election processes and their resistance to the regular workings of popular self-government. The Democrats

---

3   Wilmington *Messenger*, March 26, 30, 1897; Winston *Union-Republican*, April 1, 1897.
4   Raleigh *News and Observer*, May 12, 1897.
5   Wilmington *Messenger*, November 17, 1897.

were not content to accept the rule of law and will of the majority, as the election of 1898 would demonstrate. Consequently, Russell's Whiggish, class view of black political participation was often lost in the frenzied attacks of a Democratic press which really objected more to Republican rule than to so-called "negro rule." Democratic journals, in fact, criticized Russell from all angles, and the New Bern *Weekly Journal* even condemned his centralized power as a "demoralizing force . . . when it can be used to effect radical equality."[6]

These controversies, however, occupied relatively little of Russell's time and energy. There were corporate evils to cleanse, railroad giants to slay, and federal judges to resist. On March 10, 1897, Judge Charles H. Simonton issued a subpoena ordering the governor, attorney-general, and directors of the North Carolina Railroad to appear before the United States District Court at Greensboro on April 6. The Southern Railway Company had filed a suit against the North Carolina Railroad to prevent the cancellation of the ninety-nine-year lease. The suit, a bill in equity, was a formal complaint or petition requesting relief from potential injurious acts to the Southern's lease. In granting relief, Judge Simonton enjoined the parties cited in the subpoena from bringing suit or otherwise interfering with the Southern's possession of the North Carolina road and the lease. Daniels' *News and Observer* termed the order "government by injunction."[7]

In its suit, the Southern contended that the lease was a valid contract but that the governor intended to "impair the rights and property of the plaintiff and the value of its bonds" by bringing "vexatious and inequitable litigation" against it. Railroad officials feared that Russell would "use his power to appoint directors and a State proxy, illegally and contrary to equity, who will seek to annul said lease, and cloud the title of the plaintiff."[8]

Russell's bold response was to ignore Simonton's order to desist from acting against the Southern Railway, by summarily dismissing the state proxy (who acted as agent for the state's interests in meetings of the board of directors) and the NCRR directors. In a telegram to Simonton, Russell asserted that he had lawfully removed the railroad officials, his power to do so being in no way constrained by the injunc-

6 New Bern *Weekly Journal*, November 19, 1897.
7 Raleigh *News and Observer*, March 10, 1897.
8 *Ibid.*

tion, since such constraint would be "unauthorized, collusive and fraudulent."[9] In an interview with the Charlotte *Observer*, he sardonically derided the injunction for not compelling him to apologize to the Southern Railway, to submit his messages in advance to the Southern's managers, and to prevent the "Legislature of 1899 from doing anything they [the managers] don't like." Speaking in a more serious vein, Russell again questioned the legality of the lease which he believed amounted to a sale of the NCRR. Now the Southern wanted to avoid North Carolina's courts so that a federal equity court might handle the case, since, according to Russell, federal judges were "notoriously the partisans of plutocracy." The defiant governor alleged that the Southern was attempting to deprive the state of its right to bring suit in its own courts in order to leave North Carolina "defrauded and prostrate."[10]

The antirailroad forces in the state rushed to Russell's defense and hailed his stand against Simonton's injunction. The *Caucasian* declared: "The Courts are running the government and the railroads seem to be running the courts. . . . When a judge of the Federal Court can assume to restrain the officers of a sovereign State from taking action in the interest of a State, it is time for the people to wake up."[11] Marion Butler hurried to Raleigh "to take a hand in the most important railroad fight we have ever had in that state." He believed that the destruction of the "transportation monopoly as well as the gold trust" would determine "whether the roads will own the Government or the Government will own them."[12]

Russell moved rapidly to appoint stout antilease men to the board of directors of the NCRR. Attempting to continue the railroad fight on a nonpartisan basis, he persuaded Democrat Walter Clark, progressive justice on the state supreme court, to approach Judge Augustus W. Graham, Clark's brother-in-law, about becoming a director. Clark informed Graham that Russell wanted "to appoint a strong Board of Directors irrespective of party." Agreeing with Russell's policy, Clark asserted that "this was a fight between the people and Pierpont Morgan as to who should rule N.C.," and the governor deserved the people's

9   *Ibid.*, March 11, 1897.
10 Charlotte *Observer*, March 11, 1897; Raleigh *Caucasian*, May 27, 1897.
11 Raleigh *Caucasian*, March 18, 1897.
12 Marion Butler to J. H. Ferris, March 11, 1897, in Butler Letterbook, Marion Butler Papers, Southern Historical Collection, University of North Carolina, Chapel Hill.

full support without regard to "party fealty or party questions."[13] Consequently, Russell's handpicked board contained prominent Republicans, Populists, and Democrats.

Russell's stand against the lease and the injunction drew the fire of his old nemesis, the Raleigh *Tribune*. Describing the governor's republicanism as the "scaly kind" and his politics as "Populistic," the GOP journal chided him: "You are not a loyal Republican and have no claims upon the Republican party."[14] The combative governor ignored such attacks and directed his ire against federal judges and railroads. Calling Simonton's incessant use of injunctions "infamous, outrageous and devilish," Russell insisted that the people were not "the serfs and slaves of the bond-holding and gold-hoarding classes," the railroads, or the courts. He boldly proclaimed that he had placed himself on the side of the "producer and the toiler" and against the "coupon-clipper."[15]

Disregarding Simonton's order to appear in Greensboro on April 6, Russell sent the judge a searing message in which he denied that the state had entered "into any contract with the Southern Railway Company for the lease of the North Carolina Railroad." After declining to appear or to make North Carolina a party to the suit, the governor declared: "This is the first time . . . when corporate arrogance has arraigned a Governor for his communications to the Legislature and to the people, whose servant he is." In fact, said Russell, had he known "about the frauds and impositions put upon the State by the Southern Railway Company," his original address to the legislature would have been harsher. Challenging the court's authority, he asserted: "I deny the jurisdiction of this court or any other court to control my conduct as Governor in the execution of the laws of the State." The governor accused the Southern of concealing the real earnings of the NCRR so as to justify paying a rental rate that was not commensurate with the true value of the road. He pointed out that on lines owned outrightly by the Morgan-backed line, operating expenses consumed only 58 percent of gross earnings, whereas the NCRR purportedly needed more than 70 percent of its gross earnings to operate. Russell vowed that if

---

13   Clark to A. W. Graham, March 10, 15, 1897, in Augustus W. Graham Papers, Southern Historical Collection, University of North Carolina, Chapel Hill. Clark to Russell, March 12, 1897, in Daniel L. Russell Papers, Southern Historical Collection, University of North Carolina, Chapel Hill.
14   Raleigh *Tribune*, March 12, 17, 20, 1897.
15   Raleigh *News and Observer*, March 30, 1897.

he chose to challenge the lease on behalf of the state, the court had no jurisdiction over the lawful exercise of his duties as governor.[16]

This bravado performance forced Simonton to postpone any further hearings until June at Asheville. Meanwhile, Russell, working closely with Josephus Daniels, stepped up his attack on the Southern Railway. In April the *News and Observer* published an interview with a "well informed gentleman" (perhaps Russell himself), about the railroad situation in the South.[17] The gentleman, identified as Mr. X, claimed that J. P. Morgan was trying to gain control of every railroad from the Potomac to the Mississippi. If the financial titan successfully erected such a monopoly, suggested Mr. X, he would eliminate competition, raise freight rates, and deal a deathblow to the cotton industry of Georgia and the Carolinas. Attacking Yankee-dominated railroads and Yankee-controlled capital, Mr. X argued: "This may be termed a sort of cotton mill trust which Morgan . . . can manipulate for the benefit of rival Northern factories." This anonymous railroad expert predicted dire consequences should Morgan continue unchecked: "If Morgan could get control of the Seaboard Air Line, the Georgia Railroad, and can hold the lease of the North Carolina [Railroad], he practically has all the States between the Potomac and Mississippi rivers and north of Florida to the Ohio river, in his grip. He can squeeze merchants, manufacturers and farmers by forcing freight rates that will wring from them every dollar of profit." Only Governor Russell, according to Mr. X, had challenged Morgan's scheme and repudiated Simonton's injunction. It now remained to the Georgia and Carolina legislatures to support Russell and break up the "Railroad Trust."

This remarkable interview was a southern progressive's classic indictment of Yankee-managed railroads and northern capital and foreshadowed the reform movement of the early twentieth century. If the Populist demand for governor ownership of railroads seemed too radical, the Progressive demand for government regulation to protect merchants, manufacturers, and farmers was not. Clearly reflecting Russell's own thinking, the interview placed the renegade Republican

---

16   *Ibid.*, April 7, 1897.
17   *Ibid.*, April 18, 1897. A typewritten memorandum in the Russell Papers containing much marginalia indicates that Russell at least knew about the "interview" if he did not write it. The memorandum and published interview are nearly identical.

governor in the vanguard of the South's Progressive movement.[18]

Interviews, however, could not squash bills in equity. At Asheville in June, Simonton heard the arguments of the state and the Southern Railway. In defending the governor, state attorneys argued that the Southern's suit against the NCRR violated the Eleventh Amendment, for "suits against officials are suits against the State." Moreover, they did not believe that a bill in equity could prevent a governor from initiating litigation in a state to determine the legality of a contract. "Where relief can be obtained by a suit at law," reasoned the governor's counsel, "an equity suit cannot be maintained." The Southern's lawyers, on the other hand, contended that the lease of 1895 was valid and that the federal court had the right to hear a bill in equity since a North Carolina court might irreparably damage the contract unless a permanent injunction were brought against Tarheel officials.[19]

Alphonso Avery, the governor's advocate, briefed Russell on the hearing, stating optimistically that Simonton had been "so shaken by the arguments on our side that he would in the end dissolve the order." According to Avery, the judge was disconcerted by the prospect of denying a state the right to bring suit in its own courts. Avery predicted that Simonton would seek refuge in the "last ditch" by directing the case toward the sole question of fraud. As for the political impact of the railroad fight, the Democratic lawyer contended that western Democrats would back the governor on the "lease question and . . . make it a live issue next year . . . against those who opposed your policy last winter."[20]

Simonton's decision of June 30, 1897, determined that the lease of the North Carolina Railroad was valid and that it had been executed in conformity with the requirements of the road's charter. To settle the question of fraud, the judge appointed attorney Kerr Craig as "special master" to take testimony and then file a report. In the meantime, the restraining order remained in effect.[21]

18 Jeffrey J. Crow, " 'Populism to Progressivism' in North Carolina: Governor Daniel Russell and His War on the Southern Railway Company," *The Historian*, XXXVII (August, 1975), 666–67, hereinafter cited as Crow, "Russell's War on the Southern Railway"; Sheldon Hackney, *Populism to Progressivism in Alabama* (Princeton: Princeton University Press, 1969).
19 Charlotte *Observer*, June 9, 10, 1897.
20 Alphonso Avery to Russell, June 12, 1897, in Executive Papers of Daniel L. Russell, North Carolina Division of Archives and History, Raleigh.
21 Charlotte *Observer*, July 1, 2, 1897.

Russell reacted by calling the decision "Federalistic" and declaring that states' rights as well as private rights were being infringed by a corporate power of "railroad judges" and "railroad nabobs." The people had lost confidence in the courts, he believed, because judges habitually aligned with "railroad kings, bank barons, and money princes." The irascible governor continued: "If the plebeians and middle classes get control of this country in 1900 they may take these capitalists and corporation judges . . . and chuck them into the manure pile, a fitting sepulcher."[22]

Russell's pungent, if inelegant, denunciation of railroads and federal courts brought heated criticism. The normally staid Charlotte *Observer* chastised his "conduct and language" as governor, condemned his rhetoric as excessively brutal, and declared: "His violence and unreasonableness of temper have made him the dread of many of those who have had to be in contact with him, and have brought upon him the hatred of nearly all the members of his own party as well as of the opposition." The *Causasian*, however, applauded the governor: "The time is ripe for somebody to say something, and it appears that there is one man in the State not afraid to say it."[23]

The continuing fight with the Southern Railway represented only part of a broad range of economic reforms Russell had initiated in the months following the general assembly. Since April, 1897, he had been pressuring the railroad commission to lower railroad rates. As the *Caucasian* reported: "It is practically understood that Governor Russell, who must be commended for the fact that he has never shown any fear of the corporate power, will urge upon the Railroad Commission the advisability and necessity of reducing railroad fares and rates in the State."[24] Russell confided to his new ally Marion Butler that he was lobbying the Populist and Republican commissioners to enact rate reductions. "I am doing all I can to get these two men right," the governor said. "There are suspicions as to [A. B.] Andrews' manipulations but I am not willing to believe that either of these two men have been corrupted by that professional debaucher of public servants. I hear that he is quite confident of capturing them, or one of them."[25]

22   Raleigh *News and Observer*, July 3, 1897.
23   Charlotte *Observer*, July 8, 1897; Raleigh *Caucasian*, July 14, 1897.
24   Raleigh *Caucasian*, April 8, 1897.
25   Russell to Marion Butler, May 5, 1897, in Butler Papers.

Scheduled to convene on July 12, 1897, the railroad commission asked Governor Russell, Justice Walter Clark, and newspaper editor Josephus Daniels for their views on railroad rates and taxation. Besides calling for rate and fare reductions, Russell urged a dramatic increase in taxes paid by the railroads, demanding no less than the lines' entire profits in North Carolina. In his radical plan, the railroads' tax evaluation would be equated with 6 percent of the lines' taxable property. In 1896, for instance, the railroads reported a profit of $3.25 million in North Carolina, but they paid taxes on only $26 million worth of property. By Russell's scheme, the valuation of railroad property would automatically rise from $26 million to $54 million with the state receiving 6 percent of the latter sum, or, in other words, the entire $3.25 million profit. "Four per cent for money is reasonable," the sly governor confessed, "Five per cent is liberal. But suppose in consideration of the extraordinary expenses of some railroads when they undertake to conduct our government, control our Legislatures and Governors, appoint Federal judges and even postmasters, maintain daily newspapers and other luxuries . . . we allow them six per cent." The money, Russell pledged, would provide additional funds for North Carolina's state government and schools.[26]

Appalled by Russell's radical notions, and doubtless remembering his inaugural address prediction of government ownership of railroads, attorneys for various lines warned the commission that this scheme would cripple capitalism. One lawyer termed it a rank form of "class legislation" smacking of "government oversight" if not "government ownership."[27] The commission apparently agreed, for it not only rejected Russell's proposal but also refused to grant rate and fare reductions. The New Bern *Weekly Journal*, decrying the views of Russell, Daniels, and Clark, breathed a sigh of relief that "the spirit of Populism, altogether too prevalent in North Carolina," had finally been crushed by the railroad commission.[28]

The Democratic newspaper, however, had underestimated the resourcefulness of the "Populistic" governor. The railroad commission's failure to adopt his tax program or reduce rates particularly vexed Russell. With his lease fight momentarily buried in federal court hearings,

26   Raleigh *News and Observer*, July 11, 1897.
27   Charlotte *Observer*, July 13, 14, 1897.
28   New Bern *Weekly Journal*, July 22, 1897.

he was determined to strike a blow at the railroad monopolies and to make the commission amenable to his plans for reform. In an extraordinary maneuver, Russell removed Commissioners James W. Wilson and S. Otho Wilson from office, thereby touching off a major scandal.

Russell had well-founded grounds for dismissing the commissioners, since for several months he had known of a possible conflict of interest between the Wilsons and the Southern Railway Company. The governor's Populist adviser, John Graham, had explained to Marion Butler that the railroad commission's action in regard to rate reductions would shape Russell's course. According to Graham, S. Otho Wilson's mother had "rented or leased the '*Round Knob House*' in Western North Carolina, & . . . two thirds of this house belongs to Maj. J. W. Wilson & the other third to Col. Andrews." Since the hotel depended "entirely upon the favor of the railroad of which Col. Andrews is the head, should S. Otho vote with Maj. J. W. Wilson, & against Dr. Abbott, the republican R. R. Commissioner, in opposition to a reasonable reduction in railroad charges, no matter how conscientious he may be, it would put our party at a disadvantage."[29]

Otho Wilson, to be sure, had voted for the rate reduction, but that did not mitigate Russell's determination to control the railroad commission. Soon after the commission had rejected his proposals, rumors circulated that Russell might remove some commissioners. Under the 1891 act creating the railroad commission, the governor was empowered to suspend from office any commissioner who held stocks, bonds, or any kind of interest in a company subject to the commission's jurisdiction. The final power of removal rested with the legislature if the evidence showed a conflict of interest.

Part of the impetus for suspending the commissioners came from Justice Walter Clark. Clark loathed James W. Wilson as "a Bureau of Andrews' office" and thought that Andrews and Wilson had made the railroad commission an instrument of "corporate greed" to be used against the people. Years later Russell contended that Clark had "started the movement for the removal of the Railroad Commissioners," and as the "most active prosecutor" in the case had improperly counseled the governor, knowing that the case "would come before him as a Judge and that he would sit in judgement upon it." Clark of-

29　John Graham to Marion Butler, April 17, 1897, in Butler Papers.

fered his legal opinion on the Railroad Commission Act of 1891 and how the governor should proceed under it; more importantly, he helped Russell draft the "Show-Cause Notices" that led to the suspension of the Wilsons. In addition he suggested that the governor appoint John H. Pearson to the commission since Pearson was sympathetic to Russell's reform plans. The supreme court justice even advised Russell not to worry over "that hullabaloo about 'Impeachment,'" since J. W. Wilson was the source of it. Clark understood fully the implications of his actions, at one point imploring Russell to burn a memorandum that linked the justice to the Wilsons' case. "Please get that paper and destroy it," Clark entreated.[30]

With the able assistance of a supreme court judge, then, Russell notified the Wilsons on August 24, 1897, that they must "show cause" why they should not be suspended from office for violationg the Railroad Commission Act. Russell pointed out that the Round Knob Hotel had been unoccupied for several years when the Southern Railway designated it as a regular eating stop—the trains formerly having stopped at Hickory and Asheville instead.[31]

Russell's move, described as "brave and bold" by the *Caucasian*, prompted censure from business spokesmen across the state. The Charlotte *Observer* accused the governor and Senator Butler of trying to dictate the commission's decisions by removing recalcitrant members and appointing obsequious henchmen. "The whole business," declared the Democratic journal, "is a bit of cheap demagogy inspired by malice and having for its end personal, political gain."[32] The Republicans, as usual, were at a loss to explain Russell's behavior. Congressman Richmond Pearson, commiserating with J. W. Wilson, attributed Russell's action to the "many bad humors in his system" that had finally begun to affect his mind. "It seems clear to me," Pearson con-

30 Clark's role in this episode was not revealed until 1902 when he campaigned to become chief justice. The campaign became a mudslinging affair in which Russell evidently played no small part. He was piqued by the Democrats' attempt in the 1901 legislature to impeach two Republican supreme court justices. Russell, knowing of Clark's past indiscretions, passed the incriminating evidence to Ben Duke with instructions that it be shown to A. B. Andrews. Andrews apparently told J. W. Wilson, who in 1902 led the attack on Clark by assailing him as a disloyal Democrat and crypto-fusionist from 1894 to 1898. Clark to Marion Butler, February 8, 1897, in Butler Papers; Russell to B. N. Duke, February 19, 1901, in Benjamin Newton Duke Papers, Duke University; Raleigh *Morning Post*, April 24, May 11, 1902.
31 Russell to J. W. Wilson, August 24, 1897, Russell to S. O. Wilson, August 24, 1897, in Russell Papers.
32 Raleigh *Caucasian*, August 26, 1897; Charlotte *Observer*, August 27, 1897.

cluded, "that the conservative men of the Republican party, even those who were responsible for his nomination, will have to repudiate this wild war upon vested rights and upon civilized forms of expression and procedure." Daniels' *News and Observer* reported a movement in the GOP to force the state committee to "declare officially that the Governor is not a Republican and that the party is in no wise responsible for his act."[33]

The Wilsons denied any conflict of interest or collusion with Andrews, the vice-president of the Southern Railway. James Wilson insisted that he had sold his share of the Round Knob property "to avoid even the appearance of evil." Otho Wilson claimed that his mother was the sole owner of the hotel even though much of the furniture and supplies had been purchased in his name and shipped to his mother at a discount. But Russell remained unconvinced, and on September 24, 1897, he suspended the two commissioners. Under the law's provisions, the Wilsons were dismissed until the legislature of 1899 could settle the question of their removal or restoration. For the interim period, Russell appointed John H. Pearson, a Democrat and Clark's personal choice, and Leroy C. Caldwell, a Populist, to serve as commissioners. In the legislature of 1897 Pearson had strongly backed the Cook bill—Russell's measure to annul the lease—and was known to favor strict railroad regulation and "fair rates." Caldwell, formerly a Democrat, had not become a Populist until 1896. Once again the governor had ignored the GOP in making critical appointments.[34]

Russell's estrangement from the Republican party was no longer a source of speculation. The Raleigh *Tribune*, which included A. B. Andrews among its major stockholders, had gone bankrupt in May, 1897, but not before delivering a final blast against the "dry rot" in the Tarheel GOP caused by "Governor Russell and his little clique." The Hickory *Press* pledged its support to "the regular organization of the Republican party" but refused any "countenance to those who seek to merge Republicans with Populism." When Hiram Grant, author of the senate measure which killed the Cook bill, warned that the legislature of 1899 might impeach Russell "for general cussedness," the governor

33 Richmond Pearson to J. W. Wilson, August 27, 1897, in William C. Erwin Papers, Southern Historical Collection, University of North Carolina, Chapel Hill; Raleigh *News and Observer*, August 31, 1897.
34 Raleigh *News and Observer*, August 31, September 2, 24, 1897.

skewered his legislative antagonist with the rebuttal, "Grant is a Hessian who betrayed his constituents in order to get the smiles and favors of the monopolists."[35] Former congressman Thomas Settle declared that the Tarheel GOP was entering a crucial stage and blamed Russell for the party's woes. Russell may have been elected as a Republican, Settle admitted, but now he had "formed an alliance with outside elements, and is running things on purely Populistic lines. . . . He has gone so far that he can no longer be classed as a Republican, and all his efforts are now in the line of solidifying himself with his Populistic supporters."[36]

Settle was right; Russell and Butler had become close political allies. The *Caucasian* warmly supported the alliance, declaring: "Russell and Butler are exposing every man, no matter in what party, who proves unworthy, and are fighting for the election of a legislature that the railroads cannot control." According to the Populist journal, the "only check to the 'invasion of monopoly' has been by the Alliance and the People's party, by Gov. Russell and Senator Butler." When the state supreme court upheld Russell's removal of the railroad commissioners in December, 1897, the *Caucasian* asserted: "If the people care for their property, their rights, and their liberties, they must not fail to elect a legislature that will not only uphold the Railway Commission law, and sustain the bold and patriotic action of Governor Russell in removing the Commissioners . . . but also a legislature that will pass a law to prevent foreign corporations . . . from removing cases from our State Courts to Federal Courts by injunctions."[37]

Russell's rapprochement with Butler, however, did not sit well with many other Populists. In the view of one mid-roader, the People's party had to become the majority party instead of the balance of power in Tarheel politics. The "main idea of old 'to make more Populists' has given way to that of justification of Gov. Russell's state policy. The grand old spirit of propaganda of '88 to '93 has been lost forever. Is this lapse or signs of death?"[38]

In the view of Russell and Butler, it was a sign of regeneration. The

35 Raleigh *Tribune*, May 21, 22, 1897; Hickory *Press*, May 27, July 22, 1897; Raleigh *News and Observer*, June 24, 1897.
36 Raleigh *News and Observer*, December 9, 1897.
37 Raleigh *Caucasian*, October 14, 1897; January 6, 1898.
38 S. E. Asbury to Marion Butler, June 19, 1897, in Butler Papers.

fusionist leaders favored making the Populist party "a nucleus for bolters from both of the old parties on the railroad question." A new party alignment had become necessary, in their opinion, because both the Democrats and Republicans were split by the issue of railroad regulation whereas the Populists were nearly solid against railroads. Reportedly, the new party might not be known as the "Populists," but the campaign issues would revolve around opposition to monopolies, especially the Southern Railway "and its domination of politics in North Carolina."[39] Reform-minded Democrats such as Walter Clark and Alphonso Avery, it was further rumored, were sympathetic to the ambitious plan and had met at the governor's mansion with Russell and Butler to determine the prospects for a new party. Russell's daring assault on railroad monopolies, as manifested in his lease fight and in his dealings with the railroad commission, indicated the kind of vigorous policies the new party would undertake in an effort to accentuate economic policies and silence the racist "white line issue."[40]

In retrospect the Russell-Butler scheme might seem quixotic, but considering the post-Reconstruction experience in the South and especially in North Carolina, a new alliance was by no means farfetched. Russell after all had been elected to Congress as a Greenbacker, had seen the Readjusters triumph in Virginia in the 1880s, and closer to home had helped shape the fusionist victories of 1894 and 1896. Nationally the silver forces, though defeated in 1896, had a popular leader in William Jennings Bryan. Visionary though it may have been, a new alliance of reformers—the coalition first suggested by Russell during the legislature of 1897—was not a mere pipe dream. Indeed, Russell and Butler were determined to prove otherwise.

The Democrats, however, were already gearing up for an 1898 white-supremacy campaign. In August, 1897, they opposed the fusionist reform that allowed local school districts to raise taxes for the support of public schools. Daniels' *News and Observer*, warning voters that local control of school boards would mean black committeemen in the eastern counties supervising white teachers and pupils, argued that fusionism had to be uprooted before public education could advance. The Democrats' racist campaign succeeded, for only eleven townships adopted local taxation. Butler's *Caucasian* decried the

39   Raleigh *News and Observer*, August 11, 1897.
40   Washington *Post*, as quoted in the Raleigh *Hayseeder*, October 21, 1897.

Democratic attempt to divert the state's attention from "great economic issues" with the "nigger racket." Defending the People's party as the true white man's party and avowing his belief in "Anglo Saxon supremacy," Butler nevertheless considered himself the Negro's friend. The Afro-American, he insisted in a speech, "is not an issue in North Carolina politics, and to attempt to make him the sole issue is a fake and a delusion." As the Hickory *Mercury* explained, "The Populists will not be turned to the right or to the left by the cry of 'nigger' or the 'last legislature.' "[41]

While Butler inveighed against the Democrats' use of the race issue, Russell continued to woo Populist support and strengthen his credentials as a reformer. Russell addressed a Farmers' Alliance picnic in Wake County in August and became the first Tarheel governor to appear before the Alliancemen. Denying any political motive in attending the picnic, the governor pledged to "stand by the men who plough their own fields and pay the taxes" without regard to party. The Alliance, he pointed out, was a necessary organization for fighting "corporate power and organized wealth." In Russell's opinion, numbers and majorities were impotent without organization, and to destroy the concentrated power of corporations and trusts the farmers would have to stand united. "I will try to see to it that your side is heard," he promised. "This is one time they [the trusts] have not got the Governor." Russell also criticized the recent legislature for selling out to the monopolists who bribed lawmakers, judges, lawyers, and former governors while frustrating the people's interests. But since the legislature had adjourned, Russell declared that he found the governorship pleasant—so pleasant he hoped Pierpont Morgan would give him a lifetime appointment.[42]

It is doubtful that the great Wall Street mogul would have agreed to such a bargain, with the Southern Railway lease fight rapidly approaching a climax. Special Master Kerr Craig's hearings on the question of fraud had ranged from North Carolina to New York, where J. P. Morgan had been excused from testifying. Craig, moreover, had manacled the hands of the governor's attorneys by refusing to admit any evidence from the period after 1895, ruling it "irrelevant and incompe-

---

41 Raleigh *Caucasian*, August 12, September 16, 1897; Hickory *Mercury*, as quoted in the Winston *Union-Republican*, October 14, 1897.
42 Raleigh *News and Observer*, August 21, 1897.

tent." The North Carolina lawyers had intended to prove that A. B. Andrews and the Southern Railway had systematically suppressed any investigation of the lease by paying the old board of NCRR directors over $2,700 to lobby against the Cook bill and by funding the publication of the Raleigh *Tribune*.[43]

Thus by February, 1898, when the last hearing was held, it had become clear that Russell's allegation of fraud would not be sustained in the United States District Court. As a result, Simonton's injunction would permanently restrain North Carolina officials from challenging the lease in the state's courts. Such a prospect presaged trouble for Russell's political plans, for it left his entire fight against the lease in an unfavorable light. After a year of legal turmoil and at a cost of thousands of dollars to the state, he would have nothing to show for his efforts.

Gambling that the new party he and Butler were forging could rectify any concessions he made to the Southern Railway in the legislature of 1899, Russell quietly began probing for a compromise that would secure him some small political advantage. The key to a compromise was the Southern's offer to lease the Atlantic and North Carolina Railroad (A & NC), a state-owned line with a marginal profit. Reportedly, the offer included a thirty-year lease at a rental of 2 percent of the capital stock that was valued at $1.8 million, of which the state owned $1.2 million. In addition the Southern would buy the A & NC's rolling stock and pay all the legal fees incurred by the state in the lease fight. Governor Russell supposedly countered with a raise to 2.5 percent for rental.[44]

Before any such deal could be concluded an unexpected development seriously undermined Russell's bargaining strength. With inopportune timing, the railroad commission finally decided to lower passenger rates by as much as 20 percent. The compromise collapsed. A. B. Andrews demanded that the commission rescind the rate reductions, and in return the Southern would rent the A & NC for 2.5 percent.[45] Russell's lease fight was now entangled with his struggle to reduce railroad rates. Apparently clinging to his hope that a coalition of reformers would settle the lease and rate issues in the legislature of

43   Crow, "Russell's War on the Southern Railway," 660–61.
44   George Morton to Marion Butler, January 17, 1898, in Butler Papers; Russell to Fabius H. Busbee, May 9, 1902, in Russell Papers.
45   Raleigh *News and Observer*, February 22, 1898; Raleigh *Morning Post*, February 23, 1898.

1899 the governor's temporary solution to the dilemma was to accede to Andrews' demands and urge the newly appointed commissioners— Pearson and Caldwell—to restore the old rates. Alarmed allies of the governor pleaded with Butler to intervene. "We are absolutely dependent this off year on Russell's Rail Road policy," asserted John J. Mott. Pearson himself intimated to Butler that Russell was "making a mistake in not declaring the whole transaction off & letting the people through the next Legislature settle with the corrupt gang."[46]

Russell, however, continued to seek a settlement with the Southern Railway, proving himself a stubborn negotiator. After weeks of secret conferences, Southern President Samuel Spencer confided to his wife: "The Gov. has declined to carry out his agreements and all negotiations are off. If he continues in this mood, we will make money and finally whip him after considerable work and annoyance. I am quite satisfied with the outcome."[47] Negotiations had reached an impasse because Russell, with an eye cocked toward the 1898 campaign, planned to publish a letter in which he explained his reasons for compromising the lease question. The Southern Railway did not want him to "flagrantly inject the railway matter into politics," the governor said, but he was determined to make a strong statement calling for the legislature of 1899 to act on the lease and other railroad matters. When Russell refused to abandon his publication plan, negotiations ceased.[48]

But even as Russell was abandoning the key concession in the compromise, Leroy Caldwell was having second thoughts. In an interview with the Statesville *Landmark*, the commissioner claimed that he had "yielded to the clamor of politicians" in reducing passenger rates. He believed that the recent decision by the United States Supreme Court on the Nebraska maximum rate law undercut the North Carolina rate reduction. In the Nebraska case, the Supreme Court had ruled that no state could compel a railroad to operate at a loss within its boundaries no matter how great the road's interstate profits were. The import of Caldwell's remarks was clear: he would vote to rescind the rate reduction.[49]

---

46 John J. Mott to Marion Butler, February 24, 1898; John H. Pearson to Marion Butler, March 3, 1898, in Butler Papers.

47 Samuel Spencer to his wife, March 18, 1898, in Samuel Spencer Papers, Southern Historical Collection, University of North Carolina, Chapel Hill.

48 Charlotte *Observer*, March 19, 1898; Wilmington *Messenger*, March 19, 1898.

49 Statesville *Landmark*, as quoted in Raleigh *Morning Post*, March 24, 1898.

Russell's willingness to treat with the Southern Railway and Caldwell's anticipated "flop" on the rate question left the governor suspect
in the minds of many reformers. One disappointed Populist told Butler:
"I don't believe he could be bought but it really looks as if he can be
scared. Is it not just possible that the R.R.'s have threatened him [with
impeachment] if they secure a corporation Legislature for '99?" This
Populist still considered the governor the "people's friend," but "not the
courageous man I had taken him to be."[50]

Russell's war on the lease terminated on March 29, 1898, with a
series of resolutions passed by the board of directors of the NCRR. The
quid pro quo involving the A & NC lease and the restoration of old passenger rates was conspicuously absent. The directors asserted, however, that they would not contest the lease issue beyond Simonton's
court and would accept his ruling, which would undoubtedly exoner-
ate the Southern Railway of any fraud in obtaining the contract. In return the Southern would pay all expenses incurred by the defendant—
the NCRR—which possibly amounted to $14,000. Moreover, although
Simonton's injunction would constrain the governor, attorney-general,
and board of directors from challenging the lease, the legislature was
left free to act. In a resolution drafted by John Graham and approved
by Russell, the directors declared that the "settlement does not in any
way affect or impair the rights of the State to adopt any policy that may
be determined upon by its legislature with regard to the ownership,
management and operation of domestic railroads by foreign or nonresident corporations."[51] Therein lay the key to Russell's willingness to
compromise. The governor clearly hoped that the next legislature,
controlled by a coalition of reformers, could determine the final disposition of the lease and other railroad matters. The compromise was
more tactical than final. Since the legal battle was obviously lost, Russell at least had managed to force the Southern Railway to pay all the
legal costs of the lease fight. In no way, however, had he permitted the
Southern to hamstring the legislature or his political plans. To Russell's way of thinking, the fight for railroad reform was only beginning,
not ending.

Even so the compromise looked exceedingly feeble to many observ-

50   Charles H. Utley to Marion Butler, March 26, 1898, in Butler Papers.
51   Raleigh *Morning Post*, March 30, 1898.

ers after months of Russell's strident rhetoric and daring decisions. Charles Cook called the agreement an "excellent arrangement" and a "victory for the Governor," but Daniels' *News and Observer*, which had supported the governor in his railroad fight, charged that Russell's "surrender" established him "as an unstable, choleric and 'wobbling' officer." Even Butler's *Caucasion* hesitated a week before finally defending Russell as "honest and conscientious" and vowing that the Populists and "Governor Russell will urge the next legislature to use all lawful means to set aside the fraudulent midnight ninety-nine-year lease."[52] Walter Clark, who had been privy to many of the secret maneuverings, criticized Russell as a "*poor trader*," but he did not censure the compromise itself, only the terms the governor had exacted from the Southern Railway.[53]

Russell's compromise might have created a better impression had Caldwell not voted to restore the old passenger rates the day after the lease matter was settled. Caldwell's flop created a new 2–1 majority, there being only three members on the commission. Plainly shaken, Russell told the commissioner that by abandoning the antimonopoly forces in North Carolina he had given "color to the slanders and libels upon me." The false friends of reform would now "send out their lies, saying that I agreed with the Southern Railway Company in order to get the ninety-nine-year lease suit out of Judge Simonton's Court." Russell admitted that he had once favored the rate restoration in exchange for the Southern's lease of the A & NC at 2.5 percent. Under such an arrangement, he contended, the state would have realized several hundred thousand dollars more in income while the lease question and the reduction of rates were submitted to the people in the coming election and passed upon by the general assembly in 1899. When the Southern declined to lease the road on Russell's terms, negotiations had stopped. "Since then," the governor averred, "I have argued that the rate reduction be maintained and fought out in the courts." As for the Nebraska maximum rate case, Russell asserted, "I believe [it] to be a premeditated decision, rendered for the express purpose of emasculating the Railroad Commissions of the United States. . . . I think that our Commission and our courts ought to give to that

52   Raleigh *News and Observer*, March 30, 31, 1898; Raleigh *Caucasian*, April 14, 1898.
53   Clark to Marion Butler, March 23, 1898, in Butler Papers.

ruling the same kind of respect and obedience that was rendered by the Republican party and the antislavery men of the North to the Dred Scott decision." Russell further vowed that he would not yield to such "judicial despotism . . . usurpation and aggression." Somewhat overwhelmed, Caldwell replied simply that his vote on the rate question had had nothing to do with the compromise on the lease and that the governor had never "either by word or action, intimated or asked me to be a party to that settlement."[54]

The Russell-Caldwell encounter climaxed the Southern Railway fight. On April 13, 1898, Simonton ruled that the lease had been executed "bona fide, without fraud, covin, misrepresentation, or malpractice of any sort" on the part of the officers of the NCRR and the Southern Railway. He thereupon made the injunction against the state officers of North Carolina perpetual.[55]

Years later Josephus Daniels alleged that Russell had quit the war on the lease because of his fear of impeachment and the personal financial pressures he was experiencing. Such fears doubtless weighed upon the governor, but he certainly did not "sell out" to the railroads. He had resisted repeated attempts by the Southern Railway to bribe him with a federal judgeship and even threatened to shoot the next debaucher who approached him.[56] Russell in fact had not given up the fight for reform. The climax of the lease controversy had set the stage for the election of 1898. Despite Democratic claims to the contrary, the governor was no pliant tool of the railroads. He and Butler were prepared to take their case to the people in the coming campaign by stressing vital economic issues that would rally reformers from all parties to their standard. The Democrats, however, were desperate to return to power and had on their minds something other than a campaign centering on economic issues.

54 Raleigh *Morning Post*, March 31, 1898.
55 Benehan Cameron to Duke, May 12, 1898, in B. N. Duke Papers.
56 Josephus Daniels, *Editor in Politics* (Chapel Hill: University of North Carolina Press, 1941), 259–63; John Graham to Marion Butler, April 17, 1897, in Butler Papers; Alice Sawyer Cooper, in collaboration with Louis Goodman, "Daniel Lindsay Russell: A Family and Friend's Memoir" (MS in the Daniel L. Russell Papers, Southern Historical Collection, University of North Carolina, Chapel Hill), 61–62.

Chapter VII

"An Orgy of Deviltry the Like of Which Has Not Been Seen"

Governor Russell and the Election of 1898

"WE HAVE FALLEN on evil days in North Carolina," announced the Democratic state committee in November, 1897. "They recall the days of reconstruction. They demonstrate the truth that no Southern State can be governed with honor by the Republican party." Declaring fusion a "horror" that had engendered "negro and venal government," the Democrats called upon "all white electors who intend to vote with us in the next election and who desire the re-establishment of Anglo Saxon supremacy and honest government in North Carolina . . . to participate in all of our primaries and conventions."[1]

It required no special political prescience for Daniel Russell and Marion Butler to recognize the type of campaign the Democrats intended to wage in 1898 if given the chance. The fusionist leaders, however, believed they could thwart a white-supremacy campaign by accentuating economic policies and reform, thereby forging their new political coalition. The key to any party realignment, as they perceived the problem, was the fusion of the Populist and Democratic parties. The Republicans plainly opposed the types of reforms contemplated by Russell and Butler, especially in regard to railroad regulation. But a powerful faction in the Democratic party, identified with free silver and William Jennings Bryan on the national level, just as clearly supported these reforms—if the race issue could be avoided or played

---

1 Raleigh *News and Observer*, December 1, 1897.

down. For Russell, his flirtation with Bryan Democrats, when added to his ever-closer bond with the radical Populists, marked the height of his estrangement from the GOP. Having no other base of support, it was a gamble he felt he had to take.

In the spring of 1898 the party system in North Carolina was a maze of factions. The Republican, Populist, and Democratic parties were all split by the actions of the past two fusionist legislatures. Republicans continued to rail against the governor, while dissident Populists excoriated Butler. Populist Otho Wilson, the deposed railroad commissioner, sniped at the senator and governor in the Raleigh *Hayseeder*, calling Russell, Butler, and Democrat Alphonso Avery strange bedfellows to be building a new political alliance. Their intent, he argued, was "to disintegrate their [party] organizations and . . . build up a new conglomerate mass to be led by themselves." Russell, according to Wilson, was acting out of desperation, since he had no following in his own party and had become a "party wrecker."[2]

The continuing howl of the Democratic press about white supremacy, moreover, made black and white fusionists increasingly uneasy. State senator and Negro Republican, W. Lee Person, admitting that he and Russell had differed in the past, beseeched the governor to summon another session of the legislature in order to "rivet" the fusionist election law on the state constitution. Fearful for black "liberties and freedom," Person warned that the "Democrats are going to make desperate efforts to regain the state." If the fusionist election law fell, he concluded, "the salvation of the poor white man and the negro" would fall with it. Similarly, Judge Thomas H. Sutton, a sturdy Russell Republican, warned Senator Butler that if the Democratic use of the color line issue succeeded, the legislature of 1899 would disfranchise Populists and Republicans alike.[3]

Republicans and Populists aligned with Senator Jeter Pritchard were openly advocating fusion by March, 1898, and warning of Democratic plans to end "manhood suffrage, an honest ballot and fair count, and [the direct] election of county commissioners and magistrates by

2   Raleigh *Hayseeder*, January 27, 1898.
3   Person to Russell, February 7, March 12, 1898, in Executive Papers of Daniel L. Russell, North Carolina Division of Archives and History, Raleigh, hereinafter cited as Governor's Papers; Thomas H. Sutton to Marion Butler, January 31, 1898, in Marion Butler Papers, Southern Historical Collection, University of North Carolina, Chapel Hill.

the people." The Populists and Republicans, Otho Wilson declared, could not afford a straight party fight, for that would insure a Democratic victory.[4]

The movement to resurrect the old fusionist coalition, however, played no part in the Russell-Butler scenario. The type of alliance they envisaged would separate conservative business forces from economic reformers. Patterned after the so-called "Bryan plan," their alliance would bind together all the reform and free-silver elements in the state, no matter what previous party allegiances had been. The role of the People's party in the scheme was pivotal, and two factions were vying for its mastery. Marion Butler, backed by Secretary of State Cyrus Thompson and State Auditor Hal Ayer, was pushing the party toward fusion with Bryan Democrats as the basis of uniting the reform forces. Opposed to Butler stood Otho Wilson and Congressman Harry Skinner, an old antagonist, who preferred Republican–Populist cooperation.

Governor Russell, meanwhile, stood somewhat outside of, if not above, the battles going on in the Populist and Republican parties. Russell was not quite a Populist, but then he was not quite a Republican either. Too much the nonconformist and maverick, Russell plotted his own independent course in the face of Republican censure and Populist suspicions as to his actual motives. When President William McKinley turned down Russell's candidate for a federal appointment, the governor intimated to Butler that the president had been "gushing to me," but "you and I know how much that sort of talk amounts to as against the cramming he has had from Pritchard, Elkins, Hanna, Platt and that crowd, about my being a violent Populist and an opponent of his."[5]

Undaunted by such rebuffs, Russell continued his crusade for railroad reform. Soon after the lease controversy was compromised, the governor brought test cases for a rate reduction before the railroad commission. In explaining his complaint he acknowledged that he was challenging the Supreme Court's decision in the Nebraska maximum rate case. "It is suggested," Russell said, "that the effect of the Nebraska decision has been misconceived, and that it does not prevent

4 Winston *Union-Republican*, February 3, March 3, 10, 17, 1898; Raleigh *Hayseeder*, as quoted in the Hickory *Press*, March 31, 1898.
5 Russell to Marion Butler, April 20, 1898, in Butler Papers.

this Commission from reducing the passenger rates upon certain of the railroads in the State." The governor contended that unless a distinction were made between profits on intrastate and interstate traffic, railroad commissions would be rendered impotent. In the Nebraska case, the Supreme Court had ruled that no state could compel a railroad to operate at a loss within its boundaries no matter what the line's interstate profits. Russell's argument was that rate reductions could be instituted without forcing railroads in North Carolina to operate at a loss. For his test cases he had shrewdly chosen the North Carolina Railroad, the Wilmington and Weldon Railroad, and the Raleigh and Gaston Railroad. Each line was situated in North Carolina alone, though all were operated by larger lines. Implicit in the test cases was an attack on giant, interterritorial railroad monopolies like the Southern Railway.[6]

Russell published in *The Arena* (June, 1898) a spirited analysis of monopolies and federal courts, saying they had systematically oppressed the producing classes of the nation since the days of Alexander Hamilton and John Marshall, the two pillars of Federalism. Russell had often defended federal power as a foundation of Republicanism, and finally he had come to believe that such power could be used as a countervailing force to protect farmers and laborers against the concentrated power of big business.[7]

These unremitting attacks on monopolies did not go unnoticed in the business community. Nonetheless, in April, 1898, Daniels' *News and Observer* gingerly espoused fusion between Populists and Democrats, asserting that Republican success meant "putting the negro over the white man" in North Carolina. If the white electorate united, Negro rule would be swept aside. The Bryan organ called on the free-silver forces of the Populist and Democratic parties to combine and restore "good local government."[8] To bolster his position Daniels published a letter from William Jennings Bryan calling for the cooperation

6   Raleigh *News and Observer*, April 21, 1898. In July, 1898, the railroad commission granted a rate reduction for the Wilmington and Weldon Railroad, but prevailing rates were maintained on the other lines. An injunction prevented the implementation of the new rates, and the railroad commission was abolished by the Democratic legislature in 1899 and replaced by a corporation commission.

7   Daniel L. Russell, "Usurpations of the Federal Judiciary in the Interest of the Money Power," *The Arena* (June, 1898), 721–28.

8   Raleigh *News and Observer*, April 20, 1898.

of all silver and reform forces in North Carolina. Conservative Democrats were appalled. "For the Democrats to 'co-operate' with Butler," declared Robert Furman of the recently established Raleigh *Morning Post*, "simply means to condone all that Butlerism, including its 'twin cherry' which fulminates in the executive office, Russellism, has done to the great hurt as well as humiliation of the people."[9]

Daniels' conciliatory overtures, however, pleased the radical Populists. George Butler assured his brother Marion that this new fusion policy would attract "the best element of . . . citizens" in North Carolina who desired "*all* the remedial home legislation that our party demands." More importantly, the Democrats would divide into a "reform" faction that would come with the Populists and a "corporation" wing that would go "to the Republican Party where they properly belong." With the reform forces united, Tarheels would secure a true "white man's government."[10]

When William Jennings Bryan, National Democratic Chairman J. K. Jones, and Silver Republican Chairman Charles A. Towne issued a joint proclamation advocating the cooperation of all silver and reform forces in 1898 as the foundation for capturing the presidency in 1900, the *Caucasian* heartily endorsed that course in North Carolina. Cooperating with the Bryan Democrats, Butler carefully explained, did not mean that the Democrats would swallow the People's party. Rather, the Populists would serve as the vanguard of all reform forces.[11]

Behind the scenes Governor Russell labored assiduously to make the Russell-Butler plan, which now had large implications, a reality. Democratic Justice Walter Clark evidently remained sympathetic, hoping "to steer things so as to get the Democrats and Populists to come to a fusion in 1898."[12] Russell lobbied among the Pritchard Populists and confided to Butler: "I have been doing some work among the anti-Butler Pops and I have stopped some of their mouths and brought them over to the right side." He believed that many Populists were "willing to go in for fusion on the Congressmen and Judges and Solicitors, but there will be great difficulty in getting democratic fusion on the county tickets." One rumor held that the governor had persuaded

9   Raleigh *Morning Post*, April 25, 28, 1898.
10 George Butler to Marion Butler, May 3, 1898, in Butler Papers.
11 Raleigh *Caucasian*, May 12, 1898.
12 Russell to Duke, February 19, 1901, in Benjamin Newton Duke Papers, Duke University.

the Populist delegation from his native county of Brunswick to support fusion with the Democrats.[13]

When the Populist state convention met in May, 1898, the Butler forces prevailed despite the warnings of Harry Skinner and others. "I'm one that has stood Democratic abuse," said Skinner. "I'm one that has been ostracized. I beg of you to remember the abuse they heaped on you." The convention proceeded to endorse the recent addresses of Butler and Bryan calling for the cooperation of all silver and antimonopoly forces in North Carolina and to invite the aid of "any party or faction of a party" that held similar views. The Populist platform pledged to annul the Southern Railway's ninety-nine-year lease, protect local self-government, lower railroad rates, provide fair elections, and end government by injunction. Then in a move that illustrated their political bond with Russell, the Populists commended the honest efforts of the governor to give North Carolina "a clean and economic administration." They acclaimed his "brave fight . . . to secure . . . just and reasonable railroad fares and freights" and termed him a "true friend of the common people" against the money power.[14]

The pro-Bryan *News and Observer* interpreted the Populist convention as a repudiation of Republicanism and called upon the Democrats to "give them [the Populists] a helping hand" in uniting the Tarheel silver forces. Less hospitable to the idea of Democratic-Populist fusion was the conservative *Morning Post*. Robert Furman declared that the Populists' offer was a ploy by Butler and Russell to put the Democrats "in a hole" and divide the party. Many Populists who had voted for fusion with the Democrats, according to Furman, had "already entered into Republican–Populist fusion in their counties," and the convention bore the stamp of the Russell influence.[15]

The proffered cooperation with the Populists threatened to disrupt badly the Democratic party. Various diehard Democrats believed that the appeal to white supremacy was the only way the party could avert a disastrous rift between the silver forces and the conservative, probusiness faction. A "straight-out democracy fighting for a white man's government in North Carolina" must be the answer to the Populists, said the Wilmington *Messenger*. Another old Russell foe, the Wilmington

13 Russell to Marion Butler, April 20, 30, 1898, in Butler Papers; Wilmington *Messenger*, May 6, 1898.
14 Raleigh *News and Observer*, May 18, 19, 1898.
15 *Ibid.*, May 19, 1898; Raleigh *Morning Post*, May 19, 1898.

Morning Star, more pointedly reasoned: "The co-operation that Butler offers is not co-operation; it is a surrender of the Democratic party to the Butler contingent, a virtual endorsement of Russell and his administration and a pledge that the fusing Democrats would support Russell if he were again nominated, for Russell and Butler are sucking through the same straw now; he is classed a Populist whom the Butler faction favors and will be entitled to the Governorship under this fusion deal."[16]

When the Democratic convention assembled in late May, 1898, white supremacy, not economic reform, ruled the day. The Democrats "respectfully declined" the offer of cooperation from the Populists and promised to end "negro domination" in North Carolina.[17] They thus quashed the Russell-Butler plan, and J. C. Logan Harris, rapidly becoming Russell's closest adviser, frankly confessed: "I did not see how the democrats could do anything else than reject fusion without destroying themselves. They would have lost far more by fusion."[18] The *Caucasian* could not disguise its disappointment and bitterness. Charging that the Democratic convention had been packed with "goldbugs and railroad attorneys," the Butler organ blamed the railroads' influence for the repudiation of "Mr. Bryan's plan of co-operation [in order] to humiliate him if possible, but also to make a co-operation in 1900 more difficult, and, besides, to prevent the election of anti-monopoly legislatures in the various States during this off year."[19]

Although some Populists despaired that the party was being "run strictly in the interest of the Republican[s]," others believed that the agrarian radicals could still "co-operate with the Russell-silver faction of the Rep. party" and defeat "gold-buggism" and "Hannaism."[20] For Russell, however, the situation had become parlous. Having hitched his administration to the Populist bandwagon and consorted with pro-Bryan forces, he could hardly expect to be welcomed back to Republican circles. One pundit observed: "Governor Russell [now] wants[s] to 'fuse' with the Republicans."[21]

---

16 Wilmington *Messenger*, May 23, 1898; Wilmington *Morning Star*, as quoted in the Raleigh *Morning Post*, May 24, 1898.
17 Raleigh *News and Observer*, May 27, 1898.
18 Wilmington *Messenger*, May 28, 1898.
19 Raleigh *Caucasian*, June 2, 1898.
20 M. N. Sawyer to Marion Butler, June 28, 1898, Morrison Caldwell to Marion Butler, May 30, 1898, in Butler Papers.
21 Raleigh *Morning Post*, June 9, 1898.

Essentially a governor without a party, Russell knew that he could not control a Republican convention in 1898. He was lost somewhere between the Populist and Republican parties and feared any kind of open and formal repudiation, for neither party would wholly embrace him nor acknowledge him as its own. And impeachment, all too real for Republican Governor William W. Holden in 1871, remained a grim possibility should the legislature fall into the hands of hell-bent, Democratic zealots. Fearing the censure of the GOP, Russell, much as he had in 1888 and again in 1892, opposed calling a Republican convention. Such an assembly might become the scene of an angry showdown between "two widely divergent factions in the party," as Loge Harris pointed out, for Russell supporters would surely demand an endorsement of the administration. Hinting at possible cooperation, Populist Hal Ayer warned the GOP that "if the republican state convention did not endorse Governor Russell it would play the devil and ruin everything."[22]

Despite the Russell-Butler gambit with the Democrats, Populists and Republicans alike realized that fusion of their parties was the only possible means of beating the Democrats. James Young, whom Russell appointed colonel of North Carolina's Negro regiment during the Spanish-American War, warned Afro-Americans that the Democrats intended to "draw a bill that will disfranchise every negro in the State and yet be constitutional." Comparing America's fight for Cuban freedom with the fusionists' fight for Negro rights, Young cautioned black North Carolinians not to "let the Democrats come in between you and the Populist party and create friction."[23]

Meeting in July, 1898, the GOP state convention tepidly congratulated Governor Russell for running an economical administration but beyond that did not praise him as had the Populist convention. Openly snubbed by the Old Guard, Russell was neither seated on the podium nor invited to speak. The Republicans in their platform, however, once again asked the Populists to make a joint effort against the Democrats, stating, "We believe that the men who broke the chains of Democracy in 1894 and who restored to the whole people the right of local self gov-

22 Raleigh *News and Observer*, June 8, 9, 1898; Wilmington *Messenger*, June 9, 10, 1898.
23 Raleigh *Morning Post*, July 17, 1898. For Russell's role in the formation of the black regiment, see Willard B. Gatewood, "North Carolina's Negro Regiment in the Spanish-American War," *North Carolina Historical Review*, XLVIII (1971).

ernment and honest elections will stand together in the coming contest for the preservation of these rights." In another plank intended to appease the Populists, the GOP proposed an amendment to the state constitution "embodying the provisions of our present election law."[24]

More than ever the fusionists needed interparty harmony, for the Democrats were feverishly oiling their party machine for the coming election. In July, the Democrats chose Furnifold M. Simmons, New Bern lawyer and former congressman, to run the party's campaign. Stridently anti-Populist and anti-Republican, Simmons was a peerless strategist. To kick off the 1898 campaign he organized huge rallies throughout the state—these being "great picnic, barbecue, social and political gatherings" to which women were also invited. Simmons even set up a speakers bureau to insure that every rally had an able proponent of white supremacy to "storm the fortifications of the fusion-negro-domination enemy" and vanquish "Russellism, McKinleyism, [and] Pritchardism." In addition the new party chairman instigated "White Government Unions" to "re-establish in North Carolina the supremacy of the white race." Members of the union swore to assist in the campaign and to use only "honorable, legitimate, and proper" tactics.[25]

Behind the scenes Simmons and former governor Thomas J. Jarvis secretly solicited funds from many of the bankers, railroad executives, lawyers, and manufacturers in the state and promised that the Democrats would not raise corporation taxes if they regained power. Simmons also pledged to the denominational colleges that appropriations for state-supported institutions of higher education, especially the University of North Carolina, would not be increased. Already disconcerted by Russell's war on the railroads and the Populist-influenced legislatures since 1895, much of the business community banded together behind the Democrats.[26]

The Republicans and Populists were in disarray in the face of such a well-coordinated campaign. A fusion agreement was not struck until September, whereas Democratic orators like Charles B. Aycock, whom Simmons was grooming for the governorship, had been in the field for

---

24 Raleigh *News and Observer*, July 21, 1898.
25 *Ibid.*, July 14, 31, 1898.
26 J. Fred Rippy (ed.), *Furnifold Simmons, Statesman of the New South: Memoirs and Addresses* (Durham: Duke University Press, 1936), 23–29.

more than a month. Butler did not take the stump until nearly October; Russell never did. After two years of bitter, interparty dissension, the fusionists seemed immobilized.

Russell, Butler, and Walter Clark fretfully watched the increasing momentum of the Democratic white-supremacy campaign and its domination by business interests. According to the governor, Clark "was just as anxious to beat the Democrats as Russell or Butler . . . and told . . . all he knew that was going on in Democratic Councils." The Democratic justice, feeling betrayed by his party, declared: "The R.R.'s are *packing the nominations* & trying to elect a *Railroad legislature* with a view to repealing the R.R. Commission act . . . and assuming untrammeled sovereignty of public affairs."[27]

Russell believed that the election was a "fight for our lives . . . [for] to get a Democratic Legislature here means an orgy of deviltry the like of which has not been seen." He tried to rally the warring fusionist factions, and, eyeing his own precarious position, he warned Butler that the Democrats intended to impeach several fusionists and to perpetrate a "revolution" if they gained control of the legislature. "I do not like the looks of things in many counties," the governor confessed to the senator. "You should impress upon the Populists that this is the fight for their lives, if they lose this election their party cannot survive because they cannot vote."[28]

As the campaign heated up, the fusionists, who lacked a daily newspaper and who still bickered over economic issues, attempted to shift attention to the issues that had once harmonized Republican and Populist interests. The *Union-Republican*, denying Democratic charges that the GOP favored Negro rule, asserted that the "fully rounded meaning of nigger," as used by the Democrats, meant "a portion of the negroes, all poor white men and all illiterate white men." The Republican journal declared that "it is the purpose of the Democrats and the burden of their campaign cry to deprive a large portion of the white people of their votes."[29] The Hickory *Press*, another Republican weekly paper, played upon the same theme but emphasized the sec-

27 Russell to Duke, February 19, 1901, in B. N. Duke Papers; Clark to A. W. Graham, September, 12, 1898, in Augustus W. Graham Papers, Southern Historical Collection, University of North Carolina, Chapel Hill.
28 Russell to Duke, August 18, September 23, 1898, in B. N. Duke Papers; Russell to Marion Butler, September 25, 1898, in Butler Papers.
29 Winston *Union-Republican*, September 29, October 27, 1898.

tional and party struggles of the past. The Democratic party in North Carolina, according to the *Press*, had been the party of slaveholders in the East who deprived simple Whig farmers of the West of equal representation, state aid for railroad construction, and internal improvements. "When did the east ever come to the aid of the west?" queried the newspaper. Scoffing at the cry of "negro domination," it concluded: "Behind that hypocritical pretense is the purpose of these eastern Democrats to rob us of the right of local self-government, and to again have the rule of the boss and the work of the machine in every county."[30]

Butler's *Caucasian* also scored the Democrats for their blatant use of the race issue and for obfuscating critical economic issues with this "negro scarecrow." Butler pointed out that the Democratic platform had declared its opposition to government by injunction, "but the people of the State will take notice that the speakers sent out by the Democratic machine are not discussing this question of government by injunction, nor any other of the vital economic questions before the people. Instead they do nothing but howl 'nigger' from one end of the State to the other, hoping under the cover of the negro cry, to get men elected to the legislature who will betray the people on the question of government by injunction and other corporation reforms, as the Democratic members of the last legislature did."[31]

Negro Republicans trumpeted the alarm in the black community. Congressman George H. White personally met with President McKinley to warn him of the dangers engulfing North Carolina as a result of the "unholy war that Democrats are making on the color line." White insisted, "The cry of negro domination is a bugaboo. There has never been negro domination in any county in the State."[32] W. Lee Person, state senator, quoted Democratic Congressman W. W. Kitchin as saying, "Before we allow the negroes to control this State as they do now, we will kill enough of them that there will not be enough left to bury them." Person urged blacks to vote their sentiments even if it meant death, for "white men at the polls with their pistols showing is not a new thing in Edgecombe county."[33] Daniels' *News and Observer*, to-

---

30 Hickory *Press*, October 6, 1898.
31 Raleigh *Caucasian*, September 22, October 27, 1898.
32 Interview with George H. White, Raleigh *Morning Post*, September 13, 1898.
33 Person to the editor, Raleigh *Caucasian*, October 6, 1898.

tally dedicated now to the racist campaign and ignoring its earlier interest in economic issues, reported that Person had told blacks to go to the polls armed.[34]

To such charges as Person's the Democrats responded with intensified violence and rhetoric. Only the Republican warning of disfranchisement caused some worry, and Furnifold Simmons finally asserted that not even Afro-Americans believed that "old Republican negro bugaboo." He denied that the Democrats would take the vote away from anyone. Vowing that his party stood for "manhood suffrage," Simmons nonetheless pledged to alter the county government system "in the counties having negro majorities, thus lifting the ruthless heel of the negro from the neck of the white men who live in the negro-ridden counties of the East."[35]

Cynically manipulated by Simmons and urged on by Daniels' *News and Observer*, the white-supremacy campaign placed North Carolina on the verge of a race war. So-called Red Shirts, resurrecting one Democratic terrorist group of the Reconstruction era, appeared in the eastern and southern counties. Attired in red shirts and armed with shotguns and Winchester rifles, these Democratic horsemen roamed the counties bordering South Carolina, attended political rallies, and disrupted Republican meetings and Negro church services, terrorizing Populists, Republicans, and Negroes alike.[36]

The violent campaign kept the fusionists off the stump. In turning down a speaking engagement in Craven County, Senator Butler admitted to an anxious colleague: "I fear that I could not do you any good if the negro [Isaac H. Smith] stays on the ticket for the Legislature." Similarly, James B. Lloyd admonished Butler not to speak in any black counties where the Red Shirts might appear. "Threats are daily made here [Tarboro] of trouble," he warned. "They are saying that Mr. [W. E.] Fountain will be killed, and if trouble comes all the Pop leaders will be the first to suffer. The feeling here is intense." Lloyd stated further that unless all blacks were removed from the fusionist slate, the Democrats would take the county and townships by force.[37]

34 Raleigh *News and Observer*, September 22, 1898.
35 Charlotte *Observer*, September 25, 1898.
36 Helen G. Edmonds, *The Negro and Fusion Politics in North Carolina, 1894*–1901 (Chapel Hill: University of North Carolina Press, 1951), 148–49.
37 Marion Butler to C. S. Garner, October 8, 1898, Lloyd to Marion Butler, October 14, 15, 1898, in Butler Papers.

Throughout the fusion period Josephus Daniels' *News and Observer* never lost an opportunity to associate the Republican party with the Negro. In this January, 1897, cartoon, published on the occasion of Russell's inaugural ball, cartoonist Jennett sets the mood for the next year's campaign.

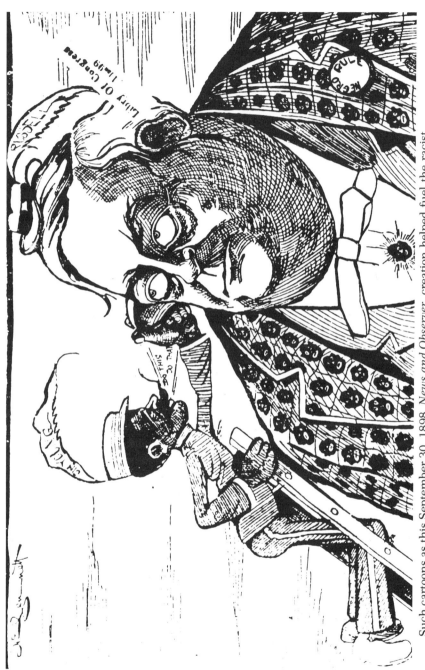

Such cartoons as this September 30, 1898, *News and Observer* creation helped fuel the racist passions of the 1898 and 1900 white supremacy campaigns.

Nowhere, however, had the pall of violence become more ominous than in Wilmington, the governor's home. For a number of months before the election certain Democratic leaders had been secretly organizing paramilitary forces to seize control of the city and oust the Republican mayor and aldermanic board.[38] Racial tensions had intensified in August, 1898, after Alex Manly, Negro editor of the Wilmington *Record*, published a provocative editorial defending his race and assailing white men who brutalized black women. Manly was responding to an article by Mrs. Rebecca Felton, a prominent Georgian, who had advocated the lynching of Negro rapists. In what whites considered an impudent reply, the black editor asserted that white women "are not any more particular in the matter of clandestine meetings with colored men than are the white men with colored women." Sneering at the notion of white men's "purity," Manly counseled white women: "Tell your men that it is no worse for a black man to be intimate with a white woman that for a white man to be intimate with a colored woman. You set yourselves down as a lot of carping hypocrites; in fact you cry aloud for the virtue of your women, when you seek to destroy the morality of ours."[39]

The Democratic press throughout the state seized on Manly's editorial as proof of the degradation that fusion had inflicted, for rarely had a North Carolina Negro spoken so forthrightly about such sensitive interracial relations. Republicans in Wilmington disavowed Manly and his newspaper. Governor Russell authorized the *Morning Post* to say in his behalf "that the negro who edits the Wilmington paper, and who wrote the vile calumny upon the wives of poor white farmers and young white ladies of culture, is not his friend or supporter, but has been his enemy throughout, and that the Governor denounces the scoundrel as severely as any can."[40] In Wilmington the black and white communities warily measured each other. For several nights after the editorial appeared, blacks gathered around the *Record*'s office to protect it from expected reprisals. Indeed, the black community rallied behind Manly, and the Negro Ministerial Union expressed its

---

38   Memoir of Thomas W. Clawson, in Thomas W. Clawson Papers, Duke University, hereinafter cited as Clawson Memoir.

39   Wilmington *Record*, August 18, 1898, North Carolina Collection, University of North Carolina, Chapel Hill.

40   Raleigh *Morning Post*, August 24, 1898.

"hearty sympathy with the efforts of The Daily Record in defending the rights of the race."[41]

Alfred M. Waddell, the Wilmington Democrat whom Russell had defeated for Congress in 1878, was canvassing the state and boldly proclaiming that the Democrats in Wilmington would seize control "if we have to choke the current of Cape Fear River with negro carcasses." Rebecca Cameron, Waddell's cousin, applauded his tactics and angrily asserted, "It has reached the point where bloodletting is needed for the health of the Commonwealth." Urging "white men to get out their shotguns," she characterized Russell as "that infamous malignant blot upon the State" and declared: "I do most earnestly trust, if it come to blows, that he [Russell] will chamber the first ball fired in that mass of val[v]ular tissue which does duty for a heart in the gubernatorial carcass."[42]

Threats were also being made against individual fusionists. In September, 1898, William H. Chadbourn, a prominent Wilmington Republican, sent a public letter to Senator Pritchard in which he stated that the Democratic "talk and palaver about the negro running riot over this city and county is a gross libel, and is doing much harm in a business way." What the Democrats really objected to, he believed, was Republican control of municipal government. Within three weeks, however, Chadbourn had posted another letter to Pritchard in which he warned of "riot, arson, and bloodshed" in Wilmington unless the GOP ticket was taken down.[43] This repudiation of the earlier letter dismayed Republican leaders. Persistent rumors held that the "Old Ring Republican" had written the second letter "either with a pistol at his head or under threats that if it was not written he would be killed." For more than a week the fanatical Wilmington *Messenger* had carried across the top of each column the enigmatic legend, "Remember the 6." On October 18, when Chadbourn's second letter appeared, the number was reduced to "5." That number was said to include the governor himself who had been personally "warned that if he goes to vote [in Wilmington] he will be killed." In fact, all five white Republican

41   Wilmington *Record*, August 24, 1898, as quoted in the Raleigh *News and Observer*, August 26, 1898.
42   Rebecca Cameron to Alfred Waddell, October 26, 1898, in Alfred M. Waddell Papers, Southern Historical Collection, University of North Carolina, Chapel Hill.
43   Both letters are conveniently printed in the Hickory *Press*, October 27, 1898.

leaders were reportedly "marked for slaughter if they seek to interfere with the election plans of those working for the success of the Democratic ticket."[44]

Disconcerted by the threats of disorder and political assassinations, Russell conferred with various fusionist leaders including Senators Pritchard and Butler, Oliver Dockery, the GOP congressional candidate in the Sixth District, and Benjamin F. Keith, a Russell appointee on the Wilmington aldermanic board. The fusionist leaders, fearful of inciting a riot, decided to abandon the political rally that had been set for Wilmington on October 29—a rally at which Russell, Butler, Pritchard, and Dockery had been scheduled to speak.[45]

Russell's activities spawned a rumor, emanating from Washington and sensationalized by the Democratic press, that he and Pritchard wanted federal troops sent to North Carolina to maintain peace and order. Reportedly, Pritchard had initiated some exploratory overtures with the GOP Congressional Committee and President McKinley's cabinet had discussed the question informally. The governor, however, could not obtain federal assistance in quelling a disturbance until state forces proved incapable of handling the situation.[46]

Nevertheless, Russell acted with purpose to stem the mounting violence. He issued an executive proclamation on October 26 enjoining "all ill-disposed" persons of every party to "desist from all unlawful practices and all turbulent conduct" and to preserve the peace. The governor had reason to believe that several counties along the southern border had been "invaded by certain armed and lawless men from another State" and that in numerous counties political meetings had been disrupted by "armed men, using threats, intimidation . . . and actual violence." Russell had information of property being destroyed, citizens being fired on from ambush, and threats of violence being made to prevent citizens from registering to vote. "Several citizens," he

44 Wilmington *Messenger*, October 15, 18, 19, 1898; Raleigh *Morning Post*, October 27, 1898; congressional hearings concerning the Sixth District contest between John D. Bellamy and Oliver Dockery, Charlotte *Observer*, April 21, 1899; "Memorandum of My Personal Recollection of the Election of 1898," by George Rountree, in Henry G. Connor Papers, Southern Historical Collection, University of North Carolina, Chapel Hill, hereinafter cited as Rountree Memoir.
45 Rountree Memoir, in Connor Papers.
46 Raleigh *News and Observer*, October 25, 1898; Raleigh *Morning Post*, October 27, 1898; New York *Times*, October 25, 1898.

revealed, "have been taken from their homes at night and whipped."[47] In a further attempt to maintain the civil and political rights of the state's citizenry, he sent Judge W. P. Bynum to Rockingham in Richmond County to gather affidavits and issue bench warrants "against parties who broke up meetings, assaulted candidates, and whipped negroes."[48]

Rather than support the governor in his plea for order, the Democratic press blasted the threat of federal troops and the Russell proclamation as a "slander" on the state. Characterizing Russell's address as a "stump speech," Daniels' *News and Observer* exploded: "It seeks to place at the door of white men the crimes of which men of his party are guilty. There has been no bad feeling in the State except such as has been engendered by Republican demogogues who have sought to inflame the passions of the negroes." The Wilmington *Messenger* blamed the racial tensions on "white radicals" and called Russell, Butler, Pritchard, and Dockery the "Bloody Four." Wilmington Democrats, said the *Messenger*, believed that "a half-dozen white men—radicals—living here, with one in Raleigh, who was of supreme power, could stop all the trouble if they pleased, and so ordered."[49]

The falsehoods propagated by the Democratic press hardly cooled the racial passions sweeping eastern North Carolina. Still determined to avert bloodshed in Wilmington, Russell worked behind the scenes with Democratic businessmen to prevent a "war between the white and black races." A committee of merchants urged the governor to suppress the Republican ticket in the port city. At first hesitant to take such an extreme measure, Russell finally relented, and the GOP ticket for New Hanover County was struck. When the Democrats further insisted that the Republican state and congressional slate be taken down, Russell refused and appealed to "conservative men" to enforce the original agreement. Assuring the governor that the agreement would be honored, the businessmen blandly asserted, "there has been no agreement, understanding, or effort looking towards the use of any force or other disorderly methods of obstructing voters."[50]

47 Proclamation of Governor Daniel L. Russell, October 26, 1898, in Governor's Papers.
48 Telegram: Russell to W. P. Bynum, n.d., *ibid*.
49 Raleigh *News and Observer*, October 26, 1898; Wilmington *Messenger*, October 28, 1898.
50 James Sprunt *et al.* to Russell, October 24, 1898, F. W. Foster to James Sprunt, October 30, 1898, Russell to James Sprunt, November 4, 1898, James Sprunt to Russell, November 4, 1898, James Sprunt *et al.* to Russell, November 5, 1898, all in Alexander Sprunt and Sons, Inc., Office Files, Duke University.

Nothing, of course, could have been further from the truth. Red Shirts apparently killed at least two Negroes in the southeastern counties; another clash of whites and blacks reportedly took place in Ashpole, near Lumberton, when a Negro was denied the right to register to vote. In Wilmington two paramilitary forces, the Red Shirts and the Rough Riders, terrorized fusionist sympathizers and blacks. The units often paraded through black localities, firing off their rifles, and a favorite tactic was to warn blacks that if they attempted to register to vote they would be discharged from their jobs. Employers supplied lists of their employees to Democratic registrars to ascertain which blacks were bold enough to exercise their franchise. In several instances, Democratic thugs reportedly beat Afro-Americans with swords.[51] In one of the last issues of the Wilmington *Record*, Manly printed a series of resolutions by an "Organization of Colored Ladies" which hailed the courage of black men who registered to vote in the face of Democratic threats and the possible loss of their jobs. The women branded any Negro who failed to register a "white livered coward who would sell his liberty and the liberty of our whole race to the demons who are even now seeking to take away the most sacred rights vouchsafed to any people."[52]

Russell, Pritchard, and Butler, in a final effort to preserve peace in Wilmington, exhorted the fusionists of New Hanover County to accept the agreement made with the merchants and vote for only state and congressional offices. In a circular appeal, the leaders declared: "Let every Republican, every Populist, every Independent, every man who is opposed to the Democratic Machine and its methods, turn out and put in his vote. If you fail to do it, the consequence may be disastrous. . . . Do not hang around the polls on Election Day, vote and go to your homes."[53]

Despite such pleas for peace and orderly democratic processes, the election in the Old North State went forward under the menacing muzzles of Winchester rifles. Robert B. Russell, Negro editor of the Maxton *Blade*, recalled the miasma of fear that had enveloped Robeson County on November 8, 1898. "The Red Shirt organization caused much unrest and alarm, and just before election day made nightly

---

51 Dockery–Bellamy hearings, Charlotte *Observer*, April 21, 1899; affidavit by M. F. Dowling, a Rough Rider, as quoted in the Winston *Union-Republican*, March 15, 1900.
52 Wilmington *Record*, as quoted in the Wilmington *Messenger*, October 21, 1898.
53 Edmonds, *Negro and Fusion*, 159–60.

raids, shot through houses, and warned negroes not to go near the polls on election day. Two or three negroes were soundly whipped. . . . On the day of the election large numbers of negro voters did not come to the polls, and those who did come were allowed to vote only till 12 o'clock." At noon the Red Shirts blocked every road leading to Maxton and drove the blacks back, brandishing their rifles, and firing "in the direction of the fleeing voters." No blacks were allowed on the streets and those who left too slowly were "severely punished." For several weeks after the election black men refused to sleep in their homes and hid in barns or forests.[54] In Wilmington many voters were challenged or their names "improperly erased from the registration books—all Republicans." In some precincts Democrats carrying guns stuffed ballot boxes and destroyed fusionist ballots.[55]

Russell traveled to Wilmington to cast his ballot, ignoring threats on his life. Accompanied by two Wilmington relatives—Walker Taylor and E. W. Sawyer—he voted without incident, but on his return to Raleigh the same afternoon he was nearly lynched. Prominent Democrats such as Cameron Morrison, future governor of North Carolina, had learned that a mob of Red Shirts would be waiting for Russell's train at Hamlet. A contingent of Red Shirts led by Morrison boarded the governor's train at Maxton to warn him of the pending danger. Distrustful, Russell was reluctant to accept Morrison's advice. Finally Morrison shoved the bulky governor into the mail-baggage car in order to hide him, and when the mob swarmed the train at Hamlet the governor was nowhere to be found.[56] In Raleigh, meanwhile, a mob of Red Shirts marched around the executive mansion shouting taunts at the governor's family.

These incidents, however, paled before the bloody aftermath to the Wilmington election. Although the Democrats would hold 134 seats in the general assembly of 1899 and the fusionists only 36, Wilmington remained under Republican rule since the terms of the mayor and aldermanic board had not expired. Such a legality was not going to deter the frenzied Democrats; bolstered by several months of preparation they staged a "revolution." White mobs burned the office of the Wil-

---

54 Dockery–Bellamy hearings, Charlotte *Observer*, April 20, 1899.
55 *Ibid.*, April 21, 1899; Dowling affidavit, Winston *Union-Republican*, March 15, 1900.
56 Alice Sawyer Cooper in collaboration with Louis Goodman, "Daniel Lindsay Russell: A Family and Friend's Memoir" (MS in the Daniel L. Russell Papers, Southern Historical Collection, University of North Carolina, Chapel Hill), 70–72.

mington *Record*, Manly's newspaper, and destroyed the press. Prominent fusionists, both black and white, were forced to flee the city, sometimes with ropes around their necks, as Democratic hoodlums roamed the streets, made house-to-house searches for fusionist leaders, and led armed attacks on alleged Negro strongholds. Black families sought refuge in forests and swamps and hid for days despite the chill November weather. Led by Alfred M. Waddell, the Red Shirts coerced the Republican officeholders into resigning. Thus the municipal government passed into the hands of Democrats who immediately swore in successors, Waddell becoming the new mayor. Although the events in Wilmington have been variously described as a race riot or race war, a *coup d'etat* executed by Democrats would be a truer description.[57]

The governor had ordered out the state militia and sent reinforcements from Clinton, Maxton, and Kinston, and he had depended upon his close friend Walker Taylor, commander of the state guard in Wilmington, to quell the disorder. Taylor, a Democrat, arrested five blacks but no whites, although white mobs "sullenly dispersed" only to gather at other points. No precise figure has ever been established as to the number of blacks killed, but contemporary accounts estimated between eleven and thirty. Only two white men were wounded. Russell refused to intervene in the *coup d'etat*, fearing that any interference might rekindle the fighting. Even as the Democrats were seizing control of the city government, the governor wired George Rountree, newly elected state assemblyman, "I will do what I can to influence Mayor and Council to resign in favor of nominees of your commercial bodies if this will help to restore order."[58]

Exhausted by the harrowing campaign and frightened by the "terrible ordeal" of the election, Russell and his wife retreated to Asheville to recuperate at the home of a friend. The governor, concerned for the safety of his fusionist ally, cautioned Marion Butler: "Is it likely that they will try to assassinate you? I hardly think so, but you had better be a little careful. My friends in Wilmington thought they would do it to me, but they didn't."[59]

57 Edmonds, *Negro and Fusion*, 158–77; Clawson Memoir, in Clawson Papers; Cronly Family Papers, Duke University; Rountree Memoir, in Connor Papers; Henry Hayden, "The Story of the Wilmington Rebellion" (MS at Duke University).
58 Report of Lt. Col. Walker Taylor to Adjutant General, November 22, 1898, *Public Documents of the State of North Carolina*, 1899, Doc. 9, p. 29–30; Russell to Rountree, n.d., in Governor's Papers; Rountree Memoir, in Connor Papers.
59 Russell to Marion Butler, November 12, 1898, in Butler Papers.

The Democratic white-supremacy campaign had shattered the visionary plan of Russell and Butler to restructure Tarheel politics. In spite of their persistent efforts, the governor and senator had never been able to shift the public's attention from the race question to fundamental economic issues. Once the Democrats had refused to cooperate with the Populists in the spring of 1898, the terms of the campaign had been set; race and race alone must determine party fealty. Consequently, many fusionists, black and white, were not allowed to vote, or their ballots were not counted. Others, notably William A. Guthrie, Populist gubernatorial candidate in 1896, and W. E. Fountain, Populist mayor of Tarboro, entered Democratic ranks. The exigencies that had blended Populist and Republican interests in 1894 and 1896 had become shrouded by the race issue, and economic issues had driven wedges between the Populist and Republican parties and just as often within them. Violence, intimidation, and to no small extent internal discord had fatally wounded fusion.

In a sense the election marked a watershed in Russell's administration. Facing a hostile Democratic legislature and being estranged from the Republican party as well, the governor was an isolated and vulnerable figure. He rarely permitted himself to become a political target after the campaign of 1898. Russell apparently even gave serious consideration to resigning, confiding to his friend, Benjamin N. Duke, that he was in "deep distress" as a result of the election. "My troubles have come," he said, "because I have been honest and unpurchaseable and have tried to help the common people." The governor feared that he and his wife could not even return to Wilmington, for the "devils are breaking up our business and it looks like we will be driven from our home." Pondering an uncertain future, he asked Duke if there might be a position available for him in New York with the American Tobacco Company. Perhaps wistfully, Russell claimed that there was no longer any danger of "deviltry from these Democrats in the way of impeachment," since that scheme had been abandoned. "I would not want to resign as Governor, until after I get rid of their Legislature," Russell intimated. "But the irritations incident to being a Republican and living in the South, are getting to be too rank to be borne."[60]

---

60   Russell to Duke, November 19, December 2, 1898, in B. N. Duke Papers.

Russell did not resign, but the bold initiatives and progressive plans for economic reform that had characterized his first two years in office had become faded dreams. The pugnacious Russell temperament remained, but his administration had suffered an agonizing death a full two years before its constitutional expiration.

Chapter VIII

"Political Liberty Is Dead in North Carolina"
The Restoration of Democratic Hegemony

WHILE THE FUSIONISTS controlled the state and Daniel Russell sat in the governor's mansion, at least the potential existed for economic reform and the elimination of the race issue. Now the Democrats had returned to power with what they considered a mandate to end the Negro citizenship that had been established during Reconstruction. In less than two years they would dismantle fusionist reforms, destroy the black electoral base that had made possible the original success of the fusionists, and frustrate the possibility of another Republican-Populist coalition. Although occasionally showing flashes of his old fire and temper, Daniel Russell for the most part watched silently and impotently as the Democrats again affixed a stultifying one-party rule on North Carolina.

Speculation centered on the "negro question"—a shibboleth for disfranchisement—as the general assembly prepared to convene in January, 1899. Republicans openly talked about a "lily-white party" and the purge of Negro loyalists. "The ruinous policy which our party has too frequently pursued," declared the Hickory *Press*, "of pushing negroes forward for office, allowing them to be too prominent in, and often even to preside over our conventions, has not only prevented thousands of good white men from affiliating with us, but has driven great numbers of those who have been life-long Republicans, to forsake us and vote the Democratic ticket." The Hendersonville *Times* added, "Politically, we believe the 'elimination' of the negro from politics will be a blessing in disguise to the Republican party," for with the "negro bug-a-boo eliminated, the whites of the South are sure to split upon economic questions."[1] Even distraught Populists considered the possibility of forming a "White Republican Party," as one of them suggested to Butler, since the Democrats had "learned that by a system of intimidation, Red Shirtism, ostracism, etc., they can frighten a very large per cent of the negroes, and Populists, and keep them silent, and thus maintain power." While such a situation prevailed, agrarian radicals might have to join the GOP *"as the least of evils."*[2]

Alarmed by the growing sentiment among the rank and file for a lily-white Republican party, Senator Jeter Pritchard commended the "devotion of the colored race to the cause of Republicanism, in the Southern States, in the face of the fierce opposition of the Democratic party." Pritchard voiced his unqualified enmity for the disfranchisement of poor and illiterate whites and blacks and urged the Democrats to fulfill their campaign pledge not to disfranchise anyone.[3]

The Democrats, however, had other intentions. Ignoring any campaign promises that had been made in the heat of battle, party journals had already announced the need for a "permanent solution of the suffrage problem." In a blunt editorial Josephus Daniels called for an end to the curse of "negro rule" by making it impossible for a "few demagogues" to gain power "by uniting the dissatisfied whites with the immense ignorant negro vote." Avowed Daniels: "The people are looking confidently to the Legislature to settle once and for all time the question of regulating suffrage."[4]

Democratic legislators were considering a variety of plans for restricting Negro suffrage. As early as 1897, Heriot Clarkson of Charlotte, who was accorded the distinction of having suggested a white-supremacy campaign, had been in touch with the disfranchisers in Mississippi. Murray F. Smith, partisan of a foremost Negro-baiter in Mississippi, James K. Vardaman, explained how his state's suffrage amendment worked. The amendment had given Mississippi a "clear, white majority," he said, and "relieved us of the negro in politics."

1 Hickory *Press*, November 24, 1898; Hendersonville *Times*, as quoted in the Raleigh *Caucasian*, November 24, 1898.
2 George T. Jones to Marion Butler, December 10, 1898, in Marion Butler Papers, Southern Historical Collection, University of North Carolina, Chapel Hill.
3 Winston *Union-Republican*, December 8, 1898.
4 Raleigh *News and Observer*, November 23, 1898.

Smith urged, "You ought, by all means if the Democrats ever get a chance in North Carolina again, to adopt some such provision."[5] Closer to home, Henry G. Connor, speaker of the house in the 1899 assembly, admitted to a colleague: "The politicians have stirred the minds and feelings of the people more deeply than they intended. . . . I find men, who would have read me out of the party in '94 now insisting that I must take the lead in working the problem [of disfranchisement] out." Connor acknowledged that the Democrats wanted a constitutional amendment to limit suffrage and "if possible, to secure the permanent and undivided political supremacy of the white man. . . . We must take the responsibility and must have the power."[6]

When the legislature convened, a cautious and defensive Governor Russell presented his biennial message. With obvious pride he pointed out that during his two years as executive the surplus in the treasury had increased by nearly $100,000. In his view, the surplus indicated an efficient use of public monies despite Democratic charges of fusionist extravagance. Moreover, the treasury had expended $135,000 not previously allocated in "extraordinary appropriations" for various state institutions. Russell believed he had demonstrated his competence and resourcefulness as an administrator. In regard to the North Carolina Railroad, the governor asserted that he had decided to cease resistance to the Southern Railway's litigation when it became apparent that the federal courts would rule in favor of the plaintiff. Even so, he had saved the state thousands of dollars in attorneys' fees, protected the rights and sovereignty of North Carolina, and had in no way precluded the present legislature from acting on the lease. Russell's most important recommendation was a call for improved public education. He urged the lawmakers to lengthen school terms and build more schools especially in rural areas. Acutely sensitive to the mood of the Democratic legislature, the governor briefly alluded to the question of "negro government." He denied that the state had ever suffered under Negro rule and as proof declared that of 818 gubernatorial appointments to civil office a grand total of eight had gone to Negroes. These figures stood in stark contrast to Democratic accusations of Negro su-

5   M. F. Smith to Heriot Clarkson, November 23, 1897, in Heriot Clarkson Papers, Southern Historical Collection, University of North Carolina, Chapel Hill.

6   H. G. Connor to George Howard, November 25, 1898, in Henry G. Connor Papers, Southern Historical Collection, University of North Carolina, Chapel Hill.

premacy. Although Russell had repeatedly appointed James Young to conspicuous posts, including state fertilizer inspector, director on a state hospital board, and colonel of the North Carolina black regiment, he had plainly evaded black demands for patronage. John G. Norwood, a Negro alderman in Wilmington, had been the only other prominent black appointee.[7]

Russell's message differed markedly from the progressive reform program he had offered in his inaugural address two years earlier. It was the last time the legislature of 1899 heard from the governor, who had no base of support and lacked the power to veto legislation repugnant to him or to the state constitution.

The Democratic legislature of 1899 literally destroyed every vestige of fusionist reform. Local self-government was ended. The assembly centralized the appointive power in its hands by stripping the governor of that important prerogative. The railroad commission was abolished and supplanted by the North Carolina Corporation Commission which was given supervision of railroads, steamboats, navigation and canal companies, telephone and telegraph companies, and banks. Ostensibly a progressive measure, the corporation commission actually replaced a reform-minded and nonpartisan commission with one dominated by the three appointed probusiness Democrats.[8] In a slap at Russell's probity the Democratic legislators even reinstated James W. Wilson and S. Otho Wilson to the railroad commission during the final weeks of its existence with the dubious judgment that the "leasing of a hotel on the side of a railroad is not such an interest as, under the statute, would have disqualified one to act as Railroad Commissioner."[9]

With a suffrage amendment in the offing, the Democrats next moved to overturn the fusionist election law. The major features of the laws of 1895 and 1897 had been the decentralization of power from the state toward the local poll and the assurance that each party would have representatives at each booth. All that changed with a new law which centralized the control of the election machinery in a state board of elections consisting of seven men appointed by the legisla-

---

7 *Public Documents of the State of North Carolina*, 1899, Doc. 1, p. 3–26.
8 For a detailed discussion of the 1899 legislature, see Helen G. Edmonds, *The Negro and Fusion Politics in North Carolina, 1894–1901* (Chapel Hill: University of North Carolina Press, 1951), 179–97.
9 Raleigh *Morning Post*, February 16, 1899.

ture. In addition the Democrats imposed an intricate and confusing registration procedure in which a prospective elector had to produce positive proof of the date and place of his birth as well as overcoming other technicalities. The new election law also changed the state election from November to August, 1900, in order to lessen the possibility of national Republican influence or interference.[10]

Although the Democrats also passed "Jim Crow" legislation codifying and mandating segregationist practices, the climax of the 1899 legislature came with the adoption of a suffrage amendment bill to be submitted to the people for ratification in 1900. On February 17, 1899, Assemblyman George Rountree introduced the suffrage amendment, noting that the "experiment of universal suffrage" had proven "impracticable," and that four years of fusion rule had shown the necessity for a restricted suffrage. Rountree rejected the notion that the proposed bill violated the Fifteenth Amendment to the federal Constitution. The men drafting the bill admittedly had sought to protect the franchise of the "unlettered" white man, but there was "no mention of any race or color, or of discrimination as such." According to the Wilmington Democrat, only "those negroes who are unfit for citizenship" would be disfranchised. He concluded that North Carolina had been "just" in its dealings with blacks but that now Negroes would have to "prepare themselves to become fit subjects to exercise the rights of suffrage."[11]

The suffrage amendment had been patterned after the one passed by Louisiana in 1898. It included a literacy test, a poll tax, and an important exception clause, the "grandfather clause," which said that no male person, or any "lineal descendant of any such person," who prior to January 1, 1867, had been able to vote in any state could be deprived of the franchise by means of the educational qualification if he registered to vote by November 1, 1908. If adopted by the electorate in 1900, the amendment would go into effect on July 1, 1902. The amendment bill easily carried both houses.

When the legislature adjourned, Senator Pritchard sounded the "bugle note of Republican opposition" to the constitutional amendment, denying that Negro domination had ever existed in North Carolina. He accused Furnifold M. Simmons of having lied about disfran-

10 *North Carolina Public Laws*, 1899, Chap. 507, pp. 658–87.
11 Raleigh *Morning Post*, February 18, 1899.

chisement during the campaign of 1898 and averred that the proposed amendment was unconstitutional in view of the Fourteenth and Fifteenth amendments. The senator warned that such a dangerous measure would "disfranchise hundreds of the honest yeomanry of the State," men who were illiterate but whose ancestors had fought for political liberty. The "false cry of negroism," Pritchard asserted, demonstrated the hypocrisy of the Democrats who sought to tyrannize North Carolina.[12] Butler's newspaper, the *Caucasian*, was quick to agree that the suffrage amendment broke the Democrats' campaign pledge and to insist that there had never been a "more flagrant violation of public faith than this."[13]

Conspicuously silent since his biennial message, Governor Russell had made no public statement about the ongoing Democratic counterrevolution. But in April the Raleigh *Progressive Farmer*, a nationally respected Populist journal, published a letter from a Mr. H who was widely believed to be J. C. L. Harris, Russell's closest adviser. Mr. H declared that the governor, who was "easily one of the best lawyers in the state," had contemplated filing a bill in equity with the United States Circuit Court as the "proper remedy" for the suffrage amendment. Borrowing a tactic used by the Southern Railway against him, Russell's suit would demand a "perpetual injunction against the secretary of state and other election officers to restrain them from submitting the proposed amendment to a vote of the people, on the distinct ground that section 5 [the "grandfather clause"] violates the 15th amendment." A bill in equity was necessary because Russell believed that it could be "clearly shown that there is no remedy in this case for the 100,000 defrauded voters, except by suit in equity in the United States courts." Until recent years, Mr. H explained, an injurious act had to be committed before an injunction was imposed, but now courts stopped certain developments, such as strikes, before they happened. Russell hesitated, however, because of several complications. He was not certain that the whole amendment would fall if section five were ruled unconstitutional. If the rest of the amendment stood, then section four—the educational and poll tax qualifications—would become operable, thereby disfranchising illiterate whites and blacks. An alter-

12   *Ibid.*, March 7, 1899.
13   Raleigh *Caucasian*, March 2, 16, 1899.

native choice for the antiamendment forces would be to ignore the courts "and undertake to destroy the Democratic party by making the amendment the paramount issue in the [1900] campaign."[14]

The question of which policy to pursue was critical. If Russell and the fusionists contested the suffrage amendment in the courts and section four remained valid, the Democrats could accuse them of striking down the exception clause and disfranchising illiterate whites. If they determined to tackle the amendment squarely in the election of 1900, the Democrats might stage another violent white-supremacy campaign. Neither alternative boded well for the fusionists despite the audacity of Russell's contemplated legal maneuver.

Perhaps more potentially disastrous was the split in the fusionist parties over the amendment. Pritchard plainly was ready to oppose the suffrage amendment at any cost, but Thomas Settle, among others, publicly announced that he would support it. All Republicans, however, probably would have agreed with Virgil Lusk of Asheville, who wrote Congressman Richmond Pearson: "That gang at Raleigh last winter calling themselves the legislature, was a disgrace to the State and a burlesque of intelligence. They had no love of country—only office, and hatred to Republicanism, because the Republican party stood in their way to the much coveted prize."[15]

The Populists were as ambivalent as the Republicans. Calling for white supremacy and the colonization of Negroes overseas, certain Populists still castigated the election law and suffrage amendment as Democratic schemes to disfranchise unlettered white men. The Hickory *Times-Mercury* claimed, "We represent the only white party in the nation. We want to take the negro not only out of politics, but out of the way. . . . so every man—white man, can vote as he pleases."[16] In November, 1899, Marion Butler finally announced his intention to take the stump against the suffrage amendment, but he denied that he was moving toward the GOP, for he still favored Bryan, free silver, and antitrust legislation. He feared, however, that if the "grandfather clause" of the suffrage amendment were ruled unconstitutional, as many as 60,000 white Tarheels would lose the vote.[17]

14   Raleigh *Progressive Farmer*, as quoted in the Raleigh *News and Observer*, April 5, 1899.
15   Virgil Lusk to Richmond Pearson, September 24, 1899, in Richmond Pearson Papers, Southern Historical Collection, University of North Carolina, Chapel Hill.
16   Hickory *Times-Mercury*, as quoted in the Raleigh *Caucasian*, September 14, 1899.
17   Raleigh *Morning Post*, October 6, November 10, 1899.

Butler might well have added another reason. It was clear that the Democrats planned another white-supremacy campaign in 1900. Populist State Auditor Hal Ayer warned Butler that unless the fusionists built "an organization that is both willing and able to suppress such tyranny and terrorism by physical force" the Democrats would again imperil political liberty in North Carolina. "Their plan does not mean argument or discussion," Ayer explained, "it means riot, slander, abuse, physical violence and general anarchy. Their plan now is to red-shirt every town in the State, and to terrorize voters through the means of such characters as can be hired to wear red-shirts, drink mean whiskey and raise commotion generally." Ayer believed that the majority sentiment in North Carolina ran against the amendment, but that it was "quite torpid and indifferent." [18] This note of alarm described the fusionists' predicament on the eve of the 1900 election. If they pitched their whole campaign against the amendment, as they evidently were determined to do, could they marshal a majority in the face of the Democrats' terrorist tactics? Daniel Russell, quietly serving out his term, did not think so.

The forum Russell chose for voicing his concerns was a shrewd one indeed—one removed from the turmoil of Tarheel politics. Invited in February, 1900, to speak at Chicago's Lincoln Day celebration, the governor sent Loge Harris to deliver a perceptive speech on "Republicanism in the South." With faintly disguised thrusts at northern Republicans and Republican administrations, Russell declared that the "experiment" of black suffrage was "plainly impossible" without federal coercion. The old Whig planter boldly imputed the difficulties surrounding Negro suffrage to the "attitude of the ruling classes in the South." He charged, "History must record it . . . that negro suffrage was brought about by the narrowness and spite of the Southern politicians, who, instead of accepting the liberal terms by the North, and uniting themselves with the party of the country [the Republicans], went with the party of opposition and of reaction. By this folly, they forced the 15th Amendment."

Unfortunately, Russell explained, the North had not provided the necessary force to make the suffrage experiment work, for the master class, which had once owned the blacks, resented Negro suffrage and

---

18 Ayer to Marion Butler, December 30, 1899, in Butler Papers.

black involvement in politics. That same class had supported slavery and secession and resisted the Civil War amendments. Now it opposed "negro suffrage and . . . negro equality in any form." The few brave souls of the slaveholding class who dared accept the war's results and ally with the Republican party had been "pursued, persecuted, and proscribed." As a result, Negro suffrage had kept white men in the old "slave belt" tied to the Democrats. But, Russell insisted, thousands of property holders and businessmen—the scions of the ruling class— objected to "Bryanism" and were truly Republican in their outlook. They supported federal power on every key issue save one—the "negro question"—and on that they demanded states' rights. The North, said Russell, had seemingly acceded on that issue, prompting him to ask, "If your War Amendments cannot be enforced, would it not be better to repeal them?"

Thus challenging northern Republicans, Russell pointed out that the Democrats proposed to nullify the Constitution with a disfranchisement amendment, thereby hoping "to keep up agitation on the negro question for the pending election." He admonished Tarheel Republicans not to permit the Democrats "to force the battle and choose the ground" with the race issue and appealed to all elements opposed to the Democratic party and its methods to refuse to accept Negro suffrage as the campaign issue. The franchise of the black man, in his opinion, was the responsibility of the "judicial and political departments of the Federal Government." With the North once more assuming its commitment to the Negro's welfare, southern Democratic triumphs would be short-lived. "The colored people," Russell asserted, "will see that their safety requires them to follow the men who give them employment. The colored tenant, if he votes at all, will vote with the owner of the land. The bugbear of negro supremacy being removed, the men of thought, of wealth, of enterprise and of action will take charge of the Republican party. In a few years under these conditions, the Republican party of North Carolina will be the party of property and intelligence."[19]

Russell's cleverly phrased address was misconstrued by many North Carolinians as blanket approval of the suffrage amendment.

19 Russell's "Republicanism in the South," in Daniel L. Russell Papers, Southern Historical Collection, University of North Carolina, Chapel Hill.

Actually, the governor had reiterated his hope that the race question could be expunged from politics and southern Republicans relieved of the burden of defending Negro suffrage. In his opinion the federal government, and more particularly northern Republicans, had promoted Negro enfranchisement, and now they had a responsibility for protecting it. Russell had not really departed from his original Whiggish view of Negro political participation firmly superintended by upper-class whites. More surprising, then, was the governor's implicit realignment with the business wing of the GOP and his brief sally at "Bryanism." After all, it was he who had consorted with Populists and Bryan Democrats. Pressed by continuing financial problems, the governor apparently wished to make peace with the business interests of the party. Indeed, Russell was still asking Ben Duke for a position in New York or a corporate legal post in North Carolina. He wrote the tobacco magnate: "I am awful anxious to make some money to pay my debts. We can get home & quit spending money. I am *badly worried* about money."[20]

The Charlotte *Observer* hailed Russell's Lincoln Day speech as "a smart and entertaining effort." The Democratic organ stated: "It is likely that he is at heart in favor of it [the amendment], for it is well known, from his former public utterances, that he has but poor opinion of the negro, and he has recently been quoted as saying, and has not denied saying, that his party's leaders are making a mistake in attempting to organize the party, as such, against the measure."[21] Russell's seeming repudiation of the GOP policy advocated by Pritchard infuriated the Old Guard. State Chairman A. E. Holton angrily responded to the speech: "The Democrats will use that. The fact is the Democrats use Russell and then charge him to the Republicans." Russell reportedly reacted to Holton's criticism with "the usual prefatory grunt" and a declaration that he "didn't expect anything else from that d——jaybird-headed f——l."[22]

Estranged as much as ever from the Republican hierarchy in North Carolina, Russell's warnings against meeting the Democrats on their own grounds—the race issue—went unheeded. In fact, the white-supremacy campaign was already in full swing. Former gover-

20 Russell to Duke, January 9, 1900, in Benjamin Newton Duke Papers, Duke University.
21 Charlotte *Observer*, February 16, 1900.
22 *Ibid.*, February 25, 1900.

nor Thomas J. Jarvis, worried by the antiamendment sentiment among western Democrats where illiteracy was high, believed that the party would be "sorely pressed" to carry the state for the amendment and its advocates. "It has in it elements of weakness which the demogogues may use among the weak and ignorant with damaging effect," Jarvis felt, and the Democrats thus had to make a "united, aggressive, heroic effort." Only a "fierce struggle" would bring victory.[23]

Again under the leadership of Furnifold Simmons, who had his eye on Butler's Senate seat for 1901, the Democratic campaign matched in ferocity the election of 1898. "White government unions" were reorganized and expanded to include county coordinators. As the campaign progressed, Simmons' rhetoric became more strident and irresponsible. He charged that Butler wanted "to stir up strife and inflame the negroes to violent resistance of the purpose of the whites to disfranchise them." If any race troubles developed, they would be the product of "agitators" like Butler. "The white people are determined to settle this negro question this year," Simmons continued, "and they are not to be deterred . . . by thinly veiled threats of negro insurrection, made by a gang of unworthy white office-seekers."[24]

Simmons sounded another ominous note in February, 1900. Worried by the fusionist argument that the courts might strike down section five of the suffrage amendment, that is, the "grandfather clause," and leave section four—the educational qualification—intact, Simmons decided that the two sections should be combined. He promised that the legislature, meeting in June, would consolidate them on the dubious legal assumption that if the one provision were ruled unconstitutional the other would also fall.[25]

This possibility caused deep consternation in Populist circles. J. F. Click, editor of the Hickory *Times–Mercury*, warned Butler that if the two sections were combined the Populists could no longer afford to run against the amendment, for the poor whites in the party, their franchise secure, would support Negro disfranchisement. Noting that poor whites already resented black suffrage and economic competition, Click contended that the suffrage amendment was a boon to both Pop-

23   Thomas J. Jarvis to F. D. Winston, December 22, 1899, Francis D. Winston Papers, Southern Historical Collection, University of North Carolina, Chapel Hill.
24   Raleigh *Morning Post*, January 28, 1900.
25   *Ibid.*, February 2, 1900.

ulists and Republicans. "But for the negro," he said, "the gold bugs and protectionists in the Democratic party would go into the Republican party bodily. It's this class of Democrats that are urging the amendment. They want it fixed so they can vote the Republican ticket without being called negro."[26]

To black leaders it was obvious that the fusionists were more interested in defending the suffrage of unlettered white men than that of Negroes. Consequently, many Negro leaders attempted to stem the rising chorus of white supremacy that echoed across the state. In January, 1900, at the annual meeting of the Emancipation Association, James E. Shepard declared, "We recognize the fact that in this country there can be no middle ground between freedom and slavery. We cannot see that the best way to make a good man is to unman him."[27] Another black leader who organized a conference of Negroes to oppose the suffrage amendment pointed out: "It has been urged that we cannot well retain our self respect nor the respect of the nation if we sit quietly by and make no protests as the negroes of Georgia did. We believe there are many white citizens in the state opposed to the amendment and by a manly yet consistent and vigorous appeal we may be enabled to enlist their services in a united effort to defeat the measure."[28]

Such moderate appeals proved useless. Charles B. Aycock, the soon-to-be-named Democratic gubernatorial candidate, announced from the stump, "There are three ways in which we may rule, by force, by fraud or by law. We have ruled by force, we can rule by fraud, but we want to rule by law."[29] When the Democratic state convention assembled in April, 1900, Aycock in his acceptance speech assailed the Russell regime. "The Republicans insist that we have never had negro rule in North Carolina, that the Republican party elects white men to office and that this fact gives us a government by white men." Russell had even boasted of appointing only eight Negroes during his tenure, but according to Aycock, who was a personal and professional friend of the governor, he missed the point that "it is the party behind the office-holder that governs and not the office-holder himself." Asserted the Democratic nominee: "There is no man in the State today more cer-

26   J. F. Click to Marion Butler, March 8, 1900, in Butler Papers.
27   Raleigh *Morning Post*, January 2, 1900.
28   B. A. Johnson to Charles Hunter, January 12, 1900, in Charles N. Hunter Papers, Duke University.
29   Raleigh *Morning Post*, March 6, 1900; Winston *Union-Republican*, March 8, 1900.

tainly conscious than Governor Russell himself that he has failed of his purpose because he had behind him the negroes of the State and not the white men." [30]

When the Populist state convention met soon after, the agrarian radicals refused to make the suffrage amendment a party question and left the issue to each man's conscience. Declaring themselves the true white man's party, the Populists damned the election law as "infamous" and termed the suffrage amendment an "evil and danger" to unlettered whites. [31]

The Republicans, following the Populist lead, nominated a full slate, but led by Senator Pritchard they affirmed their opposition to the suffrage amendment. The GOP platform characterized the amendment as a "shocking act of party perfidy" and an "impudent assault" on the federal Constitution. Russell was again snubbed by the convention, though his administration was described as "scrupulously clean, faithful and economical." [32]

The die was cast. J. C. L. Harris bitterly explained the fusionist strategy. The Republicans and Populists both put up state tickets so that the People's party could escape any association with the Negro and keep its members from voting Democratic. Fusion on the county and legislative levels, however, supposedly remained a possibility. Because Senator Butler did not want his party to "shoulder the negro and antagonize the amendment," the Populists had made the amendment a matter of individual choice. Pritchard "had decided that he could not drop the negro; that this would be turning over the negro to the tender mercies of the Democrats and worst of all would lose the negro vote in New York, Ohio, Indiana, etc." In other words, Harris believed that Pritchard was trying to protect McKinley's reelection in the more populous North, possibly at the expense of the North Carolina Republican party. [33]

Russell, of course, disagreed with Pritchard's tactics and consequently had been ignored at the GOP state convention. After the convention, Harris declared that the governor had "supreme contempt for that gang." The breach in the party, Harris confessed, had existed for

30 Charlotte *Observer*, April 12, 1900.
31 Raleigh *News and Observer*, April 19, 1900.
32 Raleigh *Morning Post*, May 3, 4, 1900.
33 Charlotte *Observer*, April 18, 1900.

some years, but the governor's outspoken disapproval of the Republicans' strategy in opposing the Democrats solely on the issue of race had made the gulf wider yet. "If the brains of the entire outfit [GOP] were concentrated," exclaimed Harris, "they would not equal in volume or quality the brain of Governor Russell."[34]

What Harris and Russell were arguing in effect was that opposition to the amendment should not be a "test of party loyalty" but rather a question of individual conscience. Believing the amendment to be unconstitutional, they felt that the federal courts would ultimately have to rule on it. To force southern Republicans to defend Negro suffrage in the face of a violent white-supremacy campaign, in their view, was not only foolhardy but disastrous.

North Carolina Republicans, in fact, were not eager to encourage Negro voting and were even more insistent that blacks refrain from running for office in 1900. Pritchard cautioned a black educator in Raleigh, "The candidacy of colored people at this time for local offices would do more to assist the Democrats in their unjust and unwarranted assertions, than all other causes combined." A. E. Holton, moreover, refused to permit joint debates between Republican and Democratic candidates since no Republican speaker could get a fair hearing with Red Shirts and shotguns again in full evidence. In addition, the Republicans declined to canvass the East or organize the black electorate there. W. S. Hyams, secretary of the GOP state committee, told Butler he need not campaign in the West, assuring the senator that the Republicans would "look after the west and are expecting you to take care of the east in the matter of sending speakers to various points."[35]

As a result, the Populists were left in the anomalous position of proclaiming themselves a "white man's party" while implicitly defending Negro suffrage. One distressed eastern Populist informed Butler that there was a "great deal of apathy on the part of the Colored Voters." Black Republicans, so he understood, complained that the Republican managers had "failed so far to put any Literature in their hands and have not offered any advice in this Campaign, and have, they feel, 'left.'" Since the GOP had abandoned the Negro, the anxious Populist

34 *Ibid.*, May 5, 1900.
35 Pritchard to Hunter, January 26, 1900, in Hunter Papers; Holton to Marion Butler, May 18, 1900, W. S. Hyams to Marion Butler, June 27, 1900, in Butler Papers.

urged Butler to prod the Republicans or "get out the [Negro] vote in sufficent numbers to beat the Dems."[36]

When the general assembly met in June, the Democrats, as Simmons had promised, combined sections four and five of the suffrage amendment so that the "grandfather clause" and the educational qualification would putatively become indivisible and the entire amendment would "stand or fall together." The Democrats also changed the election law to prohibit a judge from issuing a mandamus compelling an election officer to perform his duties except during the regular session of the supreme court, which, of course, came after the election. It was a crafty bit of chicanery by "Simmons and his ballot-box stuffing machine," said Butler's *Caucasian*.[37] The Charlotte *Observer* boldly admitted that the Democrats' ultimate goal was "to rid themselves of the danger of the rule of negroes and lower classes of whites."[38]

Confronted by the blatant racism of the Democrats and the tepid defense of Negro suffrage by the fusionists, North Carolina Negroes hardly knew where to turn. Scotland Harris, a member of the 1897 legislature and editor of the Littleton *True Reformer*, warned blacks not to vote for any Populists who were "bitter and rampant in favor of the constitutional amendment." Such Populists expected to ride into office on the shoulders of "Negro republicans . . . whose political rights they seek to abridge with one hand while they hold out the other for their votes." Harris called such duplicity "political hypocrisy in the truest sense of the word."[39] Despite such suspicions, the Butler-led Populists were making a determined bid to protect the Negro's franchise. They distributed to county and township party leaders various information sheets designed to ascertain and augment fusionist strength and also circulated hundreds of affidavits and warrants for the arrest of dishonest election officers. One affidavit specifically applied to Negroes who had been refused registration and was addressed to the United States Commissioner of the Federal District Court in North Carolina.[40]

Butler's preparations were put to the test when voter registration commenced in June. Democratic registrars illegally transcribed the names of fusionists and blacks on sheets of paper rather than entering

36   J. S. Basnight to Marion Butler, June 26, 1900, in Butler Papers.
37   Raleigh *Caucasian*, June 21, 28, 1900.
38   Charlotte *Observer*, June 6, 1900.
39   Littleton *True Reformer*, July 25, 1900.
40   Vast amounts of this material can be found in the undated portion of the Butler Papers, 1900.

them in the registration book. Negro Republicans, evidently drilled to recognize such tricks, objected to the improper procedures. In Sampson County a Democratic registrar threatened "to kick an old colored man because the old man told him he wasn't registering him according to Law."[41] In the eastern counties the Red Shirts supervised the registration and Democratic ruffians menacingly vowed that "the kinkey headed and strait haired Negroes . . . would not vote this time." One Populist reported, "The negroes are so completely frightened by their threats that we find it impossible to get them to try to register and many that has been refused registration we can not get them to file their affidavit." An embittered Greene County Populist complained, "In my opinion, the Republicans all over the East don't care much if the amendment is carried," and he added that the only Populist who had taken a stand against Democratic tactics had been shot and seriously wounded in a fight with a Democrat.[42]

Although declining to make the suffrage amendment a party test, as had the Republicans, the Populist party was compelled to defend Negro suffrage. A. E. Holton, the wily GOP party chairman, audaciously upbraided Butler for the Populists' lack of effort. "I have information that a large number of negroes in the eastern part of the state are not registering. As you know we have done very little towards organizing them leaving them to the Populists. You must stir your people, and get them to see that the colored folks are registered." Holton admitted that the Republicans were not sufficiently in touch with Negro preachers and teachers to marshal the black electorate effectively.[43]

Butler's vigorous campaign had some impact, as one account showed that at least forty-five registrars were arrested in 1900 for failure to observe proper election procedures.[44] Nevertheless, many fusionists believed that such a strategy was futile. Governor Russell seemed a forgotten figure, until shortly before the August election he denounced the arrest of the registrars and stated his belief that such tactics had ruined McKinley's chances for carrying North Carolina.

41 Claude Bell to Holton, June 29, 1900, W. F. Sissonis to Marion Butler, June 29, 1900, John Edmound to Marion Butler, June 7, 1900, *ibid.*
42 J. H. Fussell to Marion Butler, July 14, 1900, G. F. Walker to Marion Butler, July 20, 1900, W. E. Murphrey to Marion Butler, July 18, 1900, *ibid.*
43 Holton to Butler, July 17, 1900, *ibid.*
44 J. G. deRoulhac Hamilton, *History of North Carolina Since 1860*, Vol. III of R. D. W. Connor *et al.* (eds.), *History of North Carolina* (6 vols.; Chicago: Lewis Publishing Co., 1919), 313.

The fusionists, he felt, had bungled the whole campaign.[45] When asked about the suffrage amendment, the crusty governor replied: "No, I shall not vote for it. I am against it. I am against it for many reasons. One good reason is enough. . . . It is unconstitutional. It violates the Fifteenth Amendment." But in a frank assessment of the political situation, he conceded that the amendment would probably be ratified and put into operation unless voided by the federal courts. "With a free and fair vote it would be defeated, but of course, it will be adopted. There is no way to prevent it. The Democratic managers have got passion and prejudice aroused and have established a reign of terror in many localities."

Predicting that blacks would not try to register to vote "to any great extent," Russell counseled: "My advice to the colored people is to let the amendment thing alone. They are helpless. Let them leave it to the whites." He argued that open black opposition to the amendment would only exacerbate white bitterness and prejudice. As for the GOP and Senator Pritchard, the governor pointedly reminded them that he had advised against making the amendment a party issue. Now with the party apparently "wrecked," the only chance remaining for the Republicans was to strike the "machine ticket" and put up one "composed of business men and no politicians."[46]

The old maverick Republican, with his administration coming to an unhappy end, had gotten in his final licks at the Old Guard. His blunt portrayal of the political situation, however, was perhaps what moved the fusionists to make one last desperate attempt to win the election. In the final week of the campaign the Populists and Republicans fused their state tickets. According to Senator Butler, "we must have the Legislature or political liberty is dead in North Carolina." Pritchard agreed. He wrote Ben Duke almost prophetically, "this is a life and death struggle in N.C. for republican existence, and in my judgment it is the last opportunity that will be afforded us to make a stand for the cause of republicanism."[47]

The fusionist gambit was too little and too late. Violence stalked the

45 Raleigh *News and Observer*, July 18, 1900; W. H. Worth to Duke, July 18, 1900, in B. N. Duke Papers.
46 Interview with Charlotte *Observer*, July 20, 1900.
47 Circular letter by Marion Butler, n.d., in Butler Papers; Pritchard to Duke, July 21, 1900, in B. N. Duke Papers.

election, the situation once again being—as one frustrated Populist put it—"not so much nig[g]er supremisy as it is Democrat rascality."[48] In Smithfield a band of Red Shirts tore down a platform to prevent a Populist from addressing a rally, and when sympathizers tried to protect the speaker, a brawl ensued. "The red-shirters beat and drove home some of Johnston county's most respectable white men and dragged D. T. Massey, candidate for legislature, to Court square and told him he would be lynched if he did not go home," Butler reported. The Red Shirts had then threatened to destroy the office of the Smithfield *Courier*, a Republican newspaper, and kill J. D. Parker, its editor. Parker's entreaty to the governor had impelled Russell to summon the state guard from Raleigh and place it on alert until after the election.[49]

The target of Democratic abuse remained above all the Afro-American. Red Shirts whipped and intimidated Negroes throughout the eastern counties. In Richmond County a mob of them surrounded the house of a Negro farmer, demanding that he show himself. They threatened to burn the house and then fired rifles into it, but there was still no response. When the Red Shirts broke down the door they were greeted with a gun blast that seriously wounded one of them.[50] The night before the election many Negro Republicans found notes under their doors such as: "As a friend to the Colored man you stay away from the polls tomorrow; the negro that does not vote he will be saved but he that votes will smell hell."[51]

A Moore County Populist reported that there "were 36 Red Shirts around the Polls on election day" who scared many fusionists away. "On several nights before the election the Red Shirts rode around over the country firing off their Winchesters and declaring that if those opposed to the amendment tried to vote there would be trouble," he explained. Nor were instances of outright fraud uncommon. Even Attorney-General Zebulon V. Walser commented to Butler, "If they could steal here [Davidson County], when the people are all white, what could they not do in other parts of the State?"[52]

48   H. A. Windley to Marion Butler, July 24, 1900, in Butler Papers.
49   Circular letter by Marion Butler, July 31, 1900, *ibid.*; Raleigh *News and Observer*, July 22, 27, 1900.
50   J. T. Haywood to Marion Butler, August 10, 1900, in Butler Papers.
51   [?] McGidden to Marion Butler, August 13, 1900, *ibid.*
52   Undated report from Moore County (*circa* August, 1900), and Z. V. Walser to Marion Butler, August 4, 1900, *ibid.*

The demoralizing division within fusionist ranks, coupled with the Democrats' partisan election law and fear-mongering campaign, brought a smashing Democratic victory. Governor Russell, rather than vote in Wilmington, stayed in Raleigh. After the brawl in Smithfield he feared there might be further "election disorder or rioting," and if it occurred, he wanted to assume responsibility for ordering the state guard to the scene.[53] Charles B. Aycock, promising white supremacy and universal educational reforms, easily won the governorship with 186,650 votes as opposed to 126,296 for Republican Spencer B. Adams on the fusion ticket. The suffrage amendment was ratified by a vote of 182,217 to 128,285. Only thirty-one counties out of ninety-seven voted against the amendment, and they were in the central and western portions of the state. Not one of the eighteen black counties went against it. New Hanover County, scene of the Wilmington race riot in 1898, returned only two negative amendment votes and three ballots for Adams.[54] Whereas 75.3 percent of the electorate apparently turned out for the election of 1900, an estimated 33 percent of eligible black voters did not vote, a figure probably too low. Four years earlier an estimated 13 percent of the black electorate had not gone to the polls. The Populists, since they had no gubernatorial candidate, appear to have voted about three-to-two in favor of the Republican nominee. On the suffrage amendment, however, the Populists were more evenly divided with an estimated 37 percent casting ballots for it and 42 percent against.[55]

The Democratic victory was overwhelming. The Populist party had disintegrated; the GOP, having lost as much as half its voting strength with the disfranchisement of the Negro, would not elect another state officer for over seven decades. Voter turnouts that had peaked over 85 percent under the liberal fusionist election laws declined to less than 50 percent by 1904. One-party, Democratic rule had again been riveted upon North Carolina.

Daniel Russell had reached the end of a turbulent career in public office—but the Democrats had not heard the last of the cagey Republican. Already developing his own ingenious scheme for seeking re-

53   Raleigh *Morning Post*, August 2, 1900.
54   Edmonds, *Negro and Fusion*, 209–10.
55   J. Morgan Kousser, *The Shaping of Southern Politics: Suffrage Restriction and the Establishment of the One-Party South, 1880–1910* (New Haven: Yale University Press, 1974), Table 7.3, p. 186, Table 7.5, p. 194, Table 7.6, p. 195.

venge on the Democrats and simultaneously rescuing himself from
mounting financial pressures, Russell was prepared for a tranquil de-
parture from office when a final fascinating controversy climaxed his
troubled years as governor.

In late December, 1900, Republican Chief Justice William T. Faircloth of the state supreme court died, thereby giving Governor Russell
the privilege of appointing a new chief justice who would hold office
until the election of 1902. Corporate titans such as Alexander B. Andrews, vice-president of the Southern Railway and former Russell
nemesis, and Benjamin N. Duke, the Durham tobacco tycoon, feared
that Walter Clark and his truculent antitrust views might control the
supreme court unless a strongly conservative appointee were named to
the bench. The shrewd Andrews had struck upon a scheme he thought
might neutralize Clark. "The thing to do," Andrews suggested to
Duke, "is for Gov. Russell to resign and have Lt. Gov. Reynolds, who
then becomes Governor, to appoint Gov. Russell the Chief Justice. I
know this would be very gratifying to Gov. Russell, he only needs a little backing and encouragement from friends to make him agree to
pursue this course."[56]

With amazing speed, rumors of a bipartisan movement to make
Russell chief justice swept the capital. Robert Furman's *Morning Post*,
generally friendly to the Southern Railway and the American Tobacco
Company trust, applauded the idea inasmuch as the last two years of
Russell's term had been "conservative" and free of earlier partisan-
ship.[57] The building momentum for him to become chief justice as-
tounded the governor and "even his most intimate friends." He let it be
known, however, that he would not consider the appointment without
a strong endorsement by the North Carolina Bar Association. One
anonymous Democratic lawyer explained why so many Democrats
were supporting Russell, who was acknowledged to possess genuine
legal talent. "Governor Russell holds, I believe, that the State Supreme
Court cannot pass on the constitutionality of the recent amendment,
that such an act is in the province of the United States Supreme Court
alone. Hence, with Governor Russell as Chief Justice I don't believe
our amendment can be attacked in the State courts."[58]

56 Andrews to Duke, December 30, 1900, in B. N. Duke Papers.
57 Raleigh *Morning Post*, January 1, 1901.
58 Raleigh *Times*, January 2, 1900, in Russell Scrapbooks, North Carolina Collection, University of North Carolina, Chapel Hill.

The campaign to give Russell the chief justiceship cut sharply across party lines. Some of the strongest opposition emanated from the GOP, but, according to J. C. L. Harris, both Pritchard and Reynolds favored the scheme. Walter Clark, however, who reportedly coveted the position for himself, led the crusade against Russell's appointment by preventing the Raleigh bar's endorsement. Daniels' *News and Observer* charged that the railroads and corporations molded courts with "their pliant attorneys or . . . men, like Russell, who rant against them one year and the next year do their bidding. . . . They prefer a man like Russell, who, after his 'cavorting' is now docile and pulls steadily in the political harness."[59] Josiah W. Bailey, editor of the *Biblical Recorder* and future United States senator, asserted that Andrews "owned Russell body & soul" and thus wanted him on the supreme court.[60] Despite such attacks, a remarkable number of Democrats and Populists voiced their approval of the plan including Cyrus Watson, the Democratic gubernatorial nominee in 1896; Robert B. Glenn, future governor of North Carolina; George Rountree of Wilmington; Populist Justice Walter Montgomery of the state supreme court; and former congressman Harry Skinner. This broad support following decades of rancor demonstrated that Russell had earned the grudging respect of his opponents for his toughness, pugnacity, and independent spirit.

In fact it was those very attributes that most clearly showed themselves in the resolution of the justiceship question. Although under pressure from Andrews, Duke, and others to accept the post or else appoint a Republican of their choice, Russell elevated Justice David Furches to the chief justiceship and named Charles Cook to fill the vacancy. Cook, of course, had been a loyal ally to Russell for years and had led the fight against the Southern Railway in the legislature of 1897. No pliant tool of any interest group, Russell had acted with propriety and probity in refusing the post for himself and making his own appointment. "In the days when things seemed to be shaping for me to take the Chief Justiceship Cook was doing all he could for me to get it," the governor explained to Ben Duke. Reports that he did not manage the matter correctly did not disturb Russell. "*I know that I did*," he told Duke. "I made no mistake in that affair."[61]

59   Raleigh *News and Observer*, January 2, 4, 1900.
60   Josiah W. Bailey to J. C. Kilgo, June 26, 1902, in John C. Kilgo Papers, Duke University.
61   Russell to Duke, February 2, 1901, in B. N. Duke Papers.

Russell's governorship doubtless was the most trying experience of his life. Filled with high ambition and sober promise, he had never been able to overcome the interparty squabblings of the fusionists and the Democratic cry of Negro supremacy which plagued reformers throughout the South whenever one-party rule was in danger. Charles Cook provided something of an epitaph for Russell's governorship, when, writing his family shortly before Russell left office, he commented on all the governors, senators, judges, and even presidents whom he had met. None, Cook said, "had as much brains, sincerity, ability or integrity" as Russell. "I can confidently say, that he is a *gentleman*, truthful, honest, upright and just, kind, affectionate, loyal, and gentle." Although "born [an] aristocrat," Cook continued, Russell's sympathies steadfastly had remained "with the worthy and the poor. No man ever lived in the State who is least understood and worse represented. Men who have abused him are not worthy to be classed Gentlemen."[62]

---

62 Cook to Lenoir, December 23, 1900, in Charles A. Cook Papers, Southern Historical Collection, University of North Carolina, Chapel Hill.

Chapter IX

Russell's Last Foray
Origins and Politics of an Interstate Lawsuit

AS IF ALL the political woes that Russell experienced as governor of North Carolina were not enough, he also suffered economically. The state then paid its chief executive an annual salary of three thousand dollars. Governor and Mrs. Russell entertained liberally and proudly kept up the best possible Whig–Republican social appearances; he estimated that his high office cost him eleven thousand dollars a year more than he received in salary. His rice crops failed with regularity, his private debts mounted, and these circumstances, together with his desire for revenge against the Democrats and his long-standing scorn for the repudiation of state debts, led him to "invent a scheme" for making money—a great deal of money he hoped.[1]

Russell's scheme involved the bonds which North Carolina and other southern states had repudiated at the end of Reconstruction, when the Democrats had "redeemed" their respective states from "Negro–Carpetbag" rule. Russell admitted that many of the Reconstruction bond issues had been tainted with fraud; nevertheless, he felt quite strongly that not all of what he called the "hundred millions" in bond issues were fraudulent. Furthermore, he regarded as unscrupulous the wholesale repudiation by southern Democrats, who successfully hid behind the federal Constitution's Eleventh Amendment.

---

1 A more detailed account of most of the material in this chapter may be found in Robert F. Durden, *Reconstruction Bonds and Twentieth-Century Politics: South Dakota v. North Carolina (1904)* (Durham: Duke University Press, 1962).

That amendment, after 1798 and the angry reaction to *Chisholm* v. *Georgia* (1793), barred citizens of other states or of foreign nations from suing any of the sovereign states of the federal union.

Enraged northern financiers and speculators repeatedly challenged repudiation by the southern states in the last quarter of the nineteenth century. Various legal maneuvers to collect on the southern bonds were tried, but all of them, sooner or later, ran afoul of the Eleventh Amendment. Russell hit on the notion of having some of the controversial bonds donated, outright and without any strings, to a state itself. This sovereign donee, in turn, could launch a suit in equity against the repudiating southern state in the United States Supreme Court, to which tribunal the Constitution gives original jurisdiction in all controversies between states. With the validity of the bonds established by the highest federal court, Russell figured it would be easy to gain a compromise from the southern state on the remaining bonds of the series from which the donation had been made and possibly on all the state's repudiated bonds.[2]

In North Carolina's case, there existed a special group of semirepudiated, or "readjusted," bonds that had caught Governor Russell's interest. In the decades immediately preceding the Civil War, North Carolina Whigs had taken the lead in pushing the state into a bold program of state aid for railway construction. The state subscribed for $3 million worth of stock in the North Carolina Railroad, which traversed the then underdeveloped Piedmont section. To pay its subscription the state issued its "construction" bonds and to make the bonds more attractive gave them a direct lien or mortgage on the state-owned railway stock. Immediately after the war but before the Radical phase of Reconstruction had begun, North Carolina's leaders, many of whom had been antisecessionist Whigs, hoped to continue the program of railroad building despite the wreck and ruin of the war. To accomplish this at a time when the state had little or no income, the legislature of 1866–1867 authorized the issuance of state bonds which were to be secured by a second mortgage on the state-owned stock in the North

---

2   The best concise statement of Russell's scheme is in a letter he wrote on October 9, 1900, to Alfred Russell, a prominent lawyer of Detroit, Michigan, whom Governor Russell knew but to whom he was not related. This letter is published in the *North Carolina Historical Review*, XXXVIII (October, 1961), 527–34. Alfred Russell not only became associated in the bond scheme but suggested and helped procure the services of Wheeler H. Peckham of New York City, a distinguished constitutional and corporation lawyer.

Carolina Railroad. Each of these $1,000 "second mortgage" bonds, in other words, was now given a formal second lien on ten shares of the state's $100-a-share stock in the railroad. Under the difficult circumstances of the time, the state merely swapped these bonds for additional stock in the railroad and allowed the company to dispose of the second mortgage bonds for the best prices obtainable.

As these transactions were being carried out in 1868, Radical Reconstruction began. In a short span of time, North Carolina's Republican-dominated legislature authorized around $27 million worth of state bonds, mostly for railroad projects. The state actually issued over $17 million worth of what came to be known as "special tax bonds" because of a new constitutional provision requiring special taxes to pay the interest. Although the Republicans clearly had no monopoly on shady dealings in those graft-filled years, they were, at least temporarily, in power. It became, consequently, a paramount article of faith for Tarheel Democrats that the special tax bonds constituted the lead exhibit in the case against Republican "misrule."

Once North Carolina Democrats were again firmly entrenched in both the legislative and executive branches of the state government in the 1870s, they proceeded to effect a drastic financial readjustment not only by prohibiting any payment on the special tax bonds but also by scaling down the "honest" debt from the period before 1868. On the second mortgage bonds the Democratic "settlement" called for the payment of 25 percent of the principal with nothing for the coupons, despite the fact that the bonds carried on their face a second mortgage on state-owned property which other bonds placed in the same 25 percent class did not have. The first mortgage or "construction" bonds, on the other hand, received far better treatment. As a result of prolonged litigation, the state not only fully recognized them but prior to their maturity in the 1880s exchanged new 6 percent bonds for the original ones. The state also stipulated that the new bonds were given not in payment but only in extension of the old ones and without prejudice to the original bonds' lien on the state-owned railway stock.[3]

---

3   Benjamin U. Ratchford, *American State Debts* (Durham: Duke University Press, 1941), 162–96, and the same author's three articles on the North Carolina debt in the *North Carolina Historical Review*, X (1933), are the most authoritative studies. C. K. Brown, *A State Movement in Railroad Development* (Chapel Hill: University of North Carolina Press, 1928), provides a detailed account of the matters which are only summarized above.

At least one creditor of North Carolina refused to accept the state's debt arrangements of 1879. This was a New York banking firm, Schafer Brothers, that controlled 234 of the second mortgage bonds. Indignant but helpless when the southern state offered only $250 for a bond that had a face value of $1,000 in principal alone, Schafer Brothers decided to keep their bonds—and to hope. Their patient wait seemed closer to being rewarded when Governor Russell's confidential agent appeared in their New York offices in 1900 with what he claimed was a foolproof scheme for collecting the bonds.

The agent, Addison G. Ricaud, had earlier been the governor's law partner in Wilmington. But Ricaud, finding the political climate unbearably intolerant and oppressive, had left for New York in 1898, the same year the white-supremacy campaign had exploded into a bloody anti-Negro *coup* in Wilmington. After careful negotiation and without revealing the identity of his silent partner, Ricaud secured a contract from Schafer Brothers for the collection of the second mortgage bonds. It provided that he (and ultimately Russell) would receive one-third of any amount collected in excess of the 25 percent of the principal which North Carolina had for two decades offered to pay.[4]

Governor Russell feared only one snag in his scheme: how would he procure a state which would accept a donation of North Carolina bonds and sue to collect them in the Supreme Court? Ironically, sovereign states proved surprisingly obtainable for his purposes. Alfred Russell of Detroit, Michigan, a railway and corporation lawyer whom Governor Russell knew and had brought into the bond case, had no trouble getting an especially tailored bond-donation measure enacted in his state.[5] Michigan, however, was not to be the litigating state. The prime mover in the matter turned out to be none other than Marion Butler, whom the Democrats were replacing in the United States Senate with Furnifold M. Simmons. Butler, in the weeks immediately before and after his term expired in March, 1901, worked zealously to "talk up this thing" among the more approachable senators, as Russell expressed it. Butler found that his associate in many Senate battles,

---

4   Addison G. Ricaud to Russell, May 18, 19, 25, and July 23, 1900, in Daniel L. Russell Papers, Southern Historical Collection, University of North Carolina, Chapel Hill.

5   Alfred Russell to Russell, April 3, May 28, and June 1, 1901, in Russell Papers. A copy of Michigan Senate Bill 30, "To provide for the acceptance of grants, devises, bequests, donations and assignments to the State of Michigan," is also in *ibid.* Michigan's Republican governor, Aaron T. Bliss, signed the measure into law in early April, 1901.

Richard F. Pettigrew, Silver Republican of South Dakota who had also failed to be reelected, held out the best hope for quick action. Pettigrew worked through Congressman Charles H. Burke of South Dakota, and Robert W. Stewart, an influential lawyer-lobbyist of Pierre, South Dakota, and later a high offical in the Standard Oil Company. Butler promised his South Dakota friends that prompt legislation would be followed by a prompt donation of bonds to the state and assured Russell that since "Pettigrew & his rep[ublican] cong[ressman] absolutely control the situation—can control the Gov. & Attorney Genl. without extra cash," they had "a sure thing of it in S.D."[6]

Although Russell privately felt that it would "look better to have for a plaintiff a State more important than South Dakota or Nevada," his Michigan associate had not been able to produce the desired law as expeditiously as had Butler and his western allies.[7] The two aging Schafer brothers, Simon and Samuel, were increasingly eager about their second mortgage bonds, and they urged as great a speed as possible. They handed ten of the North Carolina securities to Russell in March, 1901, for donation to South Dakota. The former governor, in turn, readied his far-flung legal team for the first formal, public move—a motion from South Dakota to the United States Supreme Court for permission to file a bill of complaint against North Carolina. Moving urgently to meet a spring deadline, Russell encountered the first of what would seem an eternity of delays: under the referendum provision of the South Dakota constitution the donation act would not become effective until four months after the legislature had adjourned. The bonds, however, had already been transmitted from Russell and Congressman Burke to Governor Herreid of South Dakota. "Of course the idea

6   Russell to Marion Butler, December 22, 1900, January 30, 1901, Marion Butler to Russell, January 11, 18, 30, February 25, 26, and March 11, 1901, in Russell Papers. A copy of the agreement between Lawyer Robert W. Stewart and John L. Pyle, South Dakota's attorney-general, is also in the Russell Papers and shows that Stewart was to serve as the state's counsel in any forthcoming bond litigation and receive 10 percent and expenses from whatever amount South Dakota received. Under a subsequent agreement (September 6, 1901) between Russell, Marion Butler, and Richard F. Pettigrew the last two were each to receive 20 percent of the lawyer's contingent fee, after expenses; in addition, in the event of "recovery" on the second mortgage bonds, Pettigrew was to receive $10,000 "to satisfy the claims" of Stewart and Charles H. Burke. There is no indication in any of the documents that South Dakota's Republican governor, C. N. Herreid, participated in the happy plans for the melon-cutting. It might also be noted that in addition to South Dakota and Michigan, Nevada passed the desired donation act.

7   Russell to Wheeler Peckham, March 13, 1901, in Russell Papers. Russell signed his contract with Schafer Brothers in March, 1901, two months after his gubernatorial term expired.

of a new donation is out of the question," Ricaud reported from New York. "Simon Schafer is nervously prostrated at Atlantic City. His Brother tells me this matter has caused his trouble."[8]

Daniel Russell and his legal associates used the delay to prepare their arguments and debated through the mails some of the more difficult points involved in the case. "But I confess that I get a little nervous," Russell declared, "when I consider that we are blazing through an untrodden forest in this, that no such suit as ours has ever been brought." Why? "Because it is the only case where individuals have been co-parties with a State in a suit between two States."[9] An individual could not, of course, be a co-plaintiff with a state in a suit against a defendant state because the Eleventh Amendment forbade it. Yet a state could be a plaintiff against an individual, and if the individual were a nonresident citizen the Constitution gave the Supreme Court jurisdiction. What Russell had done was to join together as defendants the state of North Carolina and two New York citizens, each of whom owned, respectively, some of the first and second mortgage bonds. Russell had done this because in suits in equity all parties concerned in the matter must be represented, and the two New Yorkers served as representatives for both classes of bondholders. Furthermore, he arranged it so that Wheeler H. Peckham, a distinguished lawyer of New York City whose brother was on the United States Supreme Court, would appear with R. W. Stewart as counsel for the plaintiff, that is, South Dakota. Peckham's fee, however, would be secretly paid by Russell. Russell himself, together with Alfred Russell and Marion Butler, would eventually represent one Charles Salter of New York, the second mortgage bondholder.

There was a substantive point that from the first bothered Russell more than any other aspect of the case. It was a subtle matter, but the manner in which the Supreme Court decided it would determine the degree of Russell's success. The point was this: each $1,000 bond had been given a second mortgage on ten $100 shares of the state-owned railway stock. Since no particular shares of the stock had been designated, Russell hoped, but had his doubts, that the Supreme Court would not be able to select any particular one hundred shares of stock for the payment of the plaintiff and would therefore be compelled to

8   Ricaud to Russell, May 9, 1901, in Russell Papers.
9   Russell to Alfred Russell, June 24, 1901, *ibid*.

ordcr the sale of all of the stock or at least enough of it to discharge both the first and second mortgages. The state's 30,000 shares of mortgaged stock in the North Carolina Railroad had risen in value until they were worth on the market over $170 a share, or about $5,100,000 altogether. Since it would require only about $2,720,000 to pay off completely the first mortgage and about $700,000 to pay the second, Russell, as well as his fee-hungry associates, hoped for a Supreme Court ruling that would give Schafer Brothers, and therefore their lawyers, the maximum amount.

South Dakota's motion to the United States Supreme Court for permission to file a bill of complaint against North Carolina was finally submitted on November 11, 1901. The Court promptly granted the motion and ordered the defendant to appear and answer on March 3, 1902, the date being subsequently delayed until April. Governor Charles B. Aycock of North Carolina received the awesome formal tidings from the president of the United States: "For certain causes offered before the Supreme Court of the United States, having jurisdiction in equity, You are hereby commanded that, laying all other matters aside and notwithstanding any excuse, you be and appear before the Supreme Court" to answer South Dakota's bill of complaint.[10]

North Carolina's Democratic officials were more than merely surprised by the development; they were shocked and thoroughly mystified. Daniel Russell quipped: "They are less familiar with the original jurisdiction of the Supreme Court as to controversies between sovereigns than I am with the debates of the Council of Nice. About the best they could do after the first week was to walk around the streets and swear that the Court would never grant the motion, that such a thing was never heard of before. . . . I think that about all of them thought the case would have to be brought before a county squire and carried up by appeal before a jury in the county court house. But they will learn as they get older."[11]

Regardless of whether or not the "enemy" was as naive as Russell claimed, Governor Aycock at least had the good sense to keep quiet un-

10   President of the United States, via the Clerk of the Supreme Court, to the State of North Carolina, Charles Salter, and Simon Rothschilds, November 25, 1901, in Executive Papers of Charles B. Aycock, North Carolina Division of Archives and History, Raleigh, hereinafter cited as Aycock's Governor's Papers.
11   Russell to Alfred Russell, November 21, 1901, in Russell Papers.

til he understood more about the matter. Not so the state's Democratic newspapers. South Dakota's opening move, even before it became known that Russell and Butler were intimately involved, immediately stirred up a major furor in the press. The explanation for this was simple: the incident struck both the railway and bond chords that had been important in North Carolina's political life since the 1840s. Although the second mortgage bonds had been authorized by native Conservatives and not by "thieving Carpetbaggers" and their allies, many Tarheel Democrats from the very first refused to be informed correctly about the subject. The influential Raleigh *News and Observer* called the South Dakota bond suit another step in the "villainous" Southern Railway corporation's "vast conspiracy" to rule or ruin North Carolina. Haphazardly blending fact and suspicion, Josephus Daniels charged that manipulators on the inside of the Southern Railway had bought up all the bonds that were being sued on, ultimately intending to buy up the largely state-owned railway for a "song," issue bonds on it for two or three times its capital stock, and pocket several million. Southern Railway spokesmen repeatedly denied Daniels' conspiracy charge; but the company did exert very real power in North Carolina, and with the American Tobacco Company stood as a symbol for all corporate malevolence. For four years or more, even after Governor Aycock assured the public that the state's railway stock would not be sold and long after it had become clear to most people that the Southern Railway had nothing to do with the case, the *News and Observer*, followed by lesser Democratic papers, kept up its sensational charges.[12]

Whereas the bond suit at once became a major development for North Carolinians, South Dakotans heard next to nothing about their state's action. When the suit began, the western state's leading Republican paper, the Sioux Falls *Daily Argus–Leader*, carried a brief dis-

12 Raleigh *News and Observer*, November 12, 13, 1901. This paper's greatest rival, the Raleigh *Morning Post*, set about correcting the widespread opinion that the bonds were of fraudulent carpetbag origin and insisted that "all the slush as to the Southern road scheming to buy the State's stock" was "worse than nonsense" and "resorted to by the only paper in the State that will not tell the truth when it thinks its interest may be served by falsehood and slander." North Carolinians had best understand, according to the *Morning Post*, that a "lawsuit is on which cannot be whistled down the winds nor avoided by vulgar abuse and misrepresentation." Raleigh *Morning Post*, November 13, 1901. The *Morning Post* was Democratic in its politics but of the staunchly pro-Grover Cleveland and "goldbug" variety; Josphus Daniels had been and remained a fervent Bryanite. On state issues too the *News and Observer* usually differed sharply from the "Wheezy Old Railway Organ" as it called the *Morning Post*.

patch from Washington on an inside page, but the matter received no editorial comment.[13] Reconstruction bonds hit no sensitive nerves of history in the West, and also, the prominent South Dakotans involved in the bond suit had nothing to gain by publicity.

Russell, meanwhile, busied himself in preparing the elaborate, printed brief for presentation to the Supreme Court and in anticipating the arguments the North Carolina counsel, three prominent Democratic lawyers (James E. Shepherd, Charles E. Merrimon, and George Rountree), would advance. Russell prophesied, quite correctly as it turned out, that there would be a great uproar about the suit's being a fraudulent device whereby a sovereign state could be sued in defiance of the Eleventh Amendment. "All this and more will be hammered after the fashion of the 'high toned' Southern Gentleman who is never so lofty as when he is playing the pirate." The "enemy," Russell continued, would surely say the donation was only pretended, a transparent device enabling individuals to hide behind a sovereign, and "they may put in the stump speeches of Calhoun, Jeff Davis and Bob Toombs."[14]

In fact, North Carolina's long, formal answer, filed in April, 1902, began with a demand for strict proof that South Dakota owned the bonds and insisted that even if the complainant possessed them, the transfer of ownership was "purely colorable and collusive" for the purpose of evading the Eleventh Amendment. North Carolina admitted the issuance of the bonds but argued that they had not been disposed of according to the statutory requirements of newspaper advertisements and par-or-better prices for the bonds; consequently, North Carolina now argued that the mortgages allegedly made by the state treasurer on the state's railway stock were improperly executed because of the illegal procedure used in disposing of the bonds. North Carolina admitted the terms of the 1879 adjustment, as set forth in the complainant's bill, and reemphasized the state's "impoverished condition" at that time as the result of the Civil War. North Carolina further argued, getting closer to one of the points which troubled Russell, that if one Charles Salter did truly own any of the second mortgage bonds, then he should be "arrayed and treated for all purposes and especially on the question of [the Supreme Court's] jurisdiction" as a complainant in the suit rather than as a co-defendant with North Carolina.

13   Sioux Falls *Daily Argus-Leader*, November 12, 1901, and *passim*.
14   Russell to Alfred Russell, December 10, 1901, in Russell Papers.

In another argument designed to dissuade the Supreme Court from taking jurisdiction in the case, North Carolina denied any controversy, within the meaning of the Constitution, between herself and South Dakota. The southern state closed her answer with the traditional phrase that the defendant "humbly prays this Honorable Court to enter its judgment that this defendant be hence dismissed, with her reasonable costs and charges in this behalf most wrongfully sustained."[15]

"They made fools of themselves in a way that is beautiful to look at," Russell exclaimed to Butler. "It is very important that they shall remain in their present state of mind, and that they shall never know what struck them until the argument. . . . In the meantime 'The word of our guidance is mum.'"[16] The new allegations in North Carolina's answer concerning the illegal issue of the bonds bothered Russell not at all, for he had almost at his fingertips the information he needed to counter the points. What he did not have, he knew precisely how to get. Russell corroborated his own knowledge about the state's post-bellum exchange of its $1,000 bonds for $1,000 worth of railway stock by securing from Professor Kemp P. Battle, historian and former president of the University of North Carolina who had been the youthful state treasurer in 1866–1867, the statement that the "practice had been for years for the R.R. Companies to bid par for the bonds and receipts passed accordingly." Although Battle remembered that he "tried hard to comply with all the laws, and had good advisers, Gov. Worth" and others, he could not recall whether or not he had advertised, but if he had not "it was because I was advised that it was unnecessary."[17]

Battle did not remember whether he had obeyed the law by advertising the bonds, but Russell believed, or guessed, that he had. The former governor knew exactly the "right man, the man of all men in the State, to dig up" the information. This man, a prominent antiquarian and historian in Raleigh, Marshall De Lancey Haywood, shuffled through the dusty old newspapers in the state library and, sure enough, found just the advertisements Russell needed to disprove North Carolina's allegation.[18]

15   Raleigh *Morning Post* and Raleigh *News and Observer*, April 5, 1902.
16   Russell to Marion Butler, April 16, 1902, in Russell Papers.
17   Kemp P. Battle to Edm. S. Battle, April 9, 1902, *ibid.* Both Battle and the late Quaker governor, Jonathan Worth, were native Tarheels who had been Whigs but were now almost sacrosanct in the eyes of the Democratic newspapers.
18   Russell to Marshall De Lancey Haywood of Raleigh, August 5, 1902, and Russell to Alfred Russell, August 23, 1902, in Russell Papers.

Still superbly confident of most of his legal ground, Russell braced himself and his associates for the taking of testimony, which would be done by Court-appointed commissioners in New York, Washington, Raleigh, and Pierre, South Dakota. The testimony would publicly reveal for the first time that the former Republican governor of North Carolina and the former Populist senator had taken prominent roles in arranging to have their native state hauled before the nation's highest tribunal. That political bomb Russell could hardly hope to defuse. But there were some things he definitely wanted to get into the official record, as well as those he wanted to keep out. Prudently anticipating this stage of the affair, Russell had written Samuel Schafer early in 1902 telling him exactly what to say in a letter he was to write in his own hand to Congressman Burke. Although Russell himself had transmitted the ten bonds to the South Dakotan almost a year before, he wanted Schafer to appear in the record as having done it and having said that the bondholders preferred to donate the bonds to South Dakota, perhaps for the university's use, rather than accept "the pittance" North Carolina offered. Furthermore, Schafer was to say that if South Dakota succeeded in collecting the bonds, the owners of the total issue still outstanding would be most pleased to make additional donations to such "governments as may be able to collect from the repudiating state." [19]

As for things to hide, Russell cautioned R. W. Stewart in Pierre that it would be indeed unfortunate if "the enemy" procured an admission from any South Dakota official that although the state brought the suit, someone else paid the costs. "For the Lord's sake keep this out," Russell implored. "It will not look well to the Court." Russell feared that Governor Herreid might "talk too much" before the two North Carolina attorneys who were going out to Pierre for the deposition-taking. Surely Stewart could "just fix it" so that Herreid said nothing more than that Burke had handed him the bonds together with the letter from Schafer? As for Burke himself, Russell thought it would be just as well if he were not "within convenient reach just at this time." [20]

---

19   Russell to Samuel Schafer, February 13, 1902, *ibid.* For Russell's success in this move, see Schafer's letter to Burke, dated September 10, 1901, in 192 *United States Reports,* 289–90. Among other documents, which are printed there together with the arguments, the decision, and the dissent, are the relevant North Carolina laws of 1849, 1855, 1866; Treasurer Battle's 1867 endorsement on the bonds mortgaging the railway stock; and South Dakota's 1901 donation act.
20   Russell to R. W. Stewart, August 4, 8, 1902, in Russell Papers.

Russell's maneuvers paid off and the South Dakota depositions pleased him immensely. In New York, Alfred Russell and Addison Ricaud for purely political reasons wanted to conceal the fact that Russell, while still governor of North Carolina in 1900, had informally entered into negotiations about the Schafer bonds. Poor Ricaud, however, encountered difficulties in coaching Samuel Schafer and reported disgustedly that the New York depositions were successful only in establishing "the *know-nothing-ism* of our crowd." Ricaud had gone to great pains in drilling Samuel Schafer about the fact that he should "forget" when he first met Russell and "use a defective memory as an excuse for inability to answer questions." But when the nervous Mr. Shafer became rattled during the taking of his testimony and was told to produce all the letters between Russell and the Schafer Brothers, Ricaud quickly took "him in charge for 2 hours and put him straight so as to claim the privilege of atty and client."[21]

The "enemy" questioned former governor Russell himself rather closely and for the first time publicly connected his name with the bond suit. He stoutly denied that he had officially had anything to do with the suit before the signing of his contract with Schafer Brothers in March, 1901, and he slipped in one or two stump speeches against sovereigns that defrauded creditors and Democrats who repudiated honest debts.[22]

Russell arranged for Congressman Burke to be out of the District of Columbia during the taking of testimony there. Marion Butler, however, deposed that he himself had suggested to Senator Pettigrew the idea of a South Dakota donation act and that he had done so while campaigning in South Dakota for William Jennings Bryan in 1900. The Populist leader admitted that he had been employed as attorney for Schafer Brothers in January, 1901, a few weeks before his senatorial term expired, and that he had talked over the whole bond matter

21 Ricaud to Russell, September 9, 10, 1901, *ibid.* Also in the Russell Papers is the unsigned, undated memorandum of Samuel Schafer's testimony, just as Ricaud had finally written it out for him. The fact that Simon Schafer had died earlier in the year—because of worry about the second mortgage bonds according to Ricaud—proved ironically useful. As Samuel Schafer told his Ricaud-modeled story, the fact emerged that most of Russell's early dealings had been, alas, with the departed brother.

22 Charlotte *Observer*, November 8, 1902. Russell went to great lengths trying to hide the one clearly unethical step which he had taken about the bonds while governor; when eight of the second mortgage bonds were sent in for redemption by a New Yorker late in 1900, Russell arranged to have the cancellation nullified so that he could buy them with or through a banker friend. See Russell to Ricaud, November 1, 3, 1900, in Russell Papers.

with Russell shortly before the governor's own term expired in mid-January, 1901. Butler, in short, except for claiming the authorship of the donation act (and he had campaigned in South Dakota in 1900), told substantially the truth, which Russell had skirted more gingerly by clinging to misleading technicalities. That fact, plus the bitter knowledge that Butler had been the chief architect of the Tarheel Democrats' misery in the 1890s, inspired the mistaken notion which took hold in North Carolina that Marion Butler, more than anyone else, had fathered the South Dakota bond suit.

"BUTLER & RUSSELL. Their Own Evidence Convicts Them of Conduct that Will Forever Damn Them in North Carolina," declared the headline in the *News and Observer*. "Southern Railway speculating big men" were no doubt behind the traitorous pair. "The 1868-'9 gang stole more money," the Raleigh paper figured, "but if the 1895-'9 gang had been given another lease of power, it may be well doubted if the carpet-baggers of 1868-'9 would have far surpassed the disgraceful gang at the helm from '95 to '99." Butler's and Russell's bond actions were the "blackest page in the black book of their careers."[23] Lesser Democratic papers also took up the cry. One accused that Butler, "the real instigator" of the bond suit, would "do anything for the cash, provided it is against his own people." Another, blithely inaccurate about the origin of the second mortgage bonds but warming to the familiar old charges about Reconstruction, believed there was nothing surprising about Butler's and Russell's trying to collect "these old bonds that their crowd saddled upon the State when her people lay helpless and bleeding at the mercy of the gang who robbed our State and brought shame on her good name and suffering upon her people with all the evils and misgovernment and ruin."[24]

While North Carolina newspapers debated the nature and authorship of the bond suit, giving off much more political heat than historical light, Russell and his associates prepared for the dramatic, possibly decisive, argument before the Supreme Court. When that day finally came in April, 1903, the justices, through their many questions directed to the assembled counsel, showed a lively interest in the complex and unprecedented case. Justice John M. Harlan closely interro-

23 Raleigh *News and Observer*, December 19, 1902.
24 Wilkesboro *Chronicle* and Chatham *Observer* as quoted in Raleigh *News and Observer*, December 21, 28, 1902.

gated Wheeler Peckham, who appeared for South Dakota, about the proposed mode of relief, thereby indicating that the Court viewed with great seriousness the idea of foreclosing on North Carolina's rail stock.

George Rountree, prominent Democratic lawyer from Wilmington, opened for North Carolina, and Justice Harlan promptly inquired of him whether if a state repudiated a just debt another state would have cause for action. Rountree thought not; there was no precedent for the Court's taking jurisdiction in such a suit brought by one state against another; a claim that was noncollectible had no validity and did not obtain validity merely by being transferred to a state for collection.[25]

Daniel Russell appeared for the second mortgage bondholder and drew blood, at least in North Carolina Democratic circles, by his references to the "turpitude of repudiation" and the shameful depths to which North Carolina had descended in 1879. He reemphasized that the pledged railway stock had, since 1879, become worth enough on the market to pay not only the first mortgage but also the second and still leave the state almost $2 million. "And yet North Carolina retains the security . . . and is guilty of the monstrous wrong of collecting every six months the income of the stock and turning it into its treasury . . . although that income so collected every six months, in equity and in common honesty, is the property of the Complainant and the other second mortgage bond holders." There was simply no language too strong, the fiery old Republican concluded, "to denounce the turpitude of this proceeding."[26]

Reporting confidentially to Governor Aycock, George Rountree confessed that the justices had "listened patiently for a few minutes and then bombarded me with a fusillade of questions, which attempted to show that I was wrong in thinking the original Constitution did not give the Court jurisdiction over actions of debt against a state." Still Rountree believed that Justice Edward D. White and at least a couple of the others agreed with North Carolina that the individual bondholders were necessarily one with South Dakota in the action; this would mean that the Eleventh Amendment forbade the Court's taking jurisdiction. Rountree frankly admitted his "doubt about the result" but he still thought the chances were good of winning "upon the

25 Raleigh *Morning Post*, April 13, 14, 1903.
26 Raleigh *News and Observer*, April 15, 1903.

ground that the suit is necessarily one on behalf of S.D. and individuals alike."[27] Daniel Russell, Wheeler Peckham, and their associates conferred after the first day of argument and must have shared some of Rountree's estimates of the Court's thinking. At any rate, when Peckham reappeared before the Court the next day to make his concluding argument, he was reported to have declared in effect: "The claims of the individuals can be dismissed for all we care. South Dakota is not a trustee for the second mortgage bondholders."[28]

With the argument before the Court ended, the wait for the decision began. Russell optimistically reported to an old friend: "We '*wore out*' the other fellows. *They* believe they are *beat*. They are badly hacked. It looks our way; but nothing is certain till death."[29] Yet months passed and no decision was forthcoming. Alfred Russell, on tenterhooks throughout the summer of 1903 in Detroit, regretted that Wheeler Peckham, with his strategically situated brother on the Court, "would not put in writing anything he might have learned in a 'kitchen cabinet' way!"[30]

After the long suspense, the Supreme Court's order late in November, 1903, for a reargument of the bond case early in the next year came as both a disappointment and a scare to Russell and his allies. Only eight justices had heard the original argument, owing to the illness at that time of Justice William M. Day. "Informed Washingtonians" reportedly believed that the Court had divided evenly on the case and that Justice Day would probably now become the arbiter.[31]

Russell, sick and feverish anyway from a serious kidney ailment, still felt confident about the jurisdiction question. He feared the real danger might be the Court's inability to administer South Dakota's rights without substantially permitting individuals to sue a state "in the teeth" of the Eleventh Amendment. Encouragement came when Alfred Russell sent an exciting tip from Detroit: "I have ascertained, (don't ask me how,) that the doubtful questions in the mind of the Court, were, first, whether justice could be administered without the presence of the prior incumbrancers [the first mortgage bondholder,

27　Rountree to Charles Aycock, April [14?], 1903, in Aycock's Governor's Papers.
28　Raleigh *Morning Post*, April 16, 1903.
29　Russell to Duke, April 16, 1903, in Benjamin Newton Duke Papers, Duke University.
30　Alfred Russell to Russell, June 22, 1903, in Russell Papers.
31　Raleigh *Morning Post*, December 1, 1903.

although listed as a co-defendant, had not been represented by counsel in the argument]; second, whether the power of suing another State could be exercised in the case of assigned credits, that is to say, in the case of debts originating in favor of individuals, and subsequently assigned to the plaintiff state; and the Court considered that the case turned upon these two points." The Detroit attorney labeled his information "dead sure"; it was in writing and from a member of the Court, "so there is no mistake about it, but [we] must not speak of this to anybody, as the information is purely confidential."[32]

Emboldened and relieved by the valuable inside tip, Russell arranged for the brother of the clerk of the Supreme Court to appear as counsel for the first mortgage bondholder, and he and his associates prepared the strongest arguments they could devise to meet the Court's reported misgivings about a state's suing on transferred credits. The reargument early in 1904 brought a recapitulation of all the major points that had been earlier argued so exhaustively. The justices, now familiar with the intricacies of the case, questioned and discussed quite freely, furnishing abundant clues for the ever-fascinating game of guessing how they might decide. Russell spoke in court in defiance of his doctor's orders and then went almost directly to the Johns Hopkins hospital. After an emergency operation for kidney stones, he was reported several times during the next three months to be dying. Alfred Russell tried to encourage his sick friend by suggesting that the decision would be the right one; the Supreme Court was, after all, "a creditor's Court, and believes in people paying their debts."[33]

The decision, announced in February, 1904, marked a creditor's triumph—but a five-to-four, qualified one. The Court ruled, in a decision written by Justice David J. Brewer and concurred in by Justices Brown, Harlan, Holmes, and Peckham, that the Supreme Court had jurisdiction over an action brought by one state against another to enforce a property right; and, further, that where one state owned ab-

---

32   Russell to Alfred Russell, December 1, 1903, Alfred Russell to Russell, December 14, 15, 16, 17, 1903, in Russell Papers. Alfred Russell mentioned in another context almost a year later that one of his best friends was "a brother-in-law of Judge Brown [Henry B. Brown of Detroit] who gave us his vote in the South Dakota case." This may well have been the source of the earlier tip. See Alfred Russell to Russell, October 15, 1904, *ibid*.

33   Alfred Russell to Russell, January 28, 1904, *ibid*. For confirmation of this view of the Court at that time, see Fred Rodell, *Nine Men: A Political History of the Supreme Court* (New York: Random House, 1955), 169–73.

solutely bonds of another state, which were specifically secured by shares of stock belonging to the debtor state, the Court could enter a decree adjudging the amount due and providing for the foreclosure and sale of the security in case of nonpayment, "leaving the question of judgment over for any deficiency to be determined when, if ever, it arises." The Court also ruled that the motive of the gift had no effect on its validity, that the Court's jurisdiction was not affected by the fact that the bonds were originally owned by individuals, that the bonds had been legally issued and disposed of by the state, that the holder of a certain number of bonds, which had been secured by what constituted a separate and registered mortgage on a specified number of stock shares, could foreclose on the specific number of shares which secured his bonds, and that the holders of other bonds and of liens on the property were not necessary parties to the foreclosure suit and were, therefore, dismissed from further consideration in the proceedings. North Carolina should pay South Dakota $27,400 for the ten bonds on or before January 1, 1905, or suffer the foreclosure sale.[34]

Justice Edward D. White, destined soon to become chief justice, wrote a vigorous dissent in which Chief Justice Melville W. Fuller and Justices McKenna and Day joined. The dissenters argued that the Supreme Court lacked the power to render the decree the majority had entered because of the absence of essential parties, that is the private bondholders, whose presence would have prevented the Court's taking jurisdiction. "My mind cannot escape the conclusion," Justice White declared, "that if, wherever an individual has a claim, whether in contract or tort, against a State, he may, by transferring it to another State, bring into play the judicial power of the United States to enforce such claim, then the prohibition contained in the Eleventh Amendment is a mere letter, without spirit and without force."[35]

North Carolina Democrats found their only consolation in the dissenting opinion. Governor Aycock and other prominent officials expressed their great surprise and dismay at the decision, but the majority of articulate Tarheels declared at first that North Carolina would, of

---

34   192 *United States Reports*, 286 (1904); Raleigh *Morning Post*, February 5, 1904, also printed a special section carrying the full documents.

35   192 *United States Reports*, 328. Alfred Russell exulted in his belief that his "getting Peckham resulted (as I expected) in getting his bro., & I got my *old pupil, Brown. We could not have spared either one!*" Alfred Russell to Russell, May 15, 1904, in Russell Papers.

course, obey the mandate of the nation's highest tribunal. In New York, Wheeler Peckham, loftily putting the matter in proper historical perspective, regarded as "a very satisfactory feature" of the decision the fact that "it seems to have excited no particular comment; there is no rising of States or the people in hostility to the decision, as there was in the early days when the decision was rendered in Chisholm against Georgia."[36]

The distinguished Mr. Peckham, however, rather overestimated the docility of North Carolina's Democrats and underestimated their dogged ingenuity when confronted by federal mandates. A powerful faction led by Josephus Daniels and Chief Justice Walter Clark of the North Carolina Supreme Court had no intention of allowing the state to pay South Dakota the full judgment, if they could help it, and would do almost anything to prevent the state from compromising the Schafer-owned bonds at a price that would enrich Butler and Russell.[37] The *News and Observer* fumed that when the two fusionists got "the pieces of silver coming to them for the betrayal of the State that had chosen them to look after its affairs," then "they ought to have the decency to follow the example of their predecessor and go and hang themselves." North Carolina would "pay the pound of flesh denominated in the bond, but it will not permit the shedding of one drop of blood beside." The Shylock allusion became even clearer with reference to "Christian blood" and a mention of bonds owned by a New Yorker with "a Jew name."[38] The widely read Democratic organ finally calmed down enough to suggest that the only possible and honorable course for the state to follow would be to stand on the 1879 offer of 25 percent of the bond's principal ($250 per $1,000 bond) because that "just" settlement of the "wise" and "patriotic" Redeemers could not safely be questioned. Through diligent and clever political maneuvering on the part of

36 Peckham to Stewart, February 8, 1904, in Russell Papers. For the prevailing bafflement in South Dakota about the real origins of the bond case, see Sioux Falls *Daily Argus-Leader*, February 2, 4, 8, 1904.
37 Chief Justice Walter Clark's private but most influential view was that, "We are not one cent worse off by the South Dakota decision," and while the real plaintiffs had been "knocked out" South Dakota had gotten only "a right to subject equity of redemption" in 1919 when the first mortgage bonds matured. Clark, in other words, did not want North Carolina to pay the judgment but rather to let the stock be foreclosed on and sold. Clark to Graham, his brother-in-law and a prominent Democratic politician, February 8, 1904, in Aubrey L. Brooks and Hugh T. Lefler (eds.), *The Papers of Walter Clark* (2 vols.; Chapel Hill: University of North Carolina Press, 1950), Vol. II, 60–61.
38 Raleigh *News and Observer*, February 2, 1904.

Daniels, Clark, and their allies, this view, together with an ambiguous phrase about abiding "the mandates of the courts," became party dogma when the state Democratic convention of June, 1904, incorporated it into the platform.[39]

Despite the Democrats' declaration of faith in the Redeemers, Russell wanted and believed he could get a more satisfactory compromise. He had sufficiently recovered his health by the fall of 1904 to resume command of the drifting bond affair, and he had hit on one final "invention" he hoped would induce the Democrats to do business, profitable business, with Schafer Brothers. Russell deeply feared that North Carolina would submit to foreclosure on the one hundred shares of stock. That would leave the troublesome task of trying to wring a deficiency judgment from the state, since the stock could not bring more than about $17,500 and this would leave almost $10,000 still due South Dakota—and would leave Schafer Brothers exactly where they had been since 1879. The United States Supreme Court had never clarified how it could carry its judgments, as between states, into effectual execution, since it could neither compel a legislature to levy taxes nor itself levy them upon state-owned property used for public purposes.[40] Russell's new plan was for South Dakota to pass a law early in its legislative session of 1905 providing that any funds it might receive from the initial judgment against North Carolina could be used to purchase additional bonds, second mortgage bonds in fact, as a sound investment. That law, Russell figured, would either scare the Tarheel Democrats into a real compromise or else cost North Carolina so heavily that their political necks would be in jeopardy at the next state election. "If we can hold So.D. to our course with a strong steady helm," Russell predicted, "we can bring these repudiators to our feet." Marion Butler should promptly go to work on the South Dakotans and

39 *Ibid.*, June 24, 25, 1904. Among other members of the platform committee were Daniels' brother, Frank, and Augustus W. Graham.
40 Well might Russell have shied away from the question of the deficiency judgment since it dealt with one of the then unanswered questions of constitutional history and would not be settled until the Supreme Court unanimously declared in *Virginia* v. *West Virginia* (1918) that the Court's undoubted right to pronounce a judgment necessarily implied the right of the Court and the president to use appropriate means, or whatever means were at their disposal, to enforce judgment against a state. Charles Warren, *Supreme Court and Sovereign States* (Princeton: Princeton University Press, 1924), 78–79.

"let not this legislature of So.D. pass from us without getting our fortifications well erected."[41]

Having received Butler's report that Congressman Burke felt confident of arranging the legislation, Russell next launched a publicity of-
fensive. The most important of various moves he made along this line
was to write out an interview that Samuel Schafer released in New
York as his own. Russell had Schafer describe, rather pathetically,
how he and his late brother had purchased the bonds in "good faith at
a high price" (sixty-five to seventy-five cents on the dollar), had refused the pittance offered in 1879, and now felt sure that the "great"
southern state which had become so prosperous would no longer be
willing to live under the disgrace of repudiation. Schafer also explained, in response to the "Reporter's" fortunate question, that, no,
there would be no need to make further donations; since the Supreme
Court had upheld the validity of the bonds, he felt sure he could find
buyers for them.[42]

The Schafer interview mysteriously appeared in pamphlet form in
the mailbox of every North Carolina state senator, and comment in
Raleigh increased about the bond suit. Governor Aycock, failing in his
October, 1904, effort to secure a rehearing of the case, had succeeded
in gaining from the Court a delay of the deadline from January 1 to
April 1, 1905, so that the new state legislature could deal with the
question.[43] Then shortly before he left office, Aycock dispatched an
agent on a secret mission to New York, where the agent learned from
Ricaud of Russell's interest in a compromise at around $1,500 per
bond rather than the $2,740 per bond the Supreme Court had ordered
North Carolina to pay to South Dakota. The popular Aycock informed
the legislature in his last message that he felt confident that both the
judgment and the privately held bonds could be settled for much less
than their face value. He avowed his complete accord with the Demo-

---

41 Russell to Marion Butler, November 26, December 12, 20, 1904, in Russell Papers. Russell
again drafted and forwarded a bill providing what he wanted from South Dakota. See Russell
to Stewart, December 23, 1904, *ibid.*, where he holds forth on the moral justification as well
as expediency of the law.
42 A seven-page pamphlet reprinting the Schafer interview from the New York *Telegram* may
be found among Aycock's papers, in Aycock's Governor's Papers. See the Sioux Falls *Daily
Press*, January 14, 1905, for one of the strategic reprintings there. Russell's instructions to
Schafer are in Russell to W. H. Gibson, December 23, 1904, in Russell Papers.
43 Raleigh *Morning Post*, October 18, 1904; Raleigh *News and Observer*, December 7, 1904.

cratic platform of 1904 and his "entire sympathy" with the honorable adjustment proposed by the Democrats of 1879. Newly elected Governor Robert B. Glenn, in other words, inherited a nasty headache.[44]

Glenn's first, half-concealed efforts to work out a compromise failed. Ricaud, who had come down to Raleigh to join a local attorney who also represented Schafer Brothers, gave up the whole negotiation in disgust and went back to New York. The reasons for the failure were several, but chief among them was the threatening stand taken by the *News and Observer* and its allies in the legislature against paying one cent more than the Redeemers had originally offered and the "White Man's Party" had reaffirmed in 1904. Nor did this faction wish any action other than letting the state's stock be sold. Unloading its biggest guns against the Southern Railway's vast and mysterious conspiracy, the villainous fusionists connected with the bonds, and the wicked immorality of Democrats who did not obey their party's solemn pledges, Josephus Daniels and his paper effectively intimidated both Governor Glenn and those members of the legislature who opposed the policy of drifting and doing nothing about the bonds.[45]

Many North Carolinians, however, including the editors of the Raleigh *Morning Post* and the Charlotte *Observer*, simply did not like the idea of North Carolina's suffering the humiliation of foreclosure and public sale of the state-owned property.[46] Just as these papers began to speak out in emphatic editorials, which less prominent journals echoed, the Washington correspondent of the *Morning Post* wrote two significant dispatches. One reported that lawyers in the national capital did "not doubt for a moment that the Supreme Court of the United States will enforce its judgment if such an issue is presented"; and as for any deficiency judgment that might have to be dealt with, the *Post* correspondent found little doubt in Washington that the federal marshal would be authorized to levy on state-owned property that was not used for public purposes, such as railway stock. The companion story,

44 For Aycock's secret agent, who was Judge James Shepherd, one of the state's counsel in the bond case, see Ricaud to Russell, December 27, 31, 1904, in Russell Papers. For Aycock's message to the 1905 legislature, see Governor's Letterbook, North Carolina Division of Archives and History, Raleigh.
45 Raleigh *News and Observer*, January, 1905. Numerous letters from Ricaud to Russell, January, 1905, in Russell Papers, furnish an inside view of the negotiations.
46 Raleigh *Morning Post*, January 31, February 2, 3, 5, 1905.

which Congressman Burke and perhaps Marion Butler helped inspire, reported that the bond-buying law had passed the South Dakota Senate and was expected to pass the house momentarily.[47]

Assisted by the rising opposition to the do-nothing policy and the alarming reports from South Dakota, Governor Glenn acted. He first covered his *News and Observer* flank by a public declaration of his admiration and respect for that paper on the occasion of its passing the ten thousand mark in circulation. Surely with all of Josephus Daniels' great power and his genuine love for the state he would "concede the same devotion to others, though they may differ with" his views, so that the *News and Observer*, with charity as well as patriotism, could always be a mighty "power for usefulness."[48] On the same page as the governor's *billet-doux* was his special message to the legislature proposing prompt action toward adjustment of the whole matter unless the legislature wished the responsibility for the sale of the state's stock. The legislature promptly created a committee, headed by Glenn, and negotiations were resumed. Russell pinned his last hope on good news from South Dakota, but on February 16, 1905, Butler finally admitted, "there is some trouble developed in the S.D. House."[49]

The very same day that Butler sent his grim news, Governor Glenn made a bold move worthy of Daniel Russell himself: he dispatched a public letter to North Carolina's United States senators, Furnifold M. Simmons and Lee S. Overman, stating that the report of South Dakota's pending bond-buying bill sounded "so monstrous and foreign to what appears to me to be good faith in the comity between States" that he could not believe the rumor. Would the senators please ascertain the facts from their South Dakota colleagues? And if the rumor should be true, then "it is high time that in the Council Halls of the Nations, a ringing resolution should be introduced, denouncing . . . in most

47 Raleigh *Morning Post*, February 11, 12, 1905. Russell had continually begged for speedy action in South Dakota; he urged that Burke and Pettigrew should "quit the bush whacking and come out into the open, and appeal to the morality, and sense of honor and justice of that State, and then get what we want: and that is for that State to buy our bonds." The Dakotans had been assailed by "the States' Rights repudiating crowd" so why did they not hit back? Russell to Marion Butler, February 4, 1905, in Russell Papers.

48 Governor Robert B. Glenn to Josephus Daniels, in the Raleigh *News and Observer*, February 12, 1905. The editor appended a purring note about his and his paper's fighting "every day in every year for Democratic supremacy," and he never wrote another angry bond editorial or distorted news story about the bonds during the ensuing negotiations.

49 Marion Butler to Russell, February 16, 1905, in Russell Papers.

scathing terms a State that thus allows itself to be used as a catspaw by individuals to annoy and harrass another sister State."[50]

Glenn had trumped Russell's last ace. The news reached Raleigh that the bond-buying bill would not be passed because of the strong opposition that had suddenly developed within the South Dakota legislature. After a great deal of bargaining and juggling with the amount of compound interest that had to be added to $250, so that the Democrats could appear to have adhered to their 1879 and 1904 positions, the compromisers settled for $892 per bond, with North Carolina paying the full amount of $27,400 due South Dakota. Glenn boasted of how much he had saved the state and of how the bondholders had made repeated reductions in the amounts they asked, and he promptly recommended a bond issue of $250,000 to the legislature. That body, with equal promptness, passed the necessary measure and then adjourned.[51]

When Governor Glenn and the state treasurer traveled to New York to pay Samuel Schafer in late May, 1905, a large posse of fee-hungry lawyers were hot on the trail of Daniel Russell. The profit for the lawyers amounted only to about $40,800—a great deal less than the vast sums contemplated earlier. After fierce verbal battles and with Pettigrew angrily threatening a lawsuit, Russell escaped from New York with the money. He conferred again with Butler in Washington about dividing the fund and finally ended up making sure, as he candidly put it, that he received "more than the rest for manifold reasons."[52]

Undated memoranda in Russell's papers suggest that the major actors in the "business drama" received approximately the following

50 Glenn to Furnifold M. Simmons and Lee S. Overman, February 16, 1905, in Executive Papers of Robert B. Glenn, North Carolina Division of Archives and History, Raleigh, hereinafter cited as Glenn's Governor's Papers; Raleigh *Morning Post*, February 17. For South Dakota reaction to Glenn's blast, see Sioux Falls *Daily Press*'s editorials, February 19, 21, 1905, about "this fine point in interstate etiquette" which had just been discovered. The new governor in South Dakota, Samuel H. Elrod, and the growing Progressive Republican contingent in the legislature were apparently already alerted against the law by their United States senators when Glenn's manifesto made its death certain.

51 Glenn to the general assembly, March 2, 1905, in Glenn's Governor's Papers, Raleigh *Morning Post*, March 2, 7, 1905. The Raleigh *News and Observer* was still in its strangely quiescent, one could almost say drugged, condition; the Russell Papers contain too many detailed and amusing letters about the settlement to be cited here.

52 Russell to Peckham, May 29, 1905. Peckham (Peckham to Russell, June 2, 1905, in Russell Papers) emphatically disagreed with Russell and angrily but vainly insisted on at least ten thousand dollars regardless of how the rest was divided because without him in the case "it was dead sure lost."

amounts: a little over $15,000 for Russell and Ricaud together (to be divided 60–40); a bit over $5,000 each for Butler, Pettigrew, Alfred Russell, and Peckham; $2,500 for the Raleigh attorney, Fabius Busbee, who played a key role in the final negotiations; $1,000 for Congressman Burke; $500 for Senator Stewart of Nevada, who had lined up his state to accept the bonds if necessary; and the remaining $1,600 for miscellaneous payments to persons who had helped at one stage or another. Russell insisted that after all the claims on him were paid, his share of the fee amounted only to about $7,000. He did not mention that he either owned or had a large interest in at least eight of the second mortgage bonds, which together with ten of Ricaud's had been included in the 242 bonds for which North Carolina paid Schafer.

Russell's fury with the South Dakotans reached such proportions that he sent word to Glenn that North Carolina should simply not pay the judgment, let the stock go to sale, and buy it herself. He felt sure the "South Dakota crowd are wanting in legal knowledge and brains sufficient to take proceedings to collect a deficiency judgment."[53] Governor Glenn did not follow Russell's vengeful suggestion but did try in vain to compromise the judgment with South Dakota, at the $17,500 figure the rail stock was worth. When the South Dakota state constitution, among other factors, made a compromise out of the question, Glenn finally paid the full amount and thereby ended North Carolina's official role in the bond suit.[54]

The Supreme Court's decision in the bond case and North Carolina's final settlement gave a tremendous impetus to old efforts to collect on the "hundred millions" of repudiated southern bonds. A committee that Butler, Russell, and Pettigrew had earlier helped form for the purpose of pooling the old securities enjoyed a flurry of activity in

53   Russell to J. C. L. Harris, March 17, 1905, in Russell Papers. Russell and Pettigrew exchanged some classically vituperative letters, with Russell announcing at one point that Pettigrew did not know enough law "to distinguish a legal partnership from a South Dakota hay stack." Pettigrew never got the additional $10,000 which he insisted a 1901 agreement with Russell entitled him to; neither did the South Dakotan sue about the matter, probably because he did not desire publicity about the whole episode.

54   The North Carolina attorney-general rushed with a check to Chief Justice Fuller's home on the deadline, April 1, only to be informed by that dignitary that he should proceed to the home of Justice Brewer, who, after all, had written the opinion with which Fuller disagreed. Brewer assured the attorney-general that the check would not be turned over to South Dakota until the ten bonds were surrendered. The federal marshal and other officials around the Court were reported to be greatly relieved that no such steps as the unprecedented foreclosure proceedings would be needed. Raleigh *Morning Post*, April 2, 1905.

the spring of 1905. Then it collapsed because of the Russell–Pettigrew feud and Marion Butler's refusal to have anything to do with the special tax bonds of North Carolina carpetbag origin. Butler, now an ardent Republican supporter of Theodore Roosevelt, wished to return to North Carolina politics and, contrary to what he had believed about himself, wanted again to taste the power he had enjoyed in the 1890s.

Thus, while Butler did his best to dissociate himself from the whole field of repudiated bonds, a Wall Street committee headed by James G. Carlisle, former secretary of the treasury under President Cleveland, specialized in collecting North Carolina's special tax bonds and literally beat the bushes in its efforts to find a sovereign state that would accept a donation of the bonds. Governor Glenn and his successors, however, had learned their lesson from the South Dakota episode: from 1905 on the governors of North Carolina easily convinced the states of New York, Michigan, Connecticut, and Nevada, among others, that interstate comity prohibited accepting donations of the "fraudulent" bonds.

Even South Dakota in 1907 gave every indication that she regretted the late suit against North Carolina. Governor Samuel Elrod, in his last message to the South Dakota legislature, eloquently declared that he would "rather have South Dakota right, fair and just in all her transactions with her sister states than to have millions of tainted money in her treasury." Elrod explained that he had refused an offer of more North Carolina bonds from the Carlisle committee only the previous year and he urged the legislature to repeal the donation act and to refund every penny.[55] Although certain "Insurgent" or Progressive Republicans promptly introduced the recommended measure, it proved easier for some South Dakotans to claim bad consciences than for the state actually to repay North Carolina. Aside from the $2,740 plus expenses that had already been paid to R. W. Stewart as his fee, there were political reputations and sensitive egos to be considered. Too, word had come to South Dakota from one Daniel L. Russell that if North Carolina should get her "honest obligations back for nothing,"

---

55 Sioux Falls *Daily Argus-Leader*, January 8, 1907. See *ibid.*, January–February, 1909, for further agitations of the matter in South Dakota and an attempt to blame Pettigrew for it while excusing Burke and Herreid; and February 3, 1911, for the final inclusion of the "tainted money" in the general fund, from which it could presumably be spent without embarrassment.

then certainly Samuel Schafer still had "good equities" in the bonds and South Dakota would not, of course, want to make herself instrumental in "enabling North Carolina to cheat the owners of these bonds."[56] South Dakota never repaid North Carolina, thereby sparing Russell considerable embarrassment.

Although Russell failed to make the profit from his bond suit that he had once envisioned, the whole affair afforded him great satisfaction. Not only had he displayed legal skill and ingenuity of the highest order, but he had also caused abundant trouble for the Tarheel Democrats. Raised as a proud Whig to despise Democrats, Russell had spent his adult life as a Republican engaged in unrelenting combat with "the enemy." At the polls in 1898 and 1900 the Democrats had finally won, massively and for a long time to come. In the Supreme Court of the United States, however, Russell had sought and found his final revenge against Democrats and "repudiationists."

Russell cannot be easily categorized or labeled. That he "never knew the relaxation of conformity" is perhaps the truest insight into the complexities of the proud, unusual man. Louis Goodman, Russell's young law partner in Wilmington during the early years of the twentieth century, attempted to understand the man beneath the image and later recorded his impressions. Goodman judged the long lectures Russell would often give him as "worth five of the college professor's," and he vividly described his partner's style.[57] Sitting in an office chair specially constructed to hold his enormous bulk, Russell "had a way of gripping the chair, lifting up his feet and coming down on the floor with them, in a stormy display of thunderous noise. I have heard him on such occasions, cuss out clients and sometimes order them from his presence. He was not a bully. He just couldn't stand the *unsound reasoning of little minds*. However, he would do his feet the same way when he laughed in the enjoyment of a story. He would clear his throat, and say impressively, 'aha', much in the inquiring way of our 'o, yeah?'" Adept at satire, Russell frequently called people "marvels of stupidity" and "paragons of ignorance." Yet Goodman believed that be-

---

56 Russell to Charles E. DeLand of Pierre, South Dakota, January 26, February 10, 1907, in Russell Papers. Russell confided to Schafer that he did not see much chance of his scheme's amounting to anything, but if it did he expected Schafer "to treat me liberally." Russell to Samuel Schafer, February 19, 1907, *ibid*.

57 Louis Goodman to Russell, July 27, 1906, *ibid*.

neath all the strong-mindedness and violent temper lay "an element of bluster and bravado—in modern parlance called bluff in an effort to frighten."[58]

In other situations, as in his dealings with children, a softer, more compassionate side showed itself. During a period when schooling for rural white children, not to mention blacks, was virtually nonexistent in North Carolina, Russell sought a qualified black teacher for the young Negroes on his plantation in Brunswick County.[59] A young great-niece, accompanying Russell on a visit to his widowed step-mother, long remembered the "awesome formality" of the occasion and that her uncle addressed his stepmother only as "Madam."[60] The same great-niece as a young girl, once noting the noisy manner in which Russell tackled corn-on-the-cob, blurted out at the table, "Uncle sounds like one of the horses in the barn when he eats corn." She real-ized as soon as she heard her voice that she had made an outrageous remark, and crushing looks from her mother and great-aunt added to the humiliation, but she was comforted to see in Russell's face "only a mild surprise—no anger, no reproof."[61] Informed by his wife of some misfortune suffered by a neighbor or acquaintance, Russell's usual re-ply was, "What can we do to help, madam?"

Politically, Russell offered an alternative to the racial and economic policies of the Bourbon Democrats. The triumph of the fusionists in North Carolina during the 1890s and the reforms they instituted dem-onstrated the powerful attraction of their program and the direction Progressivism in the South could have taken had the race issue been quashed. As governor, Russell undertook economic reforms that ulti-mately estranged him from the Republican party but which were also boldly aimed toward the creation of a new coalition of reformers from all parties and social strata. Tarheel businessmen, already chafing un-der the discriminatory freight rates imposed by northern-controlled railroads, had as much to gain from railroad regulation as did their agrarian counterparts. Significantly, many of these same commercial interests were part of the Progressive coalition of the early twentieth

58　Louis Goodman to Mrs. Hal B. (Alice Sawyer) Cooper, July 22, 1942, *ibid.*
59　E. M. Rosafy to Russell, September 23, 1874, *ibid.*
60　Alice Sawyer Cooper, in collaboration with Louis Goodman, "Daniel Lindsay Russell: A Fam-ily and Friend's Memoir" (MS in the Daniel L. Russell Papers, Southern Historical Collec-tion, University of North Carolina, Chapel Hill), 47.
61　*Ibid.*, 93.

century, but in the 1890s they were unwilling to identify with a reform movement supported by Negro Republicans and led by a maverick governor who often talked in anticapitalist terms. That Russell espoused a reform program no more radical than such acknowledged southern Progressives as Charles B. Aycock, James K. Vardaman of Mississippi, and Hoke Smith of Georgia illustrates a much-neglected side of the reform movement in the South between 1890 and 1910. What fundamentally set Russell's brand of progressivism apart was his stand on the race issue. Southern Progressives of the early twentieth century rose to power on the crest of racial antipathies, whereas Russell, though holding distinctly paternalistic views toward the Negro and his role and place in society, also believed in protecting Negro civil and political rights. Such views were doomed by the intense racism of the late nineteenth and early twentieth centuries when repressive mechanisms such as lynching, segregation, and disfranchisement supplanted the paternalistic and accommodationist devices of an earlier age. After 1900, Russell was a man with no political future.

Having sold "Winnabow," the plantation on which he was born, in 1881, Russell kept his house in Wilmington and his plantation at Bellville, a few miles west of Wilmington and across the Cape Fear. There he tried unsuccessfully to grow rice around the turn of the century, and there he died on May 14, 1908, a few months before his sixty-third birthday.

As he sank into a final coma, Russell kept repeating a line from a nineteenth-century English operetta: "Time was made for slaves." His wife stroked his hand, murmuring, "Take your time, take your own time." Russell had once referred to "Time, the Mocker, the relentless Sphinx" while addressing a black audience, and on his deathbed the same fascination gripped his mind.[62] After funeral services in the First Presbyterian Church in Wilmington, he was buried in the Sanders family cemetery on Palo Alto plantation in Onslow County.

Scorned by the Democrats during his lifetime, Russell received no more than "mixed reviews" upon his death. Perhaps the fairest comment was that of the Charlotte *Observer*, then a conservative Democratic newspaper, which declared: "He was a striking personality—remarkable in appearance, an impressive individual in every way. He

62 *Ibid.*, 95.

was not beloved of North Carolinians but he who denies to him a high order of ability discredits himself." [63] That Russell was "not beloved by North Carolinians" was a neat understatement. He was, in fact, feared and hated as a scalawag and Republican, a thoroughgoing nonconformist who had embraced first the cause of civic and legal equality for blacks and then that of economic reforms for the agrarian majority. As if all that had not been enough, he had remained always the proud former Whig and planter—"the Knight of the Lordly Strut."

63 Charlotte *Observer*, May 15, 1908.

A Note on
the Sources

THROUGHOUT THE TEXT are numerous references to the sources used in writing this book. This essay, therefore, offers a brief discussion of the principal manuscript, newspaper, and secondary materials consulted which might prove helpful to other historians.

MANUSCRIPTS

Daniel L. Russell Papers. The Russell Papers comprise the core of this book. Housed in the Southern Historical Collection, University of North Carolina, Chapel Hill, the papers cover major episodes in Russell's life from the Civil War until his death in 1908. Even so, there are curious lacunae at crucial points such as the gubernatorial years. The collection is thin for the Civil War–Reconstruction years but has important material on the 1896 election, and it is rich and complete for Russell's bond scheme.

Marion Butler Papers. The Butler Papers, also in the Southern Historical Collection, remain the most important source on Populist-Republican politics in North Carolina during the 1890s. A vast collection, there are countless letters from national, state, and local politicians on a variety of issues. The Butler Papers are indispensable to an understanding of Populism and the fusionist program in North Carolina.

Daniel L. Russell Executive Papers, 1897–1901. The Governor's Papers, in the North Carolina Division of Archives and History, Raleigh, contain surprisingly little information on key issues during Russell's governorship. Although there are some useful materials on the lease fight in 1897, this collection yields scant information on Russell or his activities.

Benjamin Newton Duke Papers. The B. N. Duke Papers, Manuscript Department of Perkins Library, Duke University, contain a number of important personal letters from Russell. During and after his governorship Russell often reflected on his difficulties in almost confessional terms to the Republican tobacco magnate in Durham.

Thomas Settle Papers. An influential Whig-Republican family, successive generations of Settles played an active role in Republican politics from Reconstruction through the fusionist period. The Settle Papers are in the Southern Historical Collection.

Other manuscripts that proved useful and that are available at the Southern Historical Collection include the Henry G. Connor Papers, Augustus W. Graham Papers, Richmond Pearson Papers, James G. Ramsay Papers, and the Cyrus Thompson Papers.

NEWSPAPERS

Populists and Republicans in North Carolina lacked a daily newspaper that could effectively challenge the partisan Democratic dailies. During Reconstruction the Wilmington *Daily Post* operated as a Republican daily, but it was ultimately overwhelmed by the Democratic newspapers of Wilmington, the *Daily Journal*, the *Morning Star*, and the *Messenger*. The Democratic newspapers remained ardent foes of Russell throughout his career and were quick to pick up the cudgel of white supremacy in the Reconstruction and fusionist periods. The Raleigh *News and Observer* under the editorship of Josephus Daniels became the most influential newspaper in the state during the 1890s. Dubbed the "saviour of the state" by his opponents, Daniels spared no effort in promoting the Democratic party and causes he deemed important, especially white supremacy. Generally more balanced in its political coverage, if more conservative in its views, was the Charlotte *Observer*. Although a Democratic paper, the *Observer* usually eschewed the slanted, vitriolic type of news stories and editorials published by Daniels' *News and Observer*. Republicans and Populists had to depend on weekly newspapers to deliver their message. The Raleigh *Caucasian* was the organ for Marion Butler and the radical Populists, whereas the Winston *Union-Republican* served as spokesman for the Tarheel GOP. Other valuable newspaper sources were the Hickory *Press* (Republican), Raleigh *Tribune* (Republican), Raleigh *Hayseeder* (Populist), and the Raleigh *Morning Post* (Democrat).

SELECTED PRINTED STUDIES

Two recent studies of southern history have provided important insights for this book. Carl Degler's *The Other South: Southern Dissenters in the Nineteenth Century* (New York: Harper & Row, 1974) places Russell and other like-minded mavericks in the broader context of regional history over the span of a century. J. Morgan Kousser in *The Shaping of Southern Politics: Suffrage Restriction and the Establishment of the One-Party South, 1880–1910* (New Haven: Yale University Press, 1974) employs a new statistical technique—ecological regression—to estimate voting patterns of both blacks and whites. His findings indicate the persistent strength of Republicans, Independents, Populists and others who continuously challenged the Democratic hegemony.

Specialized studies on significant North Carolina personalities and topics abound. William McKee Evans' *Ballots and Fence Rails: Reconstruction on the Lower Cape Fear* (Chapel Hill: University of North Carolina Press, 1966) is an excellent study of politics and society in the region where Russell began his career. Stuart Noblin in *Leonidas LaFayette Polk: Agrarian Crusader* (Chapel Hill: University of North Carolina Press, 1949) provides the background for the Populist revolt in North Carolina. In his memoir, *Editor in Politics* (Chapel Hill: University of North Carolina Press, 1941), Josephus Daniels presents his personal view of Tarheel politics during the Populist-Progressive period. Similarly, *Furnifold Simmons, Statesman of the New South: Memoirs and Addresses* (Durham: Duke University Press, 1936), edited by J. Fred Rippy, provides Simmons' recollections about the fusionist interlude. These memoirs should be supplemented by Joseph L. Morrison, *Josephus Daniels Says . . . : An Editor's Political Odyssey from Bryan to Wilson and F. D. R., 1894–1913* (Chapel Hill: University of North Carolina Press, 1962); Richard L. Watson, Jr., "Furnifold M. Simmons: 'Jehovah of the Tar Heels?'" *North Carolina Historical*

Review, XLIV (1967); and Oliver H. Orr, Jr., *Charles Brantley Aycock* (Chapel Hill: University of North Carolina Press, 1961).

Historians dealing with the Negro experience in North Carolina owe a debt to Helen G. Edmonds' seminal work, *The Negro and Fusion Politics in North Carolina, 1894–1901* (Chapel Hill: University of North Carolina Press, 1951). Edmonds' book was the first study to challenge the Democratic myth of "negro rule" during the fusion experiment. Also pertinent are Frenise A. Logan, *The Negro in North Carolina, 1876–1894* (Chapel Hill: University of North Carolina Press, 1964); William A. Mabry, *The Negro in North Carolina Politics Since Reconstruction* (Durham: Duke University Press, 1940); Willard B. Gatewood, "North Carolina's Negro Regiment in the Spanish–American War," *North Carolina Historical Review*, XLVIII (1971); Dorothy Gay, "Crisis of Identity: The Negro Community in Raleigh, 1890–1900," *North Carolina Historical Review*, L (1973); and Jeffrey J. Crow, "'Fusion, Confusion, and Negroism': Schisms Among Negro Republicans in the North Carolina Election of 1896," *North Carolina Historical Review*, LIII (1976).

A number of recent studies have attempted to deal with persistent questions raised by the turbulent politics of the Populist-Progressive period in North Carolina. Two articles by Joseph F. Steelman examine the interdynamics of the Populist-Republican coalition as it developed in the 1890s: "Vicissitudes of Republican Party Politics: The Campaign of 1892 in North Carolina," *North Carolina Historical Review*, XLIII (1966), and "Republican Party Strategists and the Issue of Fusion with Populists in North Carolina, 1893–1894," *North Carolina Historical Review*, XLVII (1970). Also Steelman's article, "Edward J. Justice: Profile of a Progressive Legislator, 1899–1913," *North Carolina Historical Review*, XLVIII (1971), details the support of the business community for reform legislation and should be compared with Jeffrey J. Crow's findings in "'Populism to Progressivism' in North Carolina: Governor Daniel Russell and His War on the Southern Railway Company," *The Historian*, XXXVII (1975). Robert F. Durden in *The Climax of Populism: The Election of 1896* (Lexington: University of Kentucky Press, 1965) focuses on the southern Populists led by Marion Butler in that epochal campaign and the Populist denouement in North Carolina. Durden's *Reconstruction Bonds and Twentieth-Century Politics: South Dakota v. North Carolina (1904)* (Durham:

Duke University Press, 1962) provides, with all of its political nuances, a detailed account of Russell's role in a once-famous interstate lawsuit. A book by a sociologist and one by an historian offer unique insights into changing attitudes toward race relations at the turn of the century. Pierre L. van den Berghe in *Race and Racism: A Comparative Perspective* (New York: John Wiley & Sons, 1967) presents two typologies of race relations—one based on paternalism and one on conflict—to help explain the intense racism of the early twentieth century. George Fredrickson in *The Black Image in the White Mind: The Debate on Afro-American Character and Destiny, 1817–1914* (New York: Harper & Row, 1971) uses the typologies to discuss dichotomous views of the Negro in the years before World War I.

UNPUBLISHED WORKS

Many doctoral dissertations and master's theses analyze a wide scope of issues in North Carolina from the Civil War to the twentieth century. Joseph F. Steelman's "The Progressive Era in North Carolina, 1884–1917" (Ph.D. dissertation, University of North Carolina, 1955) remains the most comprehensive examination of that period and is quite useful to any student of the subject. Although somewhat unsympathetic to Populists and Republicans, Steelman acknowledges the generally conservative nature of the Democratic party in North Carolina after 1898.

An invaluable source for this book was a typewritten manuscript in the Russell Papers by Alice Sawyer Cooper, in collaboration with Louis Goodman, entitled, "Daniel Lindsay Russell, Governor of North Carolina, 1897–1901: A Family and Friend's Memoir." The recollections of Russell's last law partner and his great-niece fill a number of gaps in Russell's life and provide an intimate glimpse of the man.

Philip R. Muller's "New South Populism: North Carolina, 1884–1900" (Ph.D. dissertation, University of North Carolina, 1971) gives a careful analysis of the Tarheel Populist movement in light of the historiographical controversies that have surrounded populism in recent decades. David C. Roller in "The Republican Party in North Carolina, 1900–1916" (Ph.D. dissertation, Duke University, 1965) discusses the devastating effects of disfranchisement and white supremacy on the fusionists. Two master's theses also contain information that is germane to this study. Carroll Leslie Pegler's "The Feasibility of Populist-Republican Fusion Re-Evaluated: Marion Butler versus Jeter Pritchard" (M.A. thesis, George Washington University, 1966) supplies a detailed analysis of the careers of two leading fusionists. Rosalie F. McNeill in "The First Fifteen Months of Governor Daniel Lindsay Russell's Administration" (M.A. thesis, University of North Carolina, 1939) is helpful on legislation adopted by the general assembly of 1897.

Index

DATE DUE

GAYLORD

PRINTED IN U.S.A.